A STEP AWAY FROM PARADISE

Mount Kanchenjunga as seen from Darjeeling.

A STEP AWAY FROM PARADISE

THE TRUE STORY
OF A TIBETAN LAMA'S JOURNEY
TO A LAND OF IMMORTALITY

THOMAS K. SHOR

CITY LION
PRESS

This book was first published by

Penguin India
in 2011

While every effort has been made to find the source of the photographs,
this has not been possible in all cases; any omissions brought
to our attention will be remedied in future editions.

ISBN: 978-0-9992918-9-4
2 4 6 8 10 9 7 5 3 1

FRONT COVER PHOTOGRAPH: THE YOUNG TULSHUK LINGPA

This book is dedicated to those who dared

Tulshuk Lingpa

'Don't listen to anybody. Decide by yourself and practise madness. Develop courage for the benefit of all sentient beings. Then you will automatically be free from the knot of attachment. Then you will continually have the confidence of fearlessness and you can then try to open the Great Door of the Hidden Place.'

Tulshuk Lingpa

Sketch of Mount Kanchenjunga.

CONTENTS

Foreword

by
Jetsunma Tenzin Palmo

A Step Away from Paradise is a riveting tale of adventure, intrigue and devotion. It is an extraordinary account of Tulshuk Lingpa, a Tibetan lama who lived quite recently and received revelations concerning the Hidden Land to be found in a crack on the flanks of Mt Kanchenjunga in Sikkim, which according to Tibetan tradition is another dimension of existence beyond death, disease or suffering yet still on this very earth and accessible without the need of dying first.

I personally—as others who have read the manuscript—found it an engrossing read. After years of careful research, Thomas Shor delivers an enthralling account of the life of Tulshuk Lingpa, who was a modern day lama in search of this veritable Shangri-la along with 300 devoted followers. The author has gone to great trouble to make his research both accurate and accessible. It really is both a fascinating read, a commentary on the recent political history in Tibet and the Himalayan regions, and an aspect of Tibetan Buddhism not usually talked about. Thomas Shor, who is the author of *Windblown Clouds* about his early travels in India, is not just an excellent writer. I have attended a public lecture and presentation based on *A Step Away from Paradise* that Shor gave, and it left the audience spellbound and amazed that such events could have happened so recently.

A Step Away from Paradise deals with an aspect of Tibetan Buddhism that is in some ways more honest to the real spirit of Tibet than all the usual books on Tibetan doctrine and will, I am sure, be of interest to a wide audience. It is a fascinating account of a little-known charismatic figure that will challenge even the most sceptical mind and provide a fresh perspective on what we normally regard as 'reality'.

Like no other book I have ever read, *A Step Away from Paradise* is both unique and intriguing. Highly recommended.

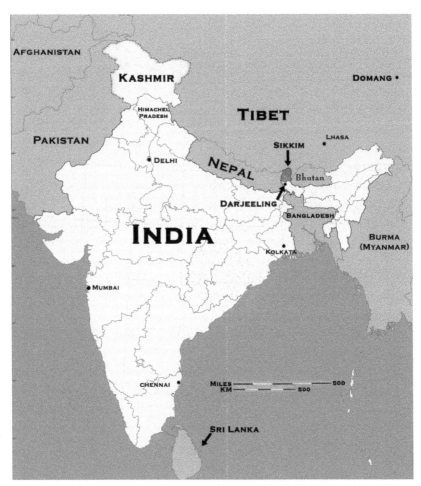

South Asia map, showing the main places in which the story takes place.

Introduction

What would have happened if Lewis Carroll had proclaimed the reality of Alice's Wonderland? What if he had gathered a following and launched an expedition?

It was autumn 1962.

The Cuban Missile Crisis threatened to end the world as we knew it. As Kennedy and Khrushchev teetered on the brink, it became startlingly clear that not only was an apocalyptic end within our technological means, it was also an immediate likelihood. The fear of incoming Soviet nuclear-tipped missiles meant schoolchildren across America were learning to duck and take cover under their desks while their parents dug bomb shelters they believed would take them to the other side of the looming apocalypse.

During those same tense days in October 1962 and half a world away, a charismatic and visionary Tibetan lama was leading over 300 followers into the snow and glaciers of the high Himalayas in order to 'open the way' to a hidden valley of immortality that Tibetan scriptures dating back to the twelfth century describe as a place of unimaginable peace and plenty that can be opened only at a time of the most dire need, when cataclysm racks the earth and there is nowhere else to run.

This book tells their true story.

CHAPTER ONE

A Crack in the World

'There is a crack in everything.
That's how the light gets in.'
Leonard Cohen

'You're a writer—you like stories? My mother-in-law has a story from when she was young, a story of a journey she took into the glaciers of the high Himalayas. You might think it's fiction—the imaginings of an old woman—but I assure you it is not. It will make you question your sense of reality.'

It was with these words that my friend Tinley set this book in motion. Tinley is a master painter of *thangkas*—the Tibetan religious scroll paintings depicting the tantric deities and various Buddhas in their myriad forms. He was crushing a blue semi-precious stone acquired from Tibet to match a patch of sky he was fixing on an antique thangka belonging to Sikkim's royal family, which was stretched taut on a wooden frame. He was sitting cross-legged on a rug in his studio in Gangtok, the capital of the Indian state of Sikkim, a once-independent Himalayan kingdom. I was sitting opposite, leaning against the wall and watching him work.

The son of Tibetan refugees, Tinley grew up at the Tibetan Refugee Self-Help Center in Darjeeling. He was around forty when I met him, and lived with his wife, son and mother-in-law on the top floor of a building called the Light of Sikkim in the centre of Gangtok. He painted, had painting apprentices and, with his wife, ran a small cyber cafe.

I had been introduced to his mother-in-law, a woman of seventy-five who was often leaning on the wide railing of their rooftop flat

Tinley Gyatso in his studio, Gangtok, Sikkim.

looking out over the city and the mountains beyond, spinning her prayer wheel and reciting mantras. Three years earlier she had shaved her head, donned a robe and become a nun in order to devote herself more fully to the religious life. Often when I visited, I would stand next to her and lean on the railing looking over the city and snow mountains beyond, stilled by her calm presence. I did not know much about her beyond that presence, since she spoke not a word of English and I speak neither Tibetan nor Bhutanese.

'How can her journey into the mountains make me question my sense of reality?' I asked Tinley.

He laughed. 'It's better she tells you herself,' he said.

'But—'

'Trust me,' Tinley said, looking up from the powder in his mortar and pestle, which was as blue as the empty Tibetan sky. He looked me in the eye: 'I tell you—it will stretch your sense of what's possible. You'll think she's spun the tale in her head. But it's entirely true.'

'What's entirely true?'

'That's for her to say!' he laughed. 'She's away for a few days now on a retreat in a monastery in western Sikkim but she'll be back tomorrow. Why don't you come the day after in the afternoon?'

I arrived at the appointed time with my tape recorder.

Tinley called his mother-in-law.

She walked into the room dressed in her nun's robes. One hand was working the beads of her mala, a Tibetan rosary, and the other she ran across the stubble of her shaved head and smiled when she saw me. I had been away from Sikkim and hadn't seen her in almost a year. She said something in Tibetan and Tinley interpreted: 'She said that since you are meeting again after such a long time, it means you still have karma together. Otherwise you wouldn't be meeting again.'

'It must be that story,' I said, laughing.

'It is a story that has changed many people's fates,' Tinley said, with an enigmatic twinkle in his eye. 'We'll see what happens to you.'

Tinley made tea. The three of us sat on the floor, and with Tinley translating she told me a story that certainly changed the course of the next four years of my life. Her story was pithy and replete with rustic details of crevasses, streams and high snow peaks—the vividness of which was remarkable for the passage of over four decades. What struck me most was the depth and passion of her faith.

She began by telling me that she was from Bhutan. She and her husband had a small farm—a few cows, chickens, and they grew their own grain. Even as a child she had heard that there was a place called Beyul

Dorje Wangmo.

Demoshong, a hidden valley in Sikkim she described as a heaven you enter through a cave, a place where you would live forever. This valley is on the slopes of Mount Kanchenjunga. In a matter-of-fact manner, as if she were telling me that she had a hundred rupees stashed under her mattress, she told me that half the wealth of this world and great stores of what she called spiritual attainment were hidden inside the mountain. 'Why do you think it is so peaceful here in Sikkim and there is so much happiness?' she asked, her eyes clear and penetrating. 'It is because we are living so close to Mount Kanchenjunga.'

Sipping her tea, spinning her prayer wheel and looking off into the distance she recalled her childhood: 'My village lama back in Bhutan used to tell us, and our parents told us too, "There is a cave, and there are people who have made it." There was a man from Tibet who went to Sikkim. He was high in the mountains when there was a big snowfall and he got lost. He saw a cave, and he went inside for refuge. It was so beautiful that he could never explain it in words. He went inside for maybe twenty minutes, and when he came out years had passed without his knowing, and zip-zip—he was old. Old age in a moment!'

Dorje Wangmo laughed, not because of the unreality of her tale but because of the incredulity she saw on my face.

'I didn't meet this man,' she said. 'I only heard his story.'

As she spun her prayer wheel thoughtfully, she explained that the story was unusual and must be based on the man's special karma. 'Usually you cannot just go there, on your own,' she said. 'It has to be "opened" by a special type of Tibetan Buddhist lama.'

Tinley explained that this special type of lama is called a *terton*, or treasure revealer. A few of these visionary lamas had attempted the opening but their karma wasn't right. Obstacles came in their way and they failed.

Dorje Wangmo was thirty-six when she heard that the lama who had all the signs had come. His name was Tulshuk Lingpa. Though he was from Tibet, he was staying at the Tashiding Monastery, which was considered the auspicious holy centre of the Kingdom of Sikkim. It was there that it was prophesied the lama would make his appearance.

She recalled for me her departure: 'A monk-brother of mine—he wasn't really my brother but all followers of the dharma are like brothers and sisters—was going to Sikkim to be there when the lama opened the way. When he told me, a tremendous feeling of longing awoke within me. I didn't want to be left out. So I told my husband "If you want to go, let's go together. If you don't want to go, I'll go by myself."

'"What?" my husband said. "You must be crazy!"'

Dorje Wangmo chuckled at the recollection and spun her prayer wheel a little faster. Her old eyes glinted.

'"It doesn't matter," I told him. "I'm going—whether you come or not."

'"Then I'll go, too," he said.

'We gave away our house and fields. We sold enough so we had the money to make the journey, and the rest we gave away. What use would we have for extra money? In Beyul there would always be food; you wouldn't have a care. And once you enter Beyul, you'll never leave. Who'd want to? Our tickets were all one-way. All tickets to Beyul are one-way.'

Dorje Wangmo laughed so long and hard it was infectious.

By the time they got to Tashiding—it took over two weeks to get there in those days—the lama had already left with his hundreds of followers to open the way. So they set off immediately, north to Mount Kanchenjunga. They stopped at Yoksum, the last village on the way, and bought enough food for the long journey: a sack each of ground corn, wheat and *tsampa*, the roasted barley flour the peoples of the high Himalayas never tire of eating. They wet the flour with tea and butter or sometimes just water, form it into balls of moist dough and pop them into their mouths.

Both the men she 'chose' for the journey, her husband and her monk-brother, were not really fit for mountain travel. They tired quickly, with the sacks of food they had to carry, the bedding and everything else. Their faith wasn't as great as hers. 'What was the weight of a bedroll,' she asked, 'when you were on your way to the Hidden Land? We had been waiting for generations.'

They found themselves on the edge of the snow. Though she was the woman, she went in front to cut the way when the snow came up to their hips. She even made steps in the snow for them.

They hadn't a clue what secret trails the lama had taken to find this hidden place, and the mountain was huge—stretching from Sikkim to Nepal and Tibet. Sometimes they came upon stones stacked on top of each other. They believed the lama left those stones to mark the way. So when they saw them, they followed them—and into the snow and windswept heights they went.

After a few days her monk-brother gave up and went back to Yoksum. He had begun to fear the heights, which made his mind play tricks on him and he began to have doubts. Now there was more for her and her husband to carry. They would take two of the sacks a kilometre ahead, hide them in a cave or cliff for safe-keeping and go back for the third. They also had with them a small bag of dried fish. But if they fried them in the fire they would smoke and the mountain gods would get upset. So they kept them in the bag in case of emergency.

The next day they met a Sikkimese couple who were felling a tree over a rushing stream to make the crossing. A baby was strapped to the woman's back. They were also looking for the lama. They had a donkey but hardly a handful of food, which impressed Dorje Wangmo greatly: only someone with tremendous faith would venture into such high mountains without food. It was because of this she agreed to continue their search together. They shared their food with them and put the sacks of food on the donkey, which made it easier especially since they had heard from some nomads that the lama was on the Nepal side—the mountain straddles the Sikkim-Nepal border—and they had to cross a high and snowy pass to get there. Soon they came upon others and yet others, all looking for the lama. The band of pilgrims became a dozen strong: three children, four women and five men.

They had to cross a glacier on their way to the pass and it became extremely dangerous. Deep cracks in the glacial ice were hidden under newly fallen snow. While they knew how to tell when the snow was hiding a crack, the donkey didn't. It stepped on to a thin layer of frozen snow and fell into a very deep crack. Held only by its lead rope it dangled over the deep, braying. Two of the sacks fell from the donkey's back and disappeared forever without a sound into the huge crack. They were able to rescue the third. It was the sack of tsampa. Then, with three of them pulling on its rope and two others grabbing its neck and legs, they were somehow able to haul the donkey to safety.

That night there was a huge snowstorm with a tremendous wind, and since they had no shelter they had to sleep huddled together beneath their jackets and blankets. They had nothing to eat but tsampa. Not even water. So they ate dry tsampa with melted snow in their mouths. Tsampa and snow—that's all they had.

The next morning they fanned out to search for shelter. Dorje Wangmo found a cave about a kilometre away into which they all could easily fit. They spent two days in that cave eating dry tsampa and melted snow while the howling wind blew blinding snow outside. The weather in high mountains, she explained, is controlled by the mountain gods, and they were clearly not happy with the intrusion of this band of human beings into their realm. They offered prayers to the gods, prostrated and burned incense.

On the third day, they awoke to sunshine. But the snow was so deep it was impossible to walk through, especially with the children. They hardly knew which way to go. Since their tsampa wouldn't last long, Dorje Wangmo decided some of them would have to go ahead and try to find the lama and his followers, or at least some nomads who could spare a little food. She chose the two strongest men to come with her. The newly fallen snow hid all but the widest crevasses, making the way all the more treacherous. They left before sunrise when the snow was the hardest and would be more likely not to give way. It was Dorje who chose the direction and broke the trail.

Tinley broke his almost simultaneous translation to interject his own observation. 'She's a powerful mother-in-law,' he said with a twinkle, 'a real warrior. Even her name Wangmo means The Powerful One.'

When they reached the first settlement in Nepal they heard that the lama and his followers were at a monastery farther down. He hadn't yet opened the secret cave. So they cut some grass for the donkey, filled a sack with cooked potatoes and climbed back over the pass to where the others were waiting in the cave. The next day, she led the others across the pass on the trail she had cut. It took two days for them to reach the lama. For a few months the lama was busy doing special pujas, or rituals, to appease the local spirits. Then he led hundreds of them high into the mountains in order to open what she called the Gate of Heaven.

With that she got up. To my amazement, night had fallen. A glance at my watch told me almost three hours had passed.

'That's how it was,' she said. 'If I were still young I'd show you the way. But now I can hardly walk. My legs hurt and my feet are swollen.' She bent down and rubbed her left knee and looked at her bare feet, gnarled with arthritis.

'Just look at my feet,' she said. 'See what time has done to them. And to think I was the one to walk in front and stamp down the snow! Now all I can do is pray.' She spun her prayer wheel, and muttering the mantra of Padmasambhava beneath her breath she left the room.

CHAPTER TWO:

Into the Rabbit Hole

'I became one of the lucky ones—
I reached my unattainable land.'
Carl Gustav Jung

When I stepped into the Gangtok night I felt elated. Just by being in Dorje Wangmo's presence, hearing her very real story, feeling the icy, snow-laden winds she described, I felt a longing awaken within me like a distant echo.

How extraordinary it is to actually meet someone with the courage not only to believe in a land of dreams but to leave everything behind for it.

'Only if you are willing to give up everything and leave forever,' she had told me, 'only then can you go to the beyul.'

Dorje Wangmo left her native Bhutan and never returned. She gladly gave up not only her possessions but was quite willing to say goodbye to everyone she had ever known, so infinitely greater was the place to which she was going.

I found myself at a high point in the city. Perhaps it was the altitude or maybe the lowness of the clouds that somehow made the sky seem more immediate, not entirely disconnected from where I stood. The firmament of stars seemed almost close enough to touch.

The moon shot free of the swiftly moving, tumbling clouds. Across a deep and broad valley rose ridges of thickly wooded hills. Ascending in the distance were the snow-clad heights of Mount Kanchenjunga. There, basking in the same silvery moonlight, were the very snowy slopes Dorje Wangmo had spoken of so vividly.

Maybe I was confounding the palpable detail with which she told her tale—vivid to the tiniest particular—for the reality of that which she sought but I felt the need to delve deeper into the story.

I went back to see Dorje Wangmo the next morning to ask if she knew of others who had gone with Tulshuk Lingpa on his journey to Beyul. She told me of two people who, in turn, told me of others, and eventually the search for those who set out for Beyul brought me to villages, monasteries and mountain retreats from Darjeeling and Sikkim in the eastern Himalayas to the western Himalayas and to Nepal. I met and spent time with most of the surviving members of the expedition, now mostly quite aged, as well as the lama's family. These extraordinary people, who gave up everything to follow their dreams, also gave freely of their time to tell me about what was for most of them the most extraordinary events of their lives.

℘   ℭ

The most important person with whom I spoke was Kunsang, Tulshuk Lingpa's only son. He provided the thread that wove together the story of Tulshuk Lingpa and his visionary expedition. Eighteen years old at the time his father departed for Beyul, Kunsang was able to offer a firsthand account of what others knew only from hearsay. Kunsang heard the stories of Tulshuk Lingpa's early life directly from him. One might expect—and even forgive—a son to exaggerate his father's deeds. But the details of his stories, no matter how fantastic, astonished me all the more by checking out when I asked others who were in a position to know. Kunsang's respect and admiration for his father was matched by his profound knowledge of Tibetan Buddhism. Deep respect did not preclude his seeing the humour and divinely inspired madness at the core of so many of the stories. With Kunsang alone I had almost fifty hours of taped interviews. When I transcribed these interviews, I was struck by the amount of time speech was rendered impossible by laughter.

I used to wonder just where to draw the line when Kunsang told his tales. Often I had the feeling he was leading me down a narrow plank over deepening water, drawing me further than

I felt comfortable to a place where logic failed. His stories often started out on firm enough ground but as the incidents built up and became increasingly fantastic, I'd suddenly find myself following with my credulity intact further than I would normally go. I would end up believing things that if told outright would sound just too fantastic to have occurred. Every time I thought Kunsang had gone too far, I'd find a corroborating detail in something someone else said. Or I'd check details of what others told me with him, and find an uncanny concurrence of facts even in the most outlandish stories.

With Kunsang, one got a taste of what his father was like, making reality of things usually relegated to the realm of fiction and imagination. He wasn't confounding fact and fiction as much as forging a new synthesis of the two.

We have been taught from the earliest age to separate fact from fiction. We can read *Alice in Wonderland* and get transported to a land of marvels. Yet while we are there, we know Wonderland doesn't really exist. By imagining it, we partake in the hidden realm of wonders the author imagined but we retain our sense of propriety. We don't redraw the line between fact and fiction; we suspend it, and we are entertained. That is certainly the prudent thing to do. We can assume it is what Lewis Carroll himself did. He could write his books about Wonderland and still maintain his position as a respected Oxford don.

Imagine what would have happened if Lewis Carroll had proclaimed the reality of Wonderland and launched an expedition? Surely he would have been thought mad as a hatter in the Oxford of his day as he would be today. The line separating fact from fiction is certainly tightly drawn and enduring—as tightly drawn as that which separates sane from insane. Cross one, and you cross the other.

℧   ℥

The first time I met Kunsang, I asked him the meaning of his father's name.

Kunsang told me that to understand the name Tulshuk Lingpa we had to go right back to Padmasambhava, the eighth-century visionary and mystic wizard often credited with bringing the dharma, or Buddhist teachings, to Tibet. Padmasambhava established the teachings by travelling through the high central Asian plateau, subduing the local deities belonging to the Bonpo (the indigenous religion of Tibet with strong shamanic elements), and turning them into protectors of the dharma.

Kunsang explained that Padmasambhava not only understood the past and had mastery of the present but could see into the future as well. He gave only the teachings that were right for the founding of Buddhism in that remote corner of the world in the eighth century. Other teachings that he knew would be better imparted at a later date, even hundreds or thousands of years later, were hidden by him. These hidden teachings are known in Tibetan as *ter* or *terma*, which means treasure. Those who find terma are known as tertons, treasure revealers.

Padmasambhava hid things like tantric scriptures. He hid certain ritual objects that, once found, would give tremendous powers. He hid great spiritual insights. But most important, Kunsang explained, he hid the secret valleys like the one in Sikkim—Beyul Demoshong. These valleys are Padmasambhava's most precious treasures, and the most difficult to find. Kunsang was both eloquent and enthusiastic about Padmasambhava's tremendous insights. Knowing the teachings of the Buddha would become endangered in Tibet, Padmasambhava also knew what would be needed and when. Some of the most important Tibetan Buddhist scriptures were protected over vast expanses of time in the changeless layers of a terton's consciousness. Terma remains hidden from the world until time itself ripens, until a particular terton takes incarnation and 'opens' it.

I told Kunsang I could imagine how Padmasambhava hid a text or even a *dorje*, the two-sided brass implement lamas use in rituals representing the thunderbolt. But when I told him I didn't understand how an insight could be hidden, especially a spiritual insight, he burst out laughing.

'You only *imagine* you can understand how Padmasambhava hid his texts! To be sure, he didn't just take a text and bury it in a cave or stuff it in a crack in a cliff. It wasn't like that at all.'

He explained how there are five places where Padmasambhava hid his terma. He hid some in the earth, this is known as *sa-ter*, he hid some in the mountains. This is *ri-ter*. Some, *chu-ter*, he

Kunsang, Tulshuk Lingpa's son.

hid in water, and yet others are called *nam-ter*. These are the treasures Padmasambhava hid in the sky. Others, *gong-ter*, he hid in the mind itself.

Hiding terma is one thing; finding it, another. As Padmasambhava hid each of the terma, he appointed a newly subdued 'protector of the dharma' to guard it and keep it hidden until that particular teaching, powerful object or insight was needed.

At the same time that he was hiding a terma in the world outside, he was also planting it inside, in the mind of one of his disciples. Not on the surface of his mind, the part that changes, that holds memories and is lost from one lifetime to another. He planted the knowledge of the terma in the unchanging layer of his disciple's mind, where the teaching would be protected.

What happens is this: when the time comes and a particular terma is needed, the right disciple takes an incarnation. He is a bit crazy. He has the ability to enter a mystic state and have revealed to him by a dharma protector or a *dakini*—a female messenger or guide—the teaching or empowerment given directly by Padmasambhava.

When a terton is given a scripture it isn't actually in the form of a book. Or not at first. Sometimes what the terton has revealed to him is only a few scratches on a stone. Other times he reaches his hand *inside* a stone and pulls out a tightly rolled scrap of yellowed paper. On it will be a few 'letters' in an alphabet only a terton can understand. He will then spend hours or even days without sleep, unfolding the meaning contained in those few characters, bringing them down—as Tulshuk Lingpa once said—from the Celestial Language into Tibetan.

Tulshuk Lingpa was a terton. Tertons are known for being crazy—and totally unpredictable. They are famous for being idiosyncratic and irrational, and by their very nature inscrutable. Illogical behaviour is their forte. They are expected to act in ways that defy the rationality to which the rest of us are bound. After all they reveal hidden treasures, and because of this they are especially revered among Tibetans and—like precious jewels—they are exceedingly rare. You cannot train to become a terton. You are born with the ability—or not. No amount of study can make you a terton. In fact, too much learning might very well take the ability right out of you. As William Blake wrote in his *The Marriage of Heaven and Hell*: 'Improvement makes straight roads, but the crooked roads without Improvement, are roads of Genius.'

Kunsang explained that his father's name was Tulshuk Lingpa. *Lingpas* are like the elites of tertons. 'They find special hidden treasures,' he said, 'therefore, they are especially crazy!'

'And the name Tulshuk,' I asked. 'Does that have significance?'

To understand that, Kunsang told me, we have to go back to Golok, north of Kham, in eastern Tibet. That is where his father was born. He was born with the name Senge Dorje, which means Lion Thunderbolt.

From the earliest age, Senge Dorje stood out as a particularly witty, intelligent and mischievous boy. He could learn despite hardly being taught. This made people suspect he was an incarnation, as often happens with boys who show special abilities. At a very early age he was sent to the Domang Gompa, a monastery in his native Golok, to be trained. This must have been in the early- or mid-1920s.

There was a great lama at that monastery known as the Domang Tulku, or reincarnation. That was his title. He was a lama who had taken reincarnation many times at the Domang Gompa, increasing his spiritual insight with each successive incarnation. His name was Dorje Dechen Lingpa. Being a lingpa, one of those rare elites of treasure revealers, he had the spark and could recognize it in the boy. He saw the boy's easy capacity for both learning and mischief. He observed that though he skipped most of his lessons, he earned the jealousy of his classmates by learning and being able to recite the ancient texts with only a single cursory reading. He began to suspect the boy had an extraordinary future ahead of him.

When the boy was at the age of losing his baby teeth, Dorje Dechen Lingpa decided to test him. He took Senge Dorje and half a dozen other young novice monks across the empty plain behind the monastery to where a chain of bare mountains rose abruptly in a series of huge cliffs. Leading them in a single file up the rock face along a treacherous way of loose scree and sheer drops, he brought them to a crack in the cliff that opened to a cave. There he sat in a circle with them in the cave's twilit interior and took out the implements of a lama's ritual life: the dorje, or double-sided brass implement that represents the thunderbolt; the *damaru*, or handheld drum made from children's skulls; and the *dilbu*, or ritual bell. Into a small brass bowl he poured a few handfuls of rice from an old leather pouch and placed it in the centre of the tight circle in which they sat.

Tibetan lamas chant sacred syllables at such a deep pitch you can feel the empty air between you vibrate. Imagine how much stronger the vibration would be if you're in a cave and tons of ancient rocks resound. If you're seven years old and an apprentice, learning both the reality of the Unseen and how to communicate with it, the lama appears to you like a wizard and the beating of his drum is heard in other worlds; then the ringing of his bell calls forth unseen beings. You sit—fear riding up your spine and spilling over into wonder and awe as the atmosphere in the cave concentrates and takes on form.

Dorje Dechen Lingpa performed a ritual that day that moved his young novices to a wide-eyed state of supernatural anticipation. When he had achieved his desired atmosphere, in which what is beyond sense reached the edge of the palpable, he took a handful of rice from the bowl. Intoning a single incantation, followed by a resounding silence, he threw the rice into the air.

In the ensuing silence the children gasped, in both fear and wonder, as the grains of rice turned into *purbas*, the daggers of Tibetan ritual, and danced before them floating and shimmering in the air.

The children all pulled back, faces marked by fear—except for one, Senge Dorje, whose face grew steady. He raised his hand and fixing his eyes on the purba closest to him, reached out and with a confidence born out of fearlessness he grasped it and held it fast.

The other children gasped in wonder and admiration at their comrade who had reached into a vision and brought back a piece; Dorje Dechen Lingpa simply smiled.

This is the story as Kunsang told it. Of course neither he nor I was there. Yet as with so many other fantastic stories in this remarkable tale, there is an element of truth in the apparent

Purbas, ritual daggers of Tibetan ritual, Ralong Gompa, Sikkim.

fantasy, a blurring of the line between fact and fiction out of which something tangible arises as if designed to make us question our assumptions. In this case it was the purba itself. For Kunsang told me that his father was to carry that purba in a cloth bag or tucked beneath his belt for the rest of his life.

When Kunsang was a young boy of eight or ten years, he used to sneak into his father's room in the middle of the night with some friends when thunderstorms were coming. Every night his father would stick the purba in a bowl of rice beside his bed, and there it would be—in the pitch-dark room—the tip glowing with the coming of the storm, sparking a moment before each bolt of lightning flashed in the sky. His friends would get so scared they'd want to scream and run away. But he'd grab on to them and force them to silence as the purba glowed and sparked next to his sleeping father.

The day after Tulshuk Lingpa got the purba, Dorje Dechen Lingpa took him on a long walk. 'I am sorry for taking that purba,' the boy said as soon as they were alone. He thought he was to be reprimanded.

Dorje Dechen Lingpa smiled inwardly.

'It's quite all right,' the lama said. 'In fact it is very good. Yesterday was a test, and you alone passed it. While I could manifest the purbas, even *I* couldn't have brought one down. The purba you brought down was nam-ter, sky treasure, treasure hidden long ago in the sky. That you got it means you are a terton. Let me see it.'

Tulshuk Lingpa had the purba tucked under his belt beneath his robes. He handed it respectfully to the lama, who examined it closely and told him to keep it safely for it would bring him much power.

Dorje Dechen Lingpa handed the purba back to the boy and spoke confidentially to him. 'I will be leaving soon,' the older lama said. 'I am going to Sikkim to try to open the way to Beyul Demoshong, the Hidden Valley where none has been. Thirty are coming with me. But the way is difficult—we must cross the plains of Tibet, braving highwaymen, cross the Himalayan passes south into Sikkim and then climb the slopes of the Mountain of the Five Heavenly Treasures, Mount Kanchenjunga. If I am successful I will never return and we may never see each other again. I want you to know something: There is a remarkable future laid out for you. You won't stay here but travel to distant lands. People from far away will know your name. If I fail to open the way, then you will be the one.'

Just before Dorje Dechen Lingpa set out on what proved to be his final journey (his attempt to open the way was unsuccessful and he was to die before returning to Golok), he presided over the coronation of the young boy at the Domang Gompa. He declared the boy a lingpa and bestowed upon him the name Tulshuk Lingpa.

Tulshuk means crazy.

৪০ ⳩

I used to go almost every afternoon to Kunsang's flat in Darjeeling to speak with him about his father. This was during a rainy monsoon. Kunsang lives with his family in the market above a restaurant, a low, one-room watering hole which was usually empty but for a few men drinking millet beer huddled around a table in the middle of which stood a single candle. Upstairs, the narrow hall that led to the doors that opened to Kunsang's flat would be pitch-dark. With water dripping from my umbrella, I'd feel my way down that darkened passage and rap my knuckles on the unseen door at the end.

Tulshuk Lingpa.

The room we met in was his bedroom as well as the family shrine and living room. Images from the Tibetan Buddhist pantheon and portraits of important Nyingma lamas draped with ceremonial scarves hung from nails along the walls. A TV stood in one corner, in front of the family altar, which glowed in the semi-darkness from the light of a single butter lamp. That lamp and the faint light coming through the windows were usually the only light by which we'd meet, for monsoon wreaked havoc with electrical lines. More often than not the electricity would be out in the whole of Darjeeling.

Kunsang would usually be sitting cross-legged on his bed when I arrived with an unbound Tibetan scripture open before him. He'd be chanting from the book, only briefly looking up as I came in to indicate the bolstered bench opposite where

I always sat. When through, he'd get up. Still chanting, he'd light a small fire of paper and wood in a convex pan that might have once been used to make chapattis, or flat breads. He would blow on it with a short pipe to get the embers glowing, then put into it the pine boughs known as *sang*, which let off billows of fragrant smoke. Opening the window he'd place the burning incense on to his neighbour's tin roof, which was immediately outside his window and protected from the rain by his own—such is the jumble of roofs in the Darjeeling market. All the while he'd be reciting a mantra while the white smoke merged with the low cloud in which the city had been immersed for days.

When he was through with his ritual, he'd carefully wrap the book in cloth, tie it with a coloured ribbon, stand up on his bed and tuck it into a shelf. Then he'd sit back on his bed with a huge smile, his gnome-like ears protruding from his head, and start laughing even before anything was said.

'So,' he'd exclaim, 'and *then* what happened?'

Over the course of innumerable afternoons he told me his father's story from beginning to end, sometimes starting at the end and working forward or backing me through fantastic episodes until I nearly knocked into reality.

Shortly after my arrival his daughter Yeshe, or more often his son Wangchuk, would arrive. They were in their twenties, spoke English well and took turns acting as my interpreter, thereby learning about their grandfather's life and the unusual way their father had grown up.

Tea would be brought by Kunsang's wife who often sat on the bed opposite and listened quietly to her husband's tales except when the story became just too funny, and we'd all be laughing with no way to stop.

Sometimes it was the Tamang Tulku, a boy of eight or nine, who brought us the tea. Tamangs are a Buddhist people from high in the Nepal Himalayas, near the Tibetan border. He was the *tulku*, or reincarnation, of a lama, though probably not a very high one. Because the Tamang Tulku was born into a family so poor they could not afford to put him in a monastery for special training, Kunsang agreed to take him on. Living with the family, he was a cross between an honoured servant, a son and a full-time clerk at the two clothing stalls they owned in a small brick shopping complex whose sign brazenly declared it 'A Shoppers' Paradise'. In exchange for taking him in in such a capacity, Kunsang was teaching him to read and write Tibetan, as well as giving him instruction in the dharma. It was only much later that Kunsang told me that the boy wasn't really a tulku, or reincarnation. I never could tell. After that I called him the Tamang non-Tulku.

Kunsang is a layperson; he does not shave his head nor does he wear a robe, except on special occasions when he wears the white robe of the tantric practitioners known as the *nagpas*. Yet he is considered by many to be a *rinpoche*. Rinpoche, meaning precious one, is the term Tibetans reserve for their high lamas. Kunsang is known as the *Dungsay* Rinpoche, the title used for the son of a high lama.

The special and almost mediumistic ability lingpas have to enter a timeless state and bring something back into time—be it a teaching in the form of ter, or treasure, or directions to a hidden valley—is often passed on from father to son. Tulshuk Lingpa's father Kyechok Lingpa had been the first in the line, and there was some expectation that Kunsang would follow. Having grown up as Tulshuk Lingpa's son, he certainly has the knowledge and experience and no doubt the education; yet Kunsang would be the first to say that he lacks that rare and special ability, which can only be given by fate and which defines the true lingpa.

Though not a lingpa, Kunsang's knowledge of the dharma—or Tibetan Buddhist teachings—is both vast and deep. Because of this, and because of his father, he has had much contact with and has taken initiation from some of the highest lamas of the day. Though devoting his life to a large extent to the dharma, he was also in business for many years. Now that his children and the Tamang Tulku have taken over the daily running of the family clothing stalls, he devotes himself even more fully to the dharma, with much of his day spent sitting cross-legged on his bed with an open *pecha*, or scripture, before him, white clouds of sang billowing to the heavens outside his window as he performs rituals for himself and his family as well as for others.

Many people come to him for teachings and to request him to perform rituals on behalf of the ill. He dispenses precious waters and other substances sanctified by ritual. Often when I arrived, there'd be others in the room listening to him discourse on some aspect of the dharma or making offerings so he'd perform a ritual for a dear one. At times, they brought sick people to him; he'd listen to symptoms, consult astrological calendars, dispense Tibetan medicines and herbal teas, and on the basis of the faith they had in him, offer them the strength to heal themselves.

Once, after the son of an old Tibetan man who was very ill had left with his little vial of blessed water, Kunsang said, 'What to do? When they come, I must do something. Though sometimes I'm busy, busy—too busy! My father was offered many monasteries. Me too. But I'm not interested. If you have your own monastery, when someone dies you have to go and do puja for the whole day. And not just one day. When people get sick, it's all the time people saying, "Rinpoche, hurry. Hurry!" And what to say? You have to go.'

Another time Kunsang said to me, 'The Tamang people told me, "You are very well educated and you are very good inside. You are a very high lama's son. So we are offering you our monastery." But I said "No, no, no."'

'This type of job—I don't like. But then they said, "Rinpoche, if you have a big monastery, you'll be a big lama with many disciples." That's what the Tamang people said. But one month has thirty days. With my own monastery, in all those days not one single day would be empty, not one moment free. This kind of job I find very *boring*.'

CHAPTER THREE

Eloping over Mountain Passes

Tibet, while maintaining its place on the map, has the reputation of being a hidden land of spiritual understanding. Though exaggerated in popular imagination, this reputation has been earned by Tibet's centuries-old vast isolation and the high attainment of its spiritual masters, considered by many to be the world's most advanced. Where better to look for a tradition of a hidden land than to that land which until recently has to the rest of the world itself been hidden? Arguably the most isolated country in the world until 1959, by its very isolation Tibet managed to guard precious pearls of ancient wisdom.

Within Tibetan tradition, we can distinguish between two types of hidden lands. One is known as the kingdom of Shambhala and, like all kingdoms, it has a history, including a known succession of kings and even a literature. Though the Kalachakra Tantra—one of the basic esoteric teachings of Tibetan Buddhism—came to Tibet via India, it is said to have originated in this hidden kingdom. Others, among them the Russian painter and writer Nicholas Roerich and his wife Helena Ivanovna, are said to have had communication with the Hidden Masters of Shambhala. The Masters are believed to be controlling the spiritual evolution of the planet from this kingdom, whose location has never been definitely pinned down. By most accounts it is hidden behind a ring of snow peaks somewhere north of western Tibet. It is believed the kingdom of Shambhala will have a definite role in the future of humanity.

When chaos, destruction and the forces of darkness threaten to overtake the planet, the king of Shambhala will lead a mighty force to eradicate the foe and found a reign of peace and spiritual enlightenment. Though many of Tulshuk Lingpa's followers referred to the land he was taking them to as Shambhala (and even Heaven, Paradise or Shangri-La), strictly speaking it was not Shambhala or any of these other places that he was speaking of. In the eighth century Padmasambhava foresaw times of tremendous darkness when greed would rule the planet and the teachings of wisdom and compassion would be in danger of becoming lost, when wars spread and poisons cover the earth, water and sky—times very much like our own. He saw the time when Tibet would be overrun by outsiders, and death and destruction would be their lot. It was with tremendous compassion and foresight for the people of Tibet that he created and then hid deep in the labyrinthine folds of the high Himalayas valleys of refuge, places of peace beyond the reach of the troubles that plague the rest of the earth. In contrast to the Kingdom of Shambhala, these are natural places, uninhabited valleys of tremendous beauty, cracks in the fabric beyond the spider web of the calculating Red Chinese or the industrialists' military might. They are beyond the range of spewing chimneys and holocausts of every description. It is even said that the time for the opening of these valleys comes when there is nowhere else to run. Some of these valleys have been 'opened', though others remain closed, having never been found. Such is Beyul Demoshong, the hidden valley in Sikkim.

Concepts about these hidden valleys vary, even amongst learned lamas. Some say that a person who is not spiritually advanced—someone without the karma to find or enter one—could climb into the high mountains, stumble upon one of these valleys and not even realize it. One could walk through a landscape that would be transformed into a place of miracle and wonder by a person of spiritual understanding, and notice nothing. William Blake once said, 'If the doors of perception were cleansed, everything would appear to man as it is, infinite.'

Tibetan lamas have been speaking of and attempting to enter Beyul Demoshong, the Hidden Land in Sikkim, since at least the eleventh century. They are quite specific. When they speak of the Hidden Land, they aren't speaking metaphorically, symbolically or of an exalted state of consciousness.

When I asked Géshipa, one of Tulshuk Lingpa's closest disciples in Sikkim, if the Hidden Land might actually not be found 'out there' but reside in the human heart, he responded with an incredulous look that spoke volumes about the gap in world views.

'What do you think?' he said. 'If the Chinese army marched in here and shot me in the heart, they'd be killing the Hidden Land?'

Let us be clear: the story of Tulshuk Lingpa and his expedition to the Hidden Land is not fiction or metaphor. Tulshuk Lingpa was no Oxford don maintaining his respectability while telling stories of an imagined land. He proclaimed a crack, and then actually set forth to step through it. If you think he must have been mad, then it was clearly no accident that the name Tulshuk Lingpa, Crazy Treasure-Revealer, was bestowed upon him at a tender age along with the prophecy that he would travel far and do great things.

හ   ශ

The second time I went to see Kunsang, the Tamang Tulku answered my knock and invited me in. Then he went down the lane to get Wangchuk from the shop to translate. They came back together. The Tamang Tulku went to the kitchen to make tea, and Wangchuk sat next to me and translated.

It was obvious that Kunsang had been thinking of what to say.

'Of course you are interested in my father's journey to the Hidden Land,' he said. 'But to gain a deep understanding of that, to understand his nature—why *he* was the one to lead the way, why he so easily gathered followers—you must know who he was. To know that we have to go right back to the beginning.'

Kunsang was sitting cross-legged on his bed. A fierce gale blew a thick rain-filled fog against the window behind him. The windowpanes rattled. He took a blanket, placed it over his knees and warmed to his subject.

'My father was born in Tibet,' he said. 'It was the year of the Fire Dragon, 1916. If you want photographs or records, of course you won't find them. The world in which he passed his childhood no longer exists.'

What he said was true. The distance between the Tibet of that day and the present is unbridgeable, a gap greater in this age of easy transportation than between any two points on the globe. In those days it probably would have taken weeks of arduous travel to go from Golok, his native place, to the closest place with regular communication with the outside world. Now you can probably get from New York to Golok within days but the Golok you would find would have nothing to do with the Golok of Tulshuk Lingpa's time.

The Chinese invasion of the 1950s destroyed all that. Even the people are gone. Of those who would have known him, many, being Khampas—renowned for their fierce resistance to the Chinese—wouldn't have survived the invasion; others survived by fleeing south over the Himalayas where they were scattered throughout India and beyond.

'What can we know of Tibet in the 1920s,' Kunsang said, 'but the stories our elders have told us? What I know of my father's early life, I heard directly from him and from his father Kyechok Lingpa. As his name indicates, my grandfather was also a lingpa—a treasure revealer. He was also based at the Domang Gompa, the monastery in Golok where my father was first tested and recognized by Dorje Dechen Lingpa.'

The Tamang Tulku brought tea, opened a tin of biscuits and sat cross-legged on the floor, his face eager to hear the story.

'Knowing my father,' Kunsang continued, 'I can only imagine that when he was a child it would have been difficult for anyone to set him on a narrow path of learning. He was sometimes found in the temple reciting esoteric mantras from memory when he was supposed to be in class. His teachers, though at first they didn't understand how this was possible, began to realize what Dorje Dechen Lingpa knew from the beginning: that Tulshuk Lingpa had an extraordinary destiny before him.

'My grandfather Kyechok Lingpa had two wives. His first wife's name was Kilo; we do not know his second wife's name. She never made it out of Tibet and it is likely she died at the hands of the Chinese.'

Lingpas often have two wives. The second wife is called a *khandro* in Tibetan—or dakini in Sanskrit—which translates to Sky Walker. She is something between a lover and an angel. Khandros are intermediaries between lingpas and the hidden realms they have special commerce with.

Tulshuk Lingpa was his father's first wife's only child. He had a half-sister and three half-brothers, his father's children by his second wife. One of these brothers was killed while being robbed by highwaymen in the high and lonely wilds of the Tibetan Plateau. Like many men from Kham, Tulshuk Lingpa's two other brothers were fierce fighters. They fought in the guerrilla army when the Chinese invaded in 1951. They were probably put in a Chinese jail from which they never emerged, a fate all too common amongst the Khampa fighters. In a futile attempt to oust the Chinese when they invaded Tibet, the American CIA started training the fierce Khampas in guerrilla warfare. Tulshuk Lingpa's halfsister Tashi Lhamo married a Tibetan man who was trained by the CIA. They escaped to Nepal and received asylum in France. Now they live and have homes in Paris, New York and Kathmandu.

Sometime in Tulshuk Lingpa's teens he left home. We know he went to Lhasa. Already, he was recognized as something extraordinary and had sponsors. Since most lamas don't work for their keep, they need sponsors to keep them. Tulshuk Lingpa had sponsors in Lhasa who were high officers with the Dalai Lama.

When Tulshuk Lingpa was about eighteen, he went to a monastery in central Tibet that was adjacent to a nunnery. Phuntsok Choeden, then a young girl, was not a nun but she lived in the nearby town, Chongay. She heard that a high lama had come to the monastery to give two or three months of Buddhist teachings. Tulshuk Lingpa was a handsome and charismatic young man with an air of magic about him. She begged her parents to let her go to the monastery to receive the teachings of this exotic lingpa from Golok. Her parents agreed, and she stayed there for about three months, by the end of which she was both in love with Tulshuk Lingpa and fired about the teachings she had received. She approached Tulshuk Lingpa as he was about to leave and told him she wanted to become a nun.

'It's not necessary for you to become a nun,' he said with a glint in his eye to the beautiful young woman who was to become Kunsang's mother. 'Come with me. Let's go together!'

This was not without its controversy, beyond the kind which might connect itself to any young couple deciding to run off together. To understand why, you have to know that Tibetan Buddhism is divided into four branches. The oldest branch,

closest to its Bonpo roots, is known as the Nyingma. Tulshuk
Lingpa was a Nyingma. Then there are the Kagyus, Sakyas and
the Geluks. The Dalai Lama is a Geluk. The young woman in
question, Phuntsok Choeden, was a Geluk. Her brothers were
high-ranking lamas at the Namgyal Monastery, the Dalai Lama's
own monastery.

'Did this create problems?' I asked. To understand what it
might mean for a Geluk to be involved with a Nyingma, just
imagine what it would be for a Catholic from a strict family to
run off with a protestant—say a Baptist.

'It wouldn't have mattered in the least to my father,' Kunsang
said. 'Such conventionalities didn't touch him. But it would have
caused a tremendous ruckus in their families. While his family
was a long and arduous journey away, my mother's was right
there. How could she explain to them that she wanted to run
away with this crazy Nyingma lama? No way! Eloping was the
only answer. They left together telling neither of their families,
travelling by foot over the high passes into India. Years later
in India when they met some lamas from the Dalai Lama's
monastery in Lhasa and asked about my mother's brothers living
there and if they were still OK, the lamas exclaimed, "You're
their sister? They thought you died years ago."'

The young couple walked south over the high Himalayan
passes into the hot plains of British India. This would have
been in the late 1930s. They moved east to west visiting the
principal Buddhist pilgrimage sites such as Bodh Gaya, where
Buddha stopped his search for a teacher and a teaching in order
to sit under a tree and examine his *own* mind until he reached
the awareness of enlightenment. They went to Sarnath, where
Buddha gave his first teachings in a deer park. Then they went to
the place in the western Himalayas that at the time was probably
the most important place specifically for Tibetan Buddhists in
India, a sacred lake called Rewalsar and known to Tibetans as
Tso Pema, in what is now the state of Himachal Pradesh but was
then part of the Punjab.

Tso Pema is sacred because of Padmasambhava. Before
Padmasambhava went to Tibet he went to Mandi, which isn't far
from Tso Pema, then known as the kingdom of Zahor. The king

of Zahor had a daughter so beautiful that maharajas from near
and far wanted her as their son's bride. Her name was Princess
Mandarava. Though the king was looking out for the best suitor,
she was drawn to the spiritual life and a life of asceticism. She
was not interested in any of the suitors her father presented
to her. Padmasambhava was a wandering ascetic—decidedly
not a suitable suitor for a princess. While passing through the

Tulshuk Lingpa,
his early days in India.

kingdom, he met Princess Mandarava and they fell in love. She became one of his two main consorts. When the king caught wind of it, he was not happy. He had his daughter stripped and wrapped in thorns and put into a pit by the river. He had Padmasambhava brought to a flat open place where he was put atop a pile of wood, which was then set aflame. Instead of perishing in the fire, Padmasambhava transformed the fire into a lake in the middle of which he appeared with his consort—the Princess Mandarava—sitting in a lotus blossom. The king was so impressed that he not only approved of their union but allowed his kingdom to be converted to the Buddhist dharma. It was after this that Padmasambhava went off to Tibet.

Tulshuk Lingpa must have been about twenty years old when they reached Tso Pema. Though he was young, he had already started to attract attention. At the monasteries clustered around the sacred lake and in the community of those who came there on pilgrimage—Tibetans and those of Tibetan origin from higher up in the mountains towards Ladakh—his spark was universally recognized. Wherever he went, people gathered who wanted to learn from him.

With thorough knowledge of the deities and all their aspects and a steady, artistic hand, it was natural that he became an accomplished thangka painter. Soon he had disciples to whom he imparted his prodigious painting skills. He was asked by the lamas of the old Nyingma monastery at Tso Pema to paint the life of Padmasambhava on the walls of the temple, an undertaking he devoted two years to.

He knew Tibetan medicine—the reading of the pulses, the use of herbs. He would perform rituals using a convex mirror made of brass and shined to a lustre in which he would see things no one else could see, and through this means he could heal people. People with epilepsy came to him, and he cured them. Wherever he went his reputation as a healer preceded him, and people came to be healed. While other tertons and high lamas would have to perform pujas many times to effect a cure, Tulshuk Lingpa would only have to perform one. It was believed that when Tulshuk Lingpa performed certain rituals many—even those in the surroundings who weren't at the ritual—would be healed. That was part of the shine that was upon him.

Having been initiated into many tantric teachings, he knew how to manipulate subtle forces—deities and demons—through ritual means. He could dispel curses, predict the future and even knew how to make and stop rain. Lay people came for his consultation; lamas came for teachings.

Kunsang explained to me that Tso Pema was a place of pilgrimage for Tibetan Buddhist people from Tibet as well as those from the upper valleys of Himachal Pradesh—Chamba, Lahaul and Spiti—which verge on Ladakh and the Tibetan Plateau. To reach these valleys one must cross dangerous passes, snowed in for much of the year. They are some of the most inaccessible places in India and—especially in those days—truly remote. Emissaries from villages in these high valleys, one more remote than the next, started arriving at Tso Pema with invitations for Tulshuk Lingpa to come to their villages and take over their monasteries. After refusing many offers, he agreed to go to a village in the Pangi Valley in Chamba district, and it was there he had his first monastery.

'He and my mother lived in Pangi for fifteen years,' Kunsang concluded. 'My sister Kamala was born there, and so was I. It is the first place I remember.'

The window behind Kunsang shuddered. The large wind-driven raindrops sounded like knuckles on the windowpanes. The cloud hit the window with a thud and it flew open. Kunsang sprang from where he was sitting cross-legged on his bed to close it.

Then he sat, dried his hands on an old face-towel and poured tea from the metal flask. The steam merged with the fog that now permeated the room.

'In this weather it is difficult to imagine the landscape of my childhood,' he said. 'Nothing could be more different from this cloud-heavy greenery. The valley in which I lived had hardly any vegetation: just steep slopes of stones, boulders and sheer rock faces rising to snow, glaciers and mountain peaks. The Chenab River, which originated in the high glacial peaks of Spiti, roared over huge rounded boulders in the valley. Above the village, on the valley's upper reaches, snow leopards stalked the wild blue sheep.'

Pangi was one of the most remote places in the Indian Himalayas. Travel in those days was by foot or by horse. It is a vast landscape and—at over 10,000 feet—the winters are harsh. The villages are few and become cut off from each other—not to mention the rest of the world—during the long winter. Life in the valley was as it had been for centuries. Whether administered by a local kingly chief, the British or independent India, what dominated life in the Pangi Valley of Kunsang's youth was metres-deep snow, avalanches and stony fields of barley.

'And for me,' he said, 'that landscape will always be imbued with my father's magic and his mastery of the ancient ways of mystics and tantrics. The world does not produce them any more.'

I was suddenly jolted back to the present again when another rainladen gust of wind blew open the window to reveal the jumble of fog-enshrouded roofs of the busy Darjeeling market. Dusk had fallen.

When Kunsang told a tale, I often felt transported to the particular plateau or mountainside he was describing. How many times did I put on my mud boots, feel my way along the pitch-black corridor, raise my umbrella to the incessant rain and descend the steep stone steps to the alley, every surface green with monsoon mould. Entering that sea of bobbing umbrellas, hemmed in between the narrow jostling alleys, it was as if I were returning from a distant journey.

I'd have a peculiar feeling, as if I were walking in two worlds.

CHAPTER FOUR

Behind the Heart of the Buddha of Compassion

Windswept Lahauli mountain peak.

One day Kunsang told me, 'My father always had followers, and always there were people who thought him mad.'

Tulshuk means crazy—but it also means fickle, mutable or changeable. So a man with a tulshuk nature would always be changing his mind—saying one thing in the morning, something else in the afternoon and contradicting both by evening. Though sober, he would get drunk, and when drunk he would act as if sober. Though a lama, he would have lovers, and when with them would still act as a lama. Though holy, he would be irreverent but while irreverent he would still retain his holiness.

One day while Tulshuk Lingpa was in Pangi, he was called by a *jinda*, or sponsor, to the village of Triloknath, also known as Karshapapa. It is famous for its temple which houses a historically important statue of Chenresig, the Buddha of Compassion.

The village was up the Chenab River Valley, a good day's journey away by horse. Lamas make their living by performing pujas, or rituals, often at people's houses. This was a big jinda, and the puja would last for days. Tulshuk Lingpa brought with him quite a few of his disciples, lamas in their own right who had gathered around him and now lived in his monastery in Pangi.

In addition to the good food that would be served to the lamas at such home pujas, there would also be quite a bit of alcohol. While smoking cigarettes was strictly prohibited for lamas, many drank. Tulshuk Lingpa was famous for drinking more than anyone else and still being able to function.

'One time, my father's disciples tested him,' Kunsang told me. 'They plied him with so much alcohol that anyone else would have passed out. They set him up straight and put a pen in his hand and a piece of paper on his lap. Though he could hardly see, he commenced to write the words from an important scripture from memory—the Tibetan letters perfectly formed and even. Every time his hand strayed from the page and he dropped the pen without even being aware, they'd put the pen back in his hand and put the tip where he had left off—and he'd continue writing. To everyone's amazement—including my own—he missed not a single letter or vocal mark. The words were formed perfectly across the page.'

This was a theme Kunsang returned to repeatedly: his father's drinking and subsequent craziness. Although I never saw Kunsang drink, his father's prowess at drinking was an endless source of wonder and laughter for him.

'Two of Tulshuk Lingpa's closest disciples, Namdrol and Sookshen, were with him at the jinda's house in Triloknath that time,' Kunsang continued, warming to his story. 'The jinda was plying them with meat and drink that night, and Tulshuk Lingpa got particularly drunk. He called Namdrol and Sookshen aside.'

'"Tonight, we have big work to do," he told them, "*big* work—but don't tell anyone. We'll have to stay awake half the night, so first you must sleep." He produced a bottle of the jinda's liquor and got his two disciples so drunk they curled up in a corner and fell into a death-like sleep.

'At two in the morning, when everyone was fast asleep, Tulshuk Lingpa got up. He shook his two disciples to wake them but so much alcohol was still coursing through their blood they would not stir. He shook them harder but still couldn't rouse them.'

With this, Kunsang sprang from where he sat on his bed and jumped to his feet. He lay on the floor, curled up no doubt like his father's drunken disciples, except that instead of sleeping he was shaking with laughter. Demonstrating with his own fist on his own skull, he continued his story from that vantage point.

'My father made a fist of his hand and rapped on their shaved skulls as if he were pounding on a door, their heads resounding like coconuts.

'Like this,' he said, and he knocked his skull as if he were knocking a door.

Chandra River Valley, Lahaul.

'This did the trick, and in a snap they were sitting up. Tulshuk Lingpa's finger to his lips reminded them of the secret nature of their rude awakening.'

This was a story Kunsang particularly loved to tell, and it must have been a dozen times that I saw Kunsang like this: lying on the floor, cracking his knuckles on his head and then rolling with laughter. He utilized pantomime, humour and dead seriousness in turn—and often with blinding speed.

Kunsang sprang back up, and like a conjurer he was suddenly sitting cross-legged on his bed. He continued: 'They followed silently, so not to wake the village dogs, and reached the village temple. Tibetan Buddhist temples and holy places have paths around them the faithful use to circumambulate, always in a clockwise direction, and recite the mantras. Called the *kora*, it is an important part of their daily life and ritual. They followed Tulshuk Lingpa, stumbling in the darkness, doing a kora of the ancient temple. The entire time Tulshuk Lingpa was looking at the temple wall. They circled the temple once; they circled it twice. The third time Tulshuk Lingpa stopped at the back of the temple and examined the temple wall.

'"I'm drunk," he said to his two disciples. "So you must help me. Last night in my dream I was visited by a dakini. She told me to look behind the heart of Chenresig."

'What the dakini's cryptic instruction meant, and how to fulfil it was up to his own tulshuk nature to figure out. That was his crazy genius.

'"Where do you think the heart of Chenresig would be?" he asked his disciples. He was referring to the Buddha of Compassion, whose statue inside the temple was on the altar on the other side of the mud and stone wall he was examining.

'Namdrol said, "Well, the statue is in the centre of the altar, and it is so big. His heart would be here," and he pointed to a place on the wall. Sookshen said, "No, I think the statue is a bit bigger than that. It would be up there," and he pointed a bit further up.

'"You're both wrong," Tulshuk Lingpa said, picking up a stone. "It would be here!" and he scratched out a circle on the dry mud wall. "Get a hammer, something we can smash the wall with!"

'"But Master," Sookshen gasped, "this isn't our temple. We can't just smash the wall."

'"Get me something to smash the wall with!"

'"But Master, where can we find a hammer? It's the middle of the night."

'While Sookshen was thus arguing with Tulshuk Lingpa, Namdrol knew what to do. He had been with Tulshuk Lingpa longer and knew that when a terton tells you to do something, you do it. You don't ask questions—no matter how tangential to logic his request might appear, no matter how irrational. He went around to the front of the temple and got the thick iron rod that was used to bar shut the temple door.

Statue of Chenresig,
Triloknath Temple.

'When he returned to the back of the temple, Tulshuk Lingpa commanded him to smash the wall.

'So he did. With one blow of tremendous force, Namdrol hit the centre of the circle Tulshuk Lingpa had drawn with the stone, and a huge chunk of the wall crashed to the ground.

'Namdrol dropped the bar with a clang, shocked at the damage his single blow had caused.

'Sookshen looked around to make sure no one had witnessed this act of vandalism.

'Tulshuk Lingpa looked into the hole as if he were looking not into a mud wall but into a hole in reality itself, his eyes as fierce and fearless as when he was a child and had grabbed the purba in the cave in Tibet. He reached into the hole and took from it a tiny rolled piece of yellowed paper. It was the size of the tip of your little finger.

'"Ter," both Namdrol and Sookshen gasped.

'Tulshuk Lingpa unrolled the paper and on it were a few

"letters", scratches really, of an alphabet only a terton could understand.

"'Now I have work to do," Tulshuk Lingpa said. "Fix the hole. You have till daybreak. No one must know what has happened here." With that, Tulshuk Lingpa left.

'Namdrol and Sookshen mixed some earth with water from a nearby stream to make mud, which they used to patch the hole in the temple wall. They smoothed their work, and then threw a layer of dust on it to hide its recent construction. Just as the sun was tingeing the sky with pink they fell asleep—exhausted—beside the temple, which is where villagers found them a little later as they came to do their morning kora of the temple.

'My father didn't sleep that night. The light was on in his room right past the time of the rising sun which he hardly noticed, so engrossed was he in unfolding the meaning contained in those few obscure letters of a language only he could understand. It took some days for him to fully unfold the meaning of the scratches found on that ancient and tiny scroll. When he was through, he had produced two pechas, or scriptures, of 300 pages each. Coming directly from Chenresig, a great and glorious heart, they told about the ending of suffering.

'What happened to this book?' I asked. 'Do you have a copy?'

'No, I don't,' Kunsang said. 'The original text, in my father's own hand, was hastily written. So he gave Namdrol the first book for him to make a copy by hand lettering it in proper Tibetan. Namdrol copied it and when he gave it back, my father gave him the second to copy. When—after a month or two—Namdrol hadn't finished copying the second book, I remember that my father became angry.

'Though I was only a boy at that time, I was curious. I went to where Namdrol was living, and he was sitting there—cross-legged on a cushion with a low table before him, copying the text. I asked him in all innocence what it was that he was copying. "I'm not supposed to tell anyone," he said, "but since you're the master's son, I can tell you. It is a very important ter that your father found," and then he told me the whole story I just told you, of the ter in the temple wall.

'What he didn't tell me was why he was taking so long to copy the second book and get it back to my father, though the truth finally did come out. After he had begun copying the second book, he had been approached by some Khampa lamas who were living in Dharamsala and had money in their pockets. They were after some of my father's ter. They said to Namdrol, "Tulshuk Lingpa has spent so much time here, he must have taken out some ter. Tell us about the ter he has taken out."

'Namdrol said, "I heard he took out some ter in Tibet but I don't know; I wasn't there."

'"Come on," they said. "Tulshuk Lingpa is such a high terton; he must have taken out ter here. Show us what you've got!"

'Only when they made it clear that their request was backed by money did Namdrol tell them about the ter he took out from the temple wall. But he said he couldn't show them.

'They pleaded with him. "Come on! Namdrol, please ..." they said. But he was not so easily persuaded to betray his teacher and his secret text. It was only when they offered him 35,000 rupees—a fortune at that time—that Namdrol's resistance crumbled. He agreed not only to show them the Chenresig ter but to make them a copy. It was because he was secretly making this second copy that he was taking so long to get my father's copy back to him. After he gave my father his copy, along with the original, he tried to get the first volume back but my father refused. The Khampa lamas never got that first volume.'

'What happened to the copies that Namdrol gave to Tulshuk Lingpa?'

'They're now at his monastery in Lahaul,' Kunsang said.

'And the originals, in Tulshuk Lingpa's own hand?'

'The originals were stuffed into a statue of Chenresig and placed into a stupa, or reliquary memorial, where they are to this day—high in the stone and snow mountains of Lahaul.'

The phone rang; Kunsang picked it up and began to speak with a relative of his wife's in Sikkim. This gave me some time to think of his story. When he hung up the phone and placed the needlework doily back on it, I asked him a question I knew was rather delicate but I had to ask. I was careful to pose the question in such a way so as not to imply doubt on my part.

'The ter your father found in the temple wall was hidden by Padmasambhava in the eighth century, right?'

'Yes,' Kunsang said, 'Very mysterious, crazy!'

'Surely the monastery in Triloknath is old,' I ventured, 'but it isn't *that* old. It took some time for Buddhism to spread to such outlying areas as Lahaul. I know that readers of this book, especially Western readers, will ask how ter hidden by Padmasambhava in the eighth century could be hidden in the wall of a monastery that was built much later, long after Padmasambhava had died.'

'The monastery in Triloknath is *extremely* old,' he said, suddenly—and for the first time since I knew him—serious. He eyed me cautiously, as if maybe I were no longer to be trusted.

'What do I tell the readers ...?'

By the tone of his voice and the look on his face I could tell he saw my point and wasn't completely satisfied with his own answer. The hypothetical Western readers needed what he didn't: an external measure of truth, one that could stand the test of doubt.

'There are 108 tertons,' Kunsang said curtly. 'They all have the same powers as Padmasambhava. One of them must have put it there.'

As if to at once put an end to that discussion and to proclaim the supremacy of madness, Kunsang jumped from his bed, lay on the floor and cracked his knuckle on his head with such force that it resounded like a coconut.

CHAPTER FIVE

Invasions and Incarnations

Each time I arrived at Kunsang's with my tape recorder, pen and paper he would get an impish smile, burst out laughing, and say, 'And *then* what happened?' But his question was clearly rhetorical. It was obvious he had been thinking of what story to tell me next. His stories weren't often linear but there was an internal, often logic-defying thread that strung the incidents of any given story together and wove the stories themselves together into a coherent whole. Since the stories of Tulshuk Lingpa's life all culminated in his setting forth for the Land of Immortality, every incident seemed designed to loosen the rational mind from its moorings.

Kunsang explained that with time, Tulshuk Lingpa's role was not just as head lama of Pangi. Not only would people go to him if they needed advice or to know their future, or if they were sick, possessed by spirits, needed a name for a child, or to learn painting and writing. People from one end of the valley to the other would come to him also to settle disputes. They would present their cases before him and ask for justice. He was the man with the best connection to the secret hidden lands of spirit and mystery from which magic and divine guidance came. Since his judgments had the authority of an oracle, his decisions were beyond dispute.

As Penzom, Kunsang's younger sister, told me in Kathmandu, 'We call the highest ranking man in the military a general; in the same way, we call the highest of the lamas a lingpa.'

One day, Tulshuk Lingpa was called upon to switch roles when a man came riding into the village on a fast steed from Klaath, a village further down the valley where the Chenab River falls through a series of gorges to Kashmir and it becomes even more rugged and lonely.

'The Muslims have invaded,' he declared as he jumped from his horse. 'They have come over the Such Pass. We must mount an army, go up the valley to Klaath and beat the Muslims back. If we don't stop them, Pangi will be next. We need at least one man from each household.' He told this to some villagers, and together with them he came to Tulshuk Lingpa.

Avenues other than open warfare are available to lingpas when it comes to overcoming foes. The Nyingma lineage (the oldest in Tibetan Buddhism) to which Tulshuk Lingpa belonged centred more on Padmasambhava than on the Buddha, whose teachings Padmasambhava brought to Tibet. Padmasambhava was a wizard and a sorcerer. He didn't go to Tibet to convert the people, using missionaries, trinkets, guns, crosses, scriptures, ideas or threats of eternal hell.

His first line of attack was on the spirit level utilizing ritual.

In an ancient tradition such as the Bonpo, which Padmasambhava came to supplant, there are both benevolent and malevolent entities—with and without bodies. There are worlds we cannot see with our natural eyes. The priests of this tradition pass between worlds, communicate with spirits, intercede on our behalf and fight brave battles in realms most people outside such a tradition would call pure imagination. Padmasambhava resembles more a shamanistic wizard than what we'd normally associate with the Buddha as he is understood in other Buddhist traditions.

Christ is the example for Christians, and the goal of Christian religion is to become more Christlike. Buddhists of the Southern School emulate Buddha by following his teachings on meditation and following a clean, simple life. In the religion of the Nyingmas, the oldest branch of Tibetan Buddhism, Padmasambhava is the example the lamas emulate. They too act as wizards, performing rituals in order to make contact with hidden realms. They too make war by fighting the malevolent entities that stand behind that which manifests here in three dimensions.

True to this tradition, Tulshuk Lingpa mounted his first offensive against the Muslim invasion by performing rituals. He called upon the deities of his tradition to fight off the Other. But it didn't work. News still came from down the Pangi Valley towards Klaath that the Muslims were coming over the Such Pass. So finally Tulshuk Lingpa said, 'I've done the rituals but they haven't worked. Now we have no other choice. If the Muslims really want to fight, we'll have to go up the valley and fight!'

That's what the man from Klaath had wanted all along. 'That's right,' he said. 'We need at least one man from every house!'

'No we don't,' Tulshuk Lingpa said. 'We must attack the Muslims but we don't need an army. We'll beat them back with only five or six of us.'

'How can we?' the others cried. 'We'll be outnumbered. We have no guns.'

'Guns are not needed!' Tulshuk Lingpa said. 'Bring your axes and your tree-cutting saws. That's all we'll need.'

Crazy as they thought he was—leading them into battle with axes and saws against an army of heavily armed Muslims—they went, only a half-dozen of them, to fight off the invaders.

The trail followed the river at the bottom of the rugged valley. When the valley narrowed to the point where both the river and the trail were pressed between two perpendicular rock faces, Tulshuk Lingpa led the way up a treacherous cliff towering over the narrow path and told the others to cut down some old, wide-girthed trees. They limbed them and left them in long sections. They found huge boulders and, leveraging them with long poles, moved them to the edge of the precipice. They left the logs teetering over the edge, awaiting the nudge that would send them and the boulders down on the invading troops. There they waited, camping at the top of the ridge.

The invaders didn't come.

After three days Tulshuk Lingpa told the men, 'I'm going back down to the trail. When I find the invaders, I'll lure them beneath the precipice. When I whistle like this,' and he whistled the call of a bird that is only found in Tibet, 'let the logs and boulders fly!' Thus saying, Tulshuk Lingpa went down into the valley. After a day and a night, not as much as a local man did he see or hear.

He called the others to come down, and when they gathered with him by the river, Tulshuk Lingpa said, 'They must be holed up in Klaath. We'll march up there and rout them out.'

'But master,' they said, 'there are only six of us. They will kill us!'

Tulshuk Lingpa knew no fear and, as if it were a test of their faith in him, they followed Tulshuk Lingpa without weapons of any sort down the stony valley to Klaath.

When they marched into Klaath—five terrified men following their white-robed general—they didn't see a soul. The village appeared deserted. Everything was locked up tight, abandoned. It was only when they heard a baby cry that they realized the population of Klaath was in hiding behind locked doors, quaking with fear, defenceless against the Muslims. Each household feared the Muslims were hiding in the next house or in the neighbouring shop, whose door was shut.

Tulshuk Lingpa himself called at each door, and those that wouldn't open to his call he kicked open with his own foot. He took rocks and smashed locks and opened every door in the village that wouldn't yield to his command. In such a way, the village came to know that the Muslims had completely deserted the village and that they were free. The only doors Tulshuk Lingpa wasn't able to make yield were the government offices', whose doors were fortified. It was only when the entire village gathered at these doors whooping with joy because they were free from the Muslim menace did the officials crack their doors open and peer out. When they saw the people gathered around Tulshuk Lingpa, they asked who he was. 'This is our guru from Pangi taking a break for war! This is our guru—now Major General!'

The people threw garlands of wildflowers around Tulshuk Lingpa's neck. The government officials mustered a marching band and they paraded their saviour through the market to let everyone know they were free. When it was over, they asked Tulshuk Lingpa if he would stay on in Klaath for a few days.

'We are afraid the Muslims were only here on a reconnaissance,' they told him. 'We fear they'll come back with greater numbers.'

'We have come here for war,' Tulshuk Lingpa called out over the crowd. 'Now that the war is over, we will perform rituals!' and so saying, he led the entire community through three days of rituals. The Muslims never came back.

ဆာ   ငာ

It is generally agreed that Padmasambhava planted within the unchanging layer of selected disciples' consciousness the knowledge of particular terma, as well as where and how to find them. So the following question naturally arises: Which of Padmasambhava's disciples was Tulshuk Lingpa the reincarnation of?

I put this question to many people close to Tulshuk Lingpa, and though they all had definite opinions, their opinions differed and there was no consensus on the most basic questions such as the number of disciples Padmasambhava had, how many of them might have ended up as tertons, how many of *them* were part of the elite known as lingpas. Rigzin Dokhampa, the senior researcher at the Namgyal Institute of Tibetology outside Gangtok with whom I spent a lot of time asking questions of doctrine and who was also a disciple of Tulshuk Lingpa, told me there were twenty-five lingpas and that Tulshuk Lingpa was the incarnation of one named Lang Palgyi Senge. When I checked this out with Kunsang, he told me flat out that Rigzin Dokhampa was wrong, and that Dorje Dechen Lingpa had *perhaps* been Lang Palgyi Senge's reincarnation. He told me that Padmasambhava gave the prophecy that Lang Palgyi Senge would be the one to have the power to open Beyul Demoshong. Others say there are a total of twenty-one beyuls. But Kunsang told me with tremendous certainty that Lang Palgyi Senge said there were eight and that Dudjom Rinpoche, Tulshuk Lingpa's root guru, was destined to open Pemako. Pemako is a beyul east of Bhutan where the Tsang Po River, after crossing Tibet, falls through a series of gorges and becomes the Brahmaputra. 'The reason Dudjom did not open Pemako,' Kunsang informed me, 'was that he was such a cautious lama. He wasn't crazy—like my father. He had the opposite nature.'

Supplying numbers for such things as the number of hidden lands or disciples of quasi-mythical beings, I found, is not a very fruitful activity. You might as well try to determine how many angels can dance on the head of a medieval pin.

Another time Kunsang told me, 'There were eight emanations of Padmasambhava, and Nyima Odser was the last. Nyima Odser said, "After me, there will be 108 tertons." Dudjom was one of the 108. It is said that at the end of time, at the time of the Great War, Dudjom will take incarnation as the king of Shambhala and lead the battle that will usher in a great age of peace.'

Once when Kunsang was trying to explain to me his father's nature and the meaning of tulshuk, he said, 'My father was just like the eighth emanation of Padmasambhava, Guru Nyima Odser. Nyima Odser was like a sadhu, a wandering holy man, never staying in one place. He was not a stable type of person. He was a crazy yogi like my father. And like my father, he drank a lot.'

The story goes that one time Nyima Odser was riding his horse across the vast Tibetan Plateau when he spied the black felt tent of an enterprising nomad who had set up a little drinking establishment.

Nyima Odser stopped his horse and started drinking chang, the thick, milky, butter and cheese millet beer of Tibet. After he'd drunk quite a few, the proprietor became nervous. A wild-looking lama riding out of the vast plane with eyes like a tiger's and now drunk beyond all measure was sure to try to pull something when it came to paying the bill.

Nyima Odser called out for another chang. 'Not until you've paid for what you've drunk,' was the proprietor's response. Though the sun was still high in the sky, it was arching towards the horizon, which in Tibet seems infinitely far away at the edge of the vast plateau, which serves as the roof of the world.

'Give me that chang and keep it flowing,' Nyima Odser said, 'and I swear on my faith in the Buddha and all the bodhisattvas that I will pay my bill the moment the sun goes down.'

The proprietor agreed, having little choice after the lama put such an oath on it.

What the nomad did not know was that Nyima Odser was an emanation of Padmasambhava and that he held control over almost everything, including the sun. In fact, his name translates to Golden Sunlight. He also didn't know that Nyima Odser had no money. He gave the lama another big bowl of chang. The lama drank it, ordered another, and while he was waiting, performed a little rite accompanied by an incantation.

As the afternoon seemed to drag on for some uncountable number of hours, the nomad had to keep supplying chang to the increasingly drunk lama; the poor man had no idea that Nyima Odser had used his mystic powers to stop the sun in its course across the sky in order to delay the moment of reckoning.

That night, night did not come. Nor did it come the next day, when the fields already started to parch. Soon the crops began to wither. It seemed to the nomad that all the moisture in Tibet was going down his customer's throat.

The highest lamas, soothsayers and oracles of Tibet gathered to divine the hidden reason the scorching sun was stuck in the sky. Their divination led them right to Nyima Odser, who was enjoying his chang outside the nomad's tent. They asked him why he had stopped the sun.

'I have no money to pay for my drinks,' he explained. 'If the sun goes down, I have to pay; that was my oath.'

When they offered to pay his bill Nyima Odser ordered one last bowl and then released the sun, which immediately fell to the horizon like an overripe cherry, releasing the land of Tibet from its grip.

'Each of the 108 tertons of Guru Padmasambhava has the power of Nyima Odser.' Kunsang concluded. 'But not all of them were as crazy as my father.'

'You say your father wasn't the incarnation of Nyima Odser,' I said. 'Do you know anything of your father's previous incarnations?'

'Verrry good question!' Kunsang said, 'Verrry interesting!'

'I told you that I was born in Pangi, where my father had his first monastery,' Kunsang began. 'Until this point, my father knew nothing of Beyul Demoshong. Yes, he was a terton, a revealer of hidden treasure. He could reach into a vision and bring back a magic dagger. He could be directed in a dream to a hidden scroll. But he was also a village lama, and as such was often asked to perform rituals in people's houses. Sometimes I'd go with him. I was young, and I'd ride in front of my father on the same horse, hanging on to the horse's mane as we negotiated narrow trails along vast stony slopes running with water from the melting snows above. Once I went with him to a house up the valley in the direction of Patanam. A few lamas from his monastery were with us. I loved going along to see new places and to be with my father. Many things happened in his presence that happened nowhere else. Being the son of a high lama, I was always treated with special deference. Even his lamas treated me with respect.

'When we were heading home, some villagers from further up the valley were going the same way, so we travelled together. We stopped for lunch by the river and were then enjoying the warmth of the mid-summer day, when someone asked my father whether he remembered anything of his previous incarnations.

'"In my last life," Tulshuk Lingpa said, "My name was Kyaray Lama. My monastery was up the valley, and my end came early.

'"An old man had fallen ill down this way, and every day I went to the man's house and performed the rituals to restore his *la*, or vital essence. The family had many fields and animals and kept me coming for over a month. Every day I'd ride my horse down the valley to this house, and every evening I'd return, usually quite sleepy from both the exertion and because of what they gave me to drink before leaving. But my horse was faithful and knew the way. Though I dozed on her back, she always brought me back home to my monastery.

'"Along my way the valley grew steep and narrow. Nobody lived there but an old woman in a house surrounded by a few meagre fields. The trail crossed through her fields, and every day she grew more and more angry at my intrusion, shaking her fist at me as I passed and shouting abuses. There was no other way up the valley. It did not matter to her that I was wearing a lama's robes.

'"One day the old woman had had enough, and she decided to kill me. After I had passed up the valley to perform my pujas, she dug a huge pit right in the middle of the trail. She covered it with branches and dried grass and waited for me to come.

'"What she didn't know was that I had secret insight. I knew what she was going to do, and that I would die. Yet I chose to let her kill me. I knew that after I died she would be so repentant that she would become a hermit, devote herself to the dharma, and reach enlightenment. I chose to sacrifice myself to her enlightenment.

'"Sure enough, there I came after nightfall. My sponsors had given me chang, and I was dozing atop my horse when suddenly the horse's foot crashed through the grass-covered branches and we tumbled into the pit. Somehow the horse was able to get back on its feet and jump out of the pit unharmed. I was killed instantly. The old woman rolled a rock on top of me and filled in the pit so no one would ever know. Then she took the branches to her house, cut them up and burned them to stay warm that night."'

Kunsang got a nostalgic look on his face.

'I still remember how it felt,' he said, 'sitting on a stone by that rushing river, the horses grazing in the background, surrounded by the other lamas, and to hear my father tell the fate of his previous incarnation. I was filled with wonder.

'Since we were coming back from a sponsor's house, we had many bottles with us; my father and the lamas were all quite drunk. One of the lamas asked him, "Master, could you still find the spot where this happened? It would be a great place of pilgrimage for us. We should do a puja for Kyaray Lama!" The others were enthused by the idea, and Tulshuk Lingpa agreed.

'"It isn't far from here," Tulshuk Lingpa told them. "Let me see if I can find the spot."

'So we packed up our lunch and went down the valley. My father rode in front; I sat in front of him on his saddle. When we got to a narrowing of the valley, my father looked around. He started speaking about fields and the old woman's house, how it was years ago and how they were now all gone. Then he jumped from the horse. He started circling the area as we all watched.

'"This is the place," he exclaimed of a stony area covered in brush. "Here!" he said. "This was the woman's house."

'Sure enough there was the stone foundation of a small house all in a tumbledown state.

'"The fields were there," he said, "and the trail went this way." He started walking into the undergrowth. Then he sat cross-legged on the ground. We stood some distance off, watching. He closed his eyes, and for a few long minutes he did not move. Then he suddenly got up and took fifteen large and deliberate steps. "Here," he said. "Dig here."

'Some of the villagers who were travelling with us had tools for digging their fields strapped to their horses' backs. They got them and set to clearing away the brush and digging a hole.

'"Wider," Tulshuk Lingpa said. "Dig deeper."

'They dug for half an hour, the men taking turns, until they came to a huge flat stone that they could only find the edges of by digging the pit wider.

'And when they'd done so, Tulshuk Lingpa said, "Turn the stone over."

'But they couldn't. It was too heavy.

'There was a village not far away. A fast horse and rider were dispatched, returning an hour later with half a dozen young men with big iron rods, and together they were able to turn the stone over.

'To our great amazement, on the underside of that stone was the imprint of the dead lama. He had died with his hand on his hip and his elbow sticking up, which was clearly impressed in the stone.

'They hoisted the rock out of the pit and set it on edge, propping it up with smaller stones. They lit pine bough incense, took out their malas, or Tibetan rosaries, and reciting the mantra of Guru Padmasambhava they circled the stone in deep reverence for my father. It is rare someone can remember a past lifetime.

'Later, my father had Lobsang write down the story of his previous birth and how he had died. Lobsang asked him how long it should be, and my father said it should be only seven or eight pages.'

'What happened to that book?' I asked.

'I do not know,' Kunsang said. 'Perhaps Lama Tashi has it. He's now the head of my father's monastery.'

'Have you ever been back to that spot?' I asked.

'No, but my aunt, Tulshuk Lingpa's younger sister, Tashi Lhamo—the one whose husband was trained by the CIA to fight the Chinese and who now lives in Paris and New York—took a journey a few years ago to the Pangi Valley in order to see this stone. She found the place but the stone had been moved. Kyaray Lama's monastery was further up the valley, and the monks of that monastery had moved the stone there. She heard that the stone was so heavy they had to break it into seven pieces, carry them on the backs of horses, and then reconstruct it. Unfortunately the way to the monastery was difficult, and my aunt was too old to make the journey.'

CHAPTER SIX

The Place of the Female Cannibal

The Place of the Female Cannibal,
Simoling [Telling], Lahaul.

There is no external mark of a truly spiritual person. You'll recognize it not by whether he or she wears a robe or a business suit, a turban or a baseball cap. How versed he is in the scriptures or whether he knows the rituals has nothing to do with it. It doesn't matter whether he eats meat or not, takes his rest on Saturday or Sunday or whether he spends his days in devotion or in the office. The mark of a person who is spiritually advanced is that he or she has natural and spontaneous compassion.

Compassion is not what the people of Telling were receiving from their neighbours in surrounding villages, who had renamed their village Simoling. Kunsang explained to me that Simoling is a Tibetan name. It translates to the Place of the Female Cannibal. It was thus renamed because people from every household in the village—perched on a steep rocky slope with glaciers above it and a roaring boulder-strewn river below in the high Himalayan region of Lahaul—found their fingers, toes, ears and noses being slowly eaten away and disappearing, the open sores refusing to heal. We would call it an epidemic of leprosy. To the people of Lahaul, it was the work of an unknown spirit who was slowly eating the villagers' flesh because of some unknown transgression against the spirit world. Outsiders believed that if you slept one night in Simoling you would awaken in the morning with a little piece of you having been nibbled away. People ceased going to the village; they would pass by it only in broad daylight.

The modern Western world view allows for unseen agents of disease in a realm invisible to the common man. This realm is visible only to specialists using specialized instruments in places marked out for such investigations. The Buddhist people of Lahaul also have their specialists: the lamas, who, like doctors, ascribe the origin of disease to realms as hidden to the layman as doctors with their microscopes and microbes. While the scientist prepares his slide for viewing in the laboratory, the lama prepares his mind for receiving the understanding that will allow him to ascribe cause to a disease.

While a Western-trained doctor would dismiss spirits as a cause of disease, he might very well be able to demonstrate to a lama the role of microbes in a disease such as leprosy. While the lama would be quite capable of understanding the physical role of microbes in disease, he wouldn't see the microbe as its root cause. He would ask a further question: Why was this particular person or community being affected at this particular time? To answer that, he would make investigations in the hidden realms he was conversant in, the realms of spirits and demons.

In the late 1940s and early 1950s, when the people of Simoling found their limbs and facial features being eaten away, it was a very remote place. To reach the village one had to cross the 13,000-foot (4000 metre) Rohtang Pass on foot or on horseback. In Tibetan, Rohtang means Plain of Corpses. Snowstorms are known to suddenly appear out of a blue sky and swoop down on the pass with the suddenness and deadly fury of a gang of mounted brigands, leaving frozen corpses and livestock in their path. This can happen any month of the year. There was no motorable road crossing the pass, let alone a clinic or health care as we know it on the other side. The steep, rock-strewn valley was cut off from the rest of the world during the six-month long winter in which travel even to neighbouring villages was impossible. The people of Lahaul lived such isolated lives that people in neighbouring villages, sometimes a kilometre away, often spoke languages that could not be mutually understood. They lived a life closer to the time of Padmasambhava than to the world of today, with mountains inhabited by gods and dramas being played out in spirit worlds that could only be understood and controlled by their 'technicians of the sacred', the lamas.

When I went to Lahaul to investigate this story, I met a man from Simoling in his early sixties by the name of Chokshi. He grew up watching his relatives being slowly gnawed away by this flesh-eating disease. Though he hadn't yet been affected, people close to him—his uncle, an aunt and many cousins, as well as uncounted neighbours—had. Many of those who hadn't yet awakened with a piece of their flesh missing abandoned their houses to the elements and fled. Desolation vied with despair. Hope was an early casualty. Even the monastery perched on the rocky slope above the village had been abandoned by the very ones who could have helped them, the lamas.

Chokshi never considered leaving. Deciding not to wait until he saw his own flesh disappear before his very eyes, he set out to find help. He went up the valley to Kardang—near the district headquarters of Keylong—to consult with the highest and most respected lama in the valley at the time, Kunga Rinpoche.

Chokshi recalled for me what happened.

'I walked up the valley to Kardang, and there I made an of-fering before Kunga Rinpoche. I told him why I was there, that so many in my village were having their limbs slowly eaten away, that we were being isolated and no one wanted to come close enough even to talk to us. The lama listened carefully, and he said he would do a *mo*, or divination, to see what course we should take.

'From the voluminous folds of his robe he produced a weathered bag, inside which there was a wooden box. He took the lid from the box to reveal two ancient bone dice. He intoned a prayer, blew on the dice, shook the box and let the dice fall on the low table before him. Noting the result on a scrap of paper with a pencil stub, he threw the dice again. He took from his shelf a pecha—a Tibetan scripture wrapped in silk cloth—and consulted it. He marked things on the paper, threw the dice again and consulted another pecha, all the time noting things on the paper. It was a full half hour before he spoke.

'"The situation in your village is extremely serious," he told

Chokshi of Simoling,
the Place of the Female Cannibal.

me, "and fraught with dangers. I am afraid it is beyond my powers to help you. But there is a high lama at the monastery in Pangi. His name is Tulshuk Lingpa. My divination shows that only he can help you."

'I had never heard of this lama, or of Pangi.

'"Where is Pangi," I asked the lama, "and how do I get there?"

'"Pangi is a two-day march from here," he told me. "But you won't find him there now. Go to Tso Pema, and look for him there."

'I'd heard of Tso Pema—Rewalsar as it's

known locally—the lake sacred to Padmasambhava. I'd never been there. In fact I only knew my village and the town of Manali, the first town in the low country just over the Rohtang Pass. Who had time to travel in those days, even on pilgrimage? But now the fate of my entire village depended on me. All of my limbs were still intact but I knew it was only a matter of time. I set out immediately for Tso Pema. Since I had no money for the bus, I walked. It took me five days.

'When I arrived in Tso Pema I asked for Tulshuk Lingpa, and someone told me to look inside the old Nyingma monastery. When I went inside, I found only a Tibetan man sitting on a scaffold putting the finishing touches to Chenresig, the Buddha of Compassion, which he was painting on the wall. He was dressed in street clothes. When I asked him for Tulshuk Lingpa, I thought he must have misunderstood me when he told me it was him I was looking for.

'We expected our lamas to be dressed in robes and to have shaved heads. Instead, he had long black hair, which was braided with a piece of red cloth and wrapped around his head as is the style of so many Tibetan men. He wore a regular pair of pants and an old shirt, both of which were spattered with the bright colours with which he was painting the gods, demons and Buddhas on the monastery wall. But there was something in his eyes; they penetrated me like two burning coals. I knew immediately that he could help my village.

'I told him I had come from far away, and that Kunga Rinpoche had sent me. Even before asking what it was about, he put his brushes into a glass of murky water and brought me to his "home". At that time he had two young children, Kamala and Kunsang. I'd never seen anything like it: he lived with his wife and children in a cave on the sharp slope above the lake. I had heard of lamas and yogis living in caves but never with their families! I was a little afraid of this man with burning eyes, the air of a great yogi and clothes of an ordinary man. One always had the feeling with him that there was more to him than he revealed.

'Phuntsok Choeden, his wife, brought us tea. Sitting on the stone floor of his cave, his kids climbing on his lap, he asked why I had come. I told him about the dire situation of my village and how Kunga Rinpoche had performed the mo and declared that only he could help us. He listened carefully, and I sensed in him a compassion that would bridge the fear that everyone else felt of even stepping foot into my village. Though his monastery in Pangi was down a side valley from Simoling three or four days' walk away, he had heard of my village and knew well why people

Tulshuk Lingpa with his ritual implements.

feared setting foot within its precinct. Without hesitation, he agreed to come. In his wife's silence I felt her fear. I knew that silence well, the silence of those who feared the dreaded disease but were too polite to voice it. It was quite natural: we felt it ourselves.

'I started the return journey to my village that day. Tulshuk Lingpa waited a few days, then took his family over the Rohtang Pass and sent them on to Pangi.'

'After having been shunned and isolated and having helplessly watched the limbs of our parents, our uncles and aunts, brothers, sisters and—finally—ourselves slowly vanishing into festering wounds, Tulshuk Lingpa's arrival gave us the hope we'd lost when this malady first arrived. His compassion enabled us to have compassion for ourselves.

'The disfigured despise themselves; the horror of someone else's leprosy gets turned on oneself when one wakes up one day and it is one's own nose that is vanishing in an open wound. A face without a nose is no less horrific if it is one's neighbour's than if it is one's own face in the mirror. We had forgotten how to love ourselves.

'And then this lama did what no one else had dared: he actually came to our village. We knew we were grotesque. We knew, when we gathered around him—fingers, hands, forearms, elbows, feet, knees and legs, noses, ears and lips in various stages of decay and disappearance, slowly eaten by festering wounds— we knew and felt for ourselves the horror of the sight. Like a doctor arriving at an accident scene, he showed not the slightest horror at our disfigurement, handling our wounds and trying to heal them with Tibetan medicine. He climbed the mountain behind the village to the monastery and moved in. We could hear the drum and human thighbone horn at all hours of the day and night. At first the rituals he performed didn't stop the course of the disease. So he went into a meditational retreat and he came out some days later having had a vision of Nagaraksha, the king of the *nagas*, or serpent gods.

'He sent someone to get his close disciples from his monastery in Pangi, Lama Namdrol, Lama Lobsang and Lama Mipham. They were very learned men. They collected the materials needed to make a sculpture, and for the next few days nobody saw them as Tulshuk Lingpa sculpted this demon king and Lama Lobsang painted it.

'When they were through, word spread through the village that we were to gather at the monastery. Tulshuk Lingpa told us the cause of our disease. Nagas, the serpent gods, are found—like serpents themselves—at springs and wet places, where trees and grasses and wildflowers grow. In Lahaul, you can tell a spring from a long way off; springs are the only naturally green places in our otherwise barren landscape. He told us that the nagas were angry at the village because the villagers had cut all the trees at the village spring and used them to construct houses. It was true. Shortly before the first of us had a sore that didn't heal and the disease started eating our bodies, greed had come over us and we had cut the trees at the spring.

'"Cutting trees at a spring," Tulshuk Lingpa explained, "puts the earth out of balance and causes disturbances in the spirit world. Your disappearing flesh is the result of the nagas' anger. It is because of that we now have the demon himself, Nagaraksha, before us."

'The sculpture was every bit as horrific as the disease itself. When I saw it,' Chokshi said, 'I shuddered. The demon sat on a lotus pedestal resting on a seething mass of serpents. Instead of legs, he had a coiled snake's tail over which he wore a tiger skin. His skin was blue, and he had snakes draped over his neck and wrapped around his arms. Nine out of his eighteen hands held snakes; the others held knives. A flayed human being was slung over his shoulders. All you could see were the feet and the legs' empty skin slit down the side. He had three tiers of heads adorned with human skulls, and the heads of snakes poked out everywhere.

'"Until now," Tulshuk Lingpa said, "the leprosy has been eradicating you. Now we will eradicate the leprosy!" So saying, the lamas started a ritual—the intensity and length of which the people of Simoling had never experienced. The chanting went on day and night as the lamas called on and mollified the angry spirits. Drums pounded, cymbals crashed, and the clarinet-like *gyalings* sounded through the night. They constructed a huge *kyilkhor*, or sand mandala, on a platform that took four people to carry. Tulshuk Lingpa drew the design on the platform and the other lamas constructed it, "painting" it with different-coloured sands. Huge caldrons of food boiled on wood fires to feed the lamas and the assembled villagers.

'The ritual lasted ten days, and when it was through, Tulshuk Lingpa called for all of us villagers to gather. He told us to bring whatever hunting rifles we had, and together we marched down to the river. The lamas brought with them the sand mandala.

'They placed dried grass on the mandala to set it aflame but before anyone could light it, it burst into flame by itself. The people were amazed and deeply moved, and they were saying, "Our lama is not crazy. This is not a drunken man! He is very powerful, most powerful!"

'Then the lamas tilted the platform and poured the sand mandala into the mountain torrent, shooting their rifles into the air and whistling shrilly as they did so to send the demons off that had been eating our flesh.

'"From this day on," Tulshuk Lingpa told us, "no leprosy will come to this village. There is nothing to fear!"

Base of Tulshuk Lingpa's sculpture of Nagaraksha,
Simoling Gompa.

'Then the people said to him, "You have sent the demon away. Where have you sent it?"

'"I have sent it to Afghanistan," he said. In Afghanistan there is a place called Simoling connected to the life of Padmasambhava.'

So it was that the flesh-eating spirit was eradicated in Simoling, and the leprosy that had been slowly eating their limbs disappeared. Their wounds healed, and no one else was affected. When I went to Simoling and surrounding villages to do research for this book, I was frankly sceptical that ritual could eradicate leprosy. All the older people remembered the incident. Every one of them attested to its truth.

The people of Simoling were so grateful that they all gathered at the monastery to show Tulshuk Lingpa their respect. The representative of the village's thirty households got up.

'We used to have sixty or seventy households,' he told the lama, 'but entire families have died of the dreaded disease you just cast out from our land—others fled. Now there are only thirty households left. With you here, we feel confident the demon will never come back. Without you, we are afraid. Therefore we would like to give you our monastery, Samdup Choekorling.'

Producing a paper stating as much, a member of each household pressed his right thumb on a pad of ink and left his print on the deed. Those without a right thumb used their left. One man used the big toe on his right foot. It was all he had.

Tulshuk Lingpa sent a horse and rider to Pangi to bring his family to Simoling. He never once returned to Pangi, despite their repeated entreaties.

CHAPTER SEVEN

Sacrifices, Sponsors and Caves

It is difficult to pin down exactly when Tulshuk Lingpa moved his family to Simoling. People in the mountains remember years by the recurring zodiac animal signs (the same twelve signs the Chinese use) but they tend to remember different things. Once I asked an old lama his age and—after thinking long and hard about it, doing calculations on his fingers—he confessed his uncertainty and said he was either eighty or ninety-two. When I asked people in Simoling when Tulshuk Lingpa moved there, I got contradictory answers. My own guess is that it was sometime in the late 1940s or early 1950s.

Kunsang remembers when they moved to Simoling, though not the year.

'I was a young boy,' he said, 'perhaps seven or eight, though I'm not really sure. All I know is that I was old enough to feel afraid of moving to this village of lepers.'

Kunsang's fear was short-lived, based on an image of the past and not on the reality of the present. For by the time he and his mother—and sister Kamala who was two years older—arrived by horseback from Pangi, the leprosy of Simoling was already a thing of the past. Though the evidence of the demoness-goddess's presence in the village was indelibly imprinted on the bodies of so many, the wounds all healed and the fear the entire valley felt towards Simoling was turned to a tremendous respect for the man who had delivered them from a fate that could have been their own.

Tulshuk Lingpa's reputation began to spread. People came from far away to be healed by him. When I asked one old man who knew Tulshuk Lingpa in those days what he thought it was that gave Tulshuk Lingpa such healing abilities, he said it was his great compassion. Lamas, too, came for his teachings, and soon the Simoling Monastery—which had been reduced to a population of one, a caretaker—was a thriving community of yogis and tantric practitioners drawn to this charismatic and learned visionary mystic. Those who had fled the village began to return; the thirty households that the village had been reduced to swelled to sixty or seventy.

Though the people of Simoling were followers of Tibetan Buddhism, they also worshipped local gods, one of whom demanded the bloody sacrifice of live goats. He is known as King Gephan. So twice a year—in May-June, and at the end of September—the people of Simoling sacrificed two goats. One of the things that distinguish Buddhism, especially the Mahayana tradition of the Tibetans, from the other religions of the region is the concept of compassion for all sentient beings. They do not perform animal sacrifices.

When Padmasambhava went to Tibet to spread the teachings of the Buddha, he had to overcome the native Bonpo religion's custom of performing animal sacrifices to appease and curry favour with the gods. Teaching them compassion for all sentient beings, Padmasambhava substituted the sacrifice of live animals for objects made of dough and mud (sometimes even painted red to represent blood), as well as flowers and bowls of clear water. In much the same vein, Tulshuk Lingpa introduced a new ritual to the village, which transformed the age-old practice of blood sacrifice into one that offered vegetable sacrifices, flowers and water. This ritual is performed in Simoling to this day, and as one lama from the monastery told me, 'We used to sacrifice four goats a year. That was over forty-five years ago. So we've saved over 180 goats.'

King Gephan is represented by a long wooden stick that is covered with multicoloured pieces of cloth. Once a year, this god is carried through the valley in a colourful procession. It makes stops in the various villages, some of which are Hindu and others Buddhist, and the people offer it live goats. This procession no longer makes a stop in Simoling but I was told that every year as it passes by the village a piece of cloth miraculously flies off the stick and blows towards the monastery as a sign of respect.

While in Simoling, Tulshuk Lingpa introduced the *Cham*, or Lama Dance. He not only stitched the costumes but sculpted the masks. He also wrote the scripture that described the dances in which the lamas don masks and costumes and play out various stories of the spirit worlds and the realms between death and rebirth. He also instituted the khandro dance in which women and even children took part. Four to five hundred people from up and down the valley would come to Simoling to watch these dances.

Namdrol, the lama who smashed the hole in the monastery wall and then sold a copy of the ter Tulshuk Lingpa found there, also learned Tibetan medicine from Tulshuk Lingpa and became famous for his ability to work with the pulses and perform cupping and bloodletting. He was one of Tulshuk Lingpa's closest and most learned disciples.

Kunsang recalled that during the lama dances, Namdrol always played the wrathful deity. He would sit cross-legged in the centre of the courtyard with his purba raised while the others danced around him. Tulshuk Lingpa would be sitting on his throne on the roof of the monastery, looking down. He would give Namdrol a sign, and Namdrol would dance once around the courtyard and sit back down. During the times of the year when there were no dances, Namdrol was known for walking down the

Two masks carved by Tulshuk Lingpa, Simoling Monastery, Lahaul.

road acting his role of the wrathful deity. He'd scare the children, then howl with laughter.

'Mipham, who was also from Lahaul, was another of my father's closest disciples,' Kunsang told me. 'He was a great practitioner of *Chod*.'

Chod, which literally means 'cutting' or 'chopping', is practised in dangerous places, like the charnel grounds at night, places where one is in constant reminder that life is fleeting. The Chod practitioner goes to the cremation ground, where the souls of demons and the dead roam. With the help of a drum, bell and horn made from a human thighbone, he calls to these beings and he visualizes his flesh being cut from his bones. He then offers his warm flesh and blood to the demons and for all who need the nourishment his body can provide. It is a profound practice of selflessness, a short road to realization.

Kunsang told me, 'When Mipham first came to my father he said, "Please guide me and teach me the rituals and understanding that will help me at the time of my death. Please help me, so I can also guide others towards non-attachment at the time of death."

'Lamas' lives are filled with ritual. It is what people expect of them; it is how they make their money. My father was in high demand, especially to do the *yangdup* puja.'

Yang means prosperity, and dup means accumulation. It is a puja lamas perform on a sponsor's behalf to help that sponsor accumulate and protect his wealth. To collect yang, prosperity, one has to collect it from different directions, levels and realms using tantric powers. It will even protect the wealth you already have.

Kunsang explained: 'Say you have a blanket. If you don't have yang, it will be of no use to you. It will get easily lost, or it will not keep you warm. Like that. So people call the lamas in to perform the yangdup puja. The higher the lama, the better and more powerful he is. My father was in constant demand to perform this puja.'

'After a while,' Kunsang concluded with a look of disdain on his face, 'I think this life of puja is very boring. That is why I don't like this kind of work.

'Mipham also didn't like this work. He used to ask Tulshuk Lingpa not to send him around to do pujas in people's houses for money. He was only interested in performing rituals for the dying and the dead. Whenever someone died, Tulshuk Lingpa would send Mipham to conduct the rituals.'

ജ   രു

Winters in Lahaul are not easy. When the snow began to fall in November or December, the Lahaulis would be entirely cut off from the outside world. For upwards of five or six months, deep and blowing snow often rendered travel to neighbouring villages impossible, let alone travel over the treacherous Rohtang Pass at over 14,000 feet. Therefore the more affluent people in Lahaul had second houses in the lower altitudes, in the comparatively lush Kullu Valley where they would go before the Rohtang Pass was blocked by snow.

Today, the situation is much the same, though recent prosperity has led to more people having houses in Kullu. There is even helicopter service between Lahaul and Kullu operated by the Indian army once every two weeks throughout the winter months. Earlier, winter was the time of almost endless local festivals and religious celebrations, which brought villagers together. Most villages in Lahaul now have only a few people staying in them for the winter, rendering life there even more isolated. Electricity has entered the valley and along with it television satellite dishes. Though as isolated from neighbouring villages as ever, they are now part of the 'global village' that stretches from Bollywood to Hollywood, skipping pretty much everything in between.

Shortly after Tulshuk Lingpa and his family moved to Simoling, he was offered a place to winter in the Kullu Valley. Until he left to open the way to Beyul Demoshong over a decade later, he and his family would spend winters in the village of Pangao in the Kullu Valley, and summers in Simoling.

Tulshuk Lingpa's sponsor, or jinda, in Pangao was known as Jinda Wangchuk. He offered Tulshuk Lingpa and his family a place to stay, and the place he offered was on a cliff towering over the Beas River. To be more exact it was the cliff itself, or rather a fissure in it—a cave in which Jinda Wangchuk paid to have walls of stone and wood constructed. He also flattened the floor. So it was that Tulshuk Lingpa spent winters with his family in a cave. It was a wild place, of eagles and snakes, a treacherous ten-minute walk along a razor-thin trail below the village of Pangao.

Tulshuk Lingpa and Jinda Wangchuk, Sikkim, early 1960s.

Kunsang told me that when Jinda Wangchuk would come to his father, he'd always have two bottles of liquor in his pockets. He used to say, 'One for the master, one for me.'

'Even though I was only a boy,' Kunsang said, 'I'd say to Jinda Wangchuk, "One bottle for my father, yeah. One for him but one for you—no. Me, you, half-half." Then Jinda Wangchuk would say, "Why not?" and share his bottle with me.'

In the course of writing this book, I found myself below the village of Pangao, crossing the cliff face to the cave where Tulshuk Lingpa and his family lived over the course of a decade.

Following a monk who beat the grass and bushes before us with a long stick to flush out any cobras, I negotiated the treacherous, razor-thin way. My heart was beating to the rhythm of vertigo, my mind reeling with the consequences of one slip of the foot (a deathly plunge into the raging Beas River flowing like a ribbon of shining mercury far below). I couldn't help but smile at the sheer divinely inspired madness of the man who would move his young family to such a place.

Kunsang recalled for me how twice a year they would make the three-day journey over the Rohtang Pass from Pangao to Simoling and back again. His mother and father each rode a horse and the kids walked, though they took turns riding when they grew tired. Following the caravan route, they made the yearly migration from their high summer home to their winter home when the sheep and goat herders were driving animals over the Rohtang Pass to and from their summer grazing grounds on the high slopes of Lahaul. Therefore they often travelled surrounded by huge herds of sheep driven by herders dressed in heavy white woollen robes tied at the waist. Sometimes they would stop with

Tulshuk Lingpa lived in a cave along these cliffs.
The monastery didn't exist in his time. Pangao, Kullu Valley.

the herders as their dogs circled their flocks and drank tea with them in the crisp and thin mountain air.

During these years, when Tulshuk Lingpa and his family went from Simoling to Pangao and back again, these two places became magnets for many of the great yogi lamas of the day. Some were obscure, others famous, and yet others were to become so. Some came as his disciples, others as his equals.

One of these Tibetan lamas, who was one of the great yogi practitioners remaining from the Tibetan tradition, was Chatral Rinpoche. He used to visit Tulshuk Lingpa in Pangao, and spent one winter in a neighbouring cave on the same cliff face.

Tarthang Tulku was twenty-five when his native Golok was taken over by the Chinese. He fled to India, where he ended up in Lahaul, at Tulshuk Lingpa's monastery. He travelled with him to Pangao as well, and later lived in a monastery down the valley from Simoling in Keylong. He then went for further studies to Sarnath. After that he moved to America where he started the Tibetan Aid Project, which helps Tibetan refugees as well as the Nyingma Institute and Dharma Publishing, which has published and distributed millions of copies of Tibetan texts.

Herbert Gunther, the well-known German scholar of Tibetan Buddhism, also spent time with Tulshuk Lingpa. Kunsang remembers that when Dr Gunther came to the Kullu Valley to pursue his studies of Tibetan religion and scriptures he stayed at the house of a big landlord who was a former colonel in the Indian army and a sponsor of Tulshuk Lingpa. He had bungalows in Manali, Kullu and Keylong. This thakur, or landowner, introduced Gunther to Tulshuk Lingpa. Gunther recognized Tulshuk Lingpa's great learning and, while probably not becoming a disciple, was his student for quite some time in both Pangao and Simoling.

'My father was always joking,' Kunsang told me. 'He used to say that because Dr Gunther didn't need a translator, he was a tulku, an incarnation. Gunther was very good at reading and writing Tibetan, though sometimes my father would help him with his grammar. To me, Dr Gunther was very old, though if I think back he must have been only forty-five or fifty. He would write his questions out in Tibetan, and my father would answer them.'

Tulshuk Lingpa's cave in Pangao; below, the Beas River.

Tulshuk Lingpa (R) with
Chatral Rinpoche.

Temple Painting depicting lama
and consort 'opening' secred cave.
Tashiding, Sikkim.

CHAPTER EIGHT

The Call

Kunsang had brought me through this much of his father's story when he suddenly said, 'Up to this point there was nothing *unusual* about my father.'

The cup of hot tea the Tamang Tulku had just handed me almost slipped from my hand, which so amused Kunsang that it took him some time to stop laughing enough to explain: 'My father was a terton, of course. He had that ability—but so have many others since the time of Padmasambhava.'

I got his point, which was one of perspective. Tibet has, after all, produced many highly developed mystics.

'Up to this point,' Kunsang continued, 'if you were writing a book about my father, what would you have described? A few incidents, the finding of ter—but others have found ter. He led an army but there have been wars since the beginning of time and no lack of people to lead them. If that were all, if he had gone on being a village lama, you wouldn't be writing a book about him.'

I had to nod my head in agreement, and wonder what he was getting at.

'My father was gifted in many arts,' Kunsang said, 'not least of which was healing. As a visionary, he communicated between worlds. Whatever he did, there was a shine. Yet up to this point, his life's work hadn't even been announced. Each terton has his particular set of treasures to uncover—be they texts, teachings or objects of great strength. Few, even among the tertons, have the destiny to discover a Heaven on Earth.

'Until now, my father had shown a tremendous ability to communicate with the hidden world of the spirits and to intercede in hidden processes for the benefit of those who came to him. His actions were marked by a sense of compassion. He developed fully the nature of the name that Dorje Dechen Lingpa bestowed upon him. Yet what was changeable and unpredictable in his outward behaviour, what appeared inconsistent, capricious and erratic, was but the outward appearance of a man whose mind was attuned to other things, and who was a visionary.

'Despite being a visionary who was tuned to the inner world to a greater degree than most, he was not oblivious to the outer world, not even to the world of politics. For shortly after the Chinese invaded Tibet in 1951 and marched through his native Golok, in eastern Tibet, on their way to the Tibetan capital of Lhasa, stories drifted like a miasma over the mountains from the Tibetan Plateau beyond, stories of the massacres and suffering caused by the invasion. He immediately foresaw the consequences—the Chinese takeover, the carnage, the smashing of the monasteries, the imprisonment of monks and lamas and the flight of the Dalai Lama.

'In fact, Tulshuk Lingpa predicted troubles for the fourteenth Dalai Lama twenty years before he fled. This was before my father came to India, when he was in Lhasa with lamas from the Dalai Lama's monastery. The present incarnation of the Dalai Lama, the fourteenth, was yet to be found. Tulshuk Lingpa told these lamas that he didn't think when they found the boy that the boy's future would be good. "Shut up!" they said. "You mustn't speak like that about His Holiness." Some years later, those same lamas found themselves in exile along with the Dalai Lama. Tulshuk Lingpa ran into one of them in India and asked if he remembered his earlier prediction. Pressing his palms to his forehead and bowing, the lama silently acknowledged both Tulshuk Lingpa's foresight and the tragedy of its coming to pass.

'Tulshuk Lingpa saw the deteriorated condition of Tibet first hand when he returned there to rescue his parents. With a few of his closest disciples, among them Namdrol and Sookshen, he travelled across north India to the Kingdom of Sikkim and crossed the Nathula Pass to the Chumbi Valley in Tibet. They went to Dromo, where his parents had been waiting with two nieces and a nephew for five months.'

Tulshuk Lingpa's father, Kyechok Lingpa, was a formidable character. A lingpa himself—wearing the white robes of a nagpa, his hair twisted in a huge bun on top of his head—he had been part of the Domang Gompa and had never had a monastery of his own. Now he received his own *gompa* in Patanam, a few days' walk up the valley from Simoling. His wife, Kilo, was no less formidable. In Kunsang's words, 'She was huge, like a woman from Iraq—Iran.'

It was in October or November some years later that Tulshuk Lingpa and his family were in Simoling getting ready to make their yearly migration to Pangao when they got word that Kyechok Lingpa had died. Tulshuk Lingpa and his family went by horse to Patanam and Tulshuk Lingpa oversaw the cremation of

Tulshuk Lingpa (R) and his father, Kyechok Lingpa.

his father. When the death ceremonies were through, he brought his mother back with him to live in Simoling and Pangao. Though his father's followers made countless requests for him to come to Patanam to perform rituals there, he never returned. 'If you need help,' he told them, 'you can always come to Simoling.'

The Chinese invasion of Tibet affected Tulshuk Lingpa profoundly. Not only did he see it for himself when he went to get his parents but with the continual flood of refugees from Tibet coming through Ladakh and Lahaul on their way to Kullu and beyond, he heard of the increasingly dire conditions. The dharma itself was in danger. The Chinese were smashing monasteries and torturing lamas, throwing them into jail and killing them.

To a yogi and mystic such as Tulshuk Lingpa, the most important thing is having the time and space to do spiritual practice. Tibet, with its vast isolation and empty spaces, had been a natural place of spiritual attainment; it had produced many of the world's most highly developed mystics who had handed down and preserved an ancient tradition of attaining spiritual understanding and *bodhichitta*, loving kindness. In the isolation of the cliff face in Pangao and in the monastery in Simoling, Tulshuk Lingpa found that even surrounded by family he could continue to develop his practice. Yet he saw that for so many others death and cataclysm was their lot, and increasingly they had nowhere to go.

This was not the first time in history that Tibet had been overrun. In the twelfth and thirteenth centuries the Mongols invaded from the north and, as in the 1950s, both the Tibetan people and the dharma were in grave danger. It is in texts dating from the Mongol invasions that Tibetan scholars find the first mention of beyuls in the Tibetan literature, the first stories of tertons searching for and opening hidden valleys in the Himalayas.

As conditions worsen, times ripen for the opening of a beyul. Just as when a flower is in need of pollination the bees come, so it is that when there is nowhere else to run conditions arise for a beyul's opening. It was for those times that Padmasambhava hid secret lands and planted the seeds that would create the conditions for their opening in future centuries.

Imagine the insight needed to foresee conditions in a future age. It is like a chess master who with his first move already foresees his last. Only someone with tremendous and even miraculous understanding of the interconnected nature of all things could create the conditions in which the worsening times would naturally coincide with the incarnation of the right terton, whose insight would ripen in his consciousness just when it became necessary for the crack to form.

Tulshuk Lingpa started performing certain rituals and making offerings to the dakinis so the way to a beyul would be revealed. He wasn't necessarily asking that he be the one to open it; to him that wasn't important. What was important was that a place of refuge be found for the Tibetans.

One night, while in Simoling, Tulshuk Lingpa had a vision that occurred neither in his sleep nor in what we usually term waking consciousness. Khandro Yeshe Tsogyal, the consort of Padmasambhava, appeared before Tulshuk Lingpa and spoke to him sternly: 'Listen to every word I say,' she commanded. 'Listen to every word, and do not miss a single detail. Tibet is being overrun and those who aren't slaughtered have nowhere to go. The time is coming for the opening of the beyul in Sikkim. You have work to do, and you must do this work carefully. You will be the one to open it.'

She told him in great detail the way to the hidden valley, that he was to go to Sikkim, and go up this particular valley, turn left up a side valley at this particular landmark, and perform this ritual for the appeasing of the spirit owners of the land and the spirits of Beyul. She told him in exacting detail, and repeated important landmarks, imploring him not to forget a single one. 'In the future,' she said to him, 'I will come to your dreams, and I will keep reminding you. We have a tremendous work.'

Tulshuk Lingpa had visions of the time that Padmasambhava hid the ter, which he later wrote about in his *neyik*, or guidebook to the beyul, titled *The Great Secret Talk of the Dakinis Showing the Way to Demoshong*.

At the time of the hiding of the ter, Lang Palgyi Senge bowed down before Padmasambhava and offered a mandala containing various precious jewels. He requested of Padmasambhava the following in a befitting manner:

'Hail compassionate guru. In the future, at the time when the subjects of Tibet are all suffering, if it becomes necessary for us to escape to the hidden place, please tell us the signs of the time; advise us and give us clear prophecy.'

This he persistently requested.

Then the great guru said,

'Listen all of you bright attendants; what I have to tell you is meant to protect all the sentient beings of the future.

'At the twilight of time [literally the 'red string of time', a metaphor derived from the last red line of the setting sun along the vast Tibetan horizon], have no doubt that the infinite meaning of the ter will burst out.

'At the end of the bad times, the whole world will be the subjects of the black devils of lust, hatred, and delusion. The good customs will perish and everyone will practise evil deeds. Tibetans, by the power of their own bad karma, will be scattered throughout all districts and countries and go into the hands of the butchers.

'Most will die of famine and by weapons. The remaining followers of Buddhism will soon be forsaken. Evil people will especially hate the practitioners of the dharma. Those who follow the wrong path will be appreciated by every-body. At that time the elements will become unbalanced and diseases will increase. Crops and cattle will degener-ate; internal fights and quarrelling will increase. Poisonous and chemical weapons will shake the earth.

'The evil ghost of China will influence everybody into hating dharma practitioners. They will be the enemies of the great souls and criticize them. There will be no hap-piness and only suffering, whether the people be high or low. As in a pit of fire, there will be nowhere to run. Suf-fering will increase day by day, month by month, and year by year.

'How pitiful the suffering of beings.

'When those bad times arise, the precious hidden place will be in Sikkim. It will be the place to protect and save all Tibetans.

'Abandon having two minds about going to the abode of such a great secret tantric master, Padmasambhava, which is the place to protect Tibetans.'

This was the ancient prophecy concerning the hidden land of Beyul Demoshong, which Tulshuk Lingpa had revealed to him one night in Simoling. From that time onwards, Tulshuk Lingpa started speaking of the beyul: describing it, telling his disciples that one day they would go to the valley hidden in Sikkim and they would never return.

Some immediately thought him mad; others asked him persistently, 'Master, when are we going?' But it isn't as easy as just going to the right place. A beyul is different from anywhere else you might try to go in that you can't just place yourself before the gate and walk through. It is a land that exists on no map. No co-ordinates of latitude and longitude bound it. It must be 'opened'. To open it, certain conditions must be fulfilled.

The first thing needed is the right lama, the one whose fate it is to open the way, the one who has had planted in the unchanging levels of his consciousness the key to its opening. The other thing is timing. The lama must make the attempt at the proper time. Even if the right lama doesn't divine the right time, he will meet with only obstructions. It is the greatest of human feats to open a hidden land. Conditions must be perfect. One hair's breadth away, failure—and even death—is the result.

Kunsang remembers when his father first started speaking of Beyul. 'It was a long time from when my father had his first vision of Khandro Yeshe Tsogyal to the time we went to Sikkim,' Kunsang told me. 'I was just a kid. My father used to describe Beyul, how there would be no war of any kind, how you'd have enough clothing and food, and you'd have nothing to worry about. He spoke of Beyul's natural beauty—the waterfalls and pools of nectar. When he spoke like this people used to say, "When you go, take us with you." Everybody wanted to go to Shangri-La.

'He was such a persuasive speaker that all he had to do was speak of Beyul, and whoever was listening would see it in their mind's eye and long to go there—immediately! But always he'd say the time wasn't right. Some thought he was crazy. Others understood the importance of timing. Yet even they grew impatient. My father used to drink. He would get drunk and say, "I have to go to Sikkim. I have to open the gates to Shangri-La!" Some would just say, "Tulshuk Lingpa is drunk again! He always says he has to go to Sikkim but he never goes." Others would say, "Come on. Let's go!" Always my father would say, "One day, we go. We definitely go." Even those who thought he was crazy, when they heard him speak of Beyul, when he read from the prophecy, they couldn't help themselves from wanting to go. They'd say, "We want to go too. Hurry, hurry. How do we get there?" My father would say, "I know the way but I'm not telling!" Sometimes, when people came from far away to hear him speak of Beyul, he'd tell them, "When you come here the next time, I won't be here. I'll be gone to the Hidden Valley!"'

But certain things had to fulfil themselves first.

To open the way to a beyul, tertons also need help from the spirit world. They must communicate with and appease through ritual the *sadag*, the spirit owners of the land, and the *shipdak*, the local deities. They also need a good connection with the dakinis. Dakini is a Sanskrit term meaning Sky Walker. The Tibetan is khandro. Much is communicated to tertons by way of khandros, who appear in their dreams and visions. Khandros can also take human form and become the terton's spiritual as well as physical consort, a sort of spiritual bride. In fact, for the terton to perform certain tasks, he must have a khandro with him. She provides the link with the deepest strata of the spiritual realms, acting as an intermediary and guide. To open a beyul, the khandro must be with him.

'Therefore,' Kunsang said with a smile, 'it should have been no surprise that once my father had his vision of Beyul, young ladies would be seen entering his room surrounded by an air of mystery. You can be sure it caused a sensation. The only thing was that I and my sister and my mother—we didn't know about the necessity of a khandro. It wasn't so easy on us.

'You see, we began to see one or sometimes two of them—beautiful, well-dressed young ladies—going into my father's room when he was alone but their faces used to be covered. They never used to show their faces. They would go into my father's room, and they would *never* come out.'

'What do you mean they would never come out?' I asked.

'Yes, that's how we knew they were khandros,' Kunsang said.

'Let me get this straight,' I said. 'You used to see beautiful young women entering your father's room, and they would disappear?'

'Crazy!' Kunsang exclaimed. 'But that's how it was. They weren't really women, you see; they were khandros. Before they came, my father would always do a certain ritual to call the khandros, called a *lungten*. He would go into a prophetic trance. When he came to again, he would just know the khandros would be coming and he'd tell everybody to leave. We'd leave but we'd watch his door. Then we'd see them come: sometimes one, sometimes two, in fine dresses but always with their faces covered. No matter how many people watched, we'd never see them leave.'

'Doesn't it seem more likely,' I blurted out indelicately, 'that they just stayed there till morning? Couldn't it have been his way of having women?'

'If this was the case,' Kunsang said sharply, 'then somebody would have seen them leave. Everybody saw them enter, and we were all on the watch but we never once saw them leave.'

'What was the purpose of their visits?' I asked, looking down at my pad of paper and trying to keep a straight face.

'They gave him prophecies, teachings and instructions. One time when he came out of trance, instead of sending everyone away, he had us get his two closest disciples, Namdrol and Mipham. He explained to them that he'd received instructions that there was a khandro in human form who would stay with him and travel with him to Sikkim when he opened Beyul. She would be known by having a mole on the side of her breast and two on her back. So he sent them on a mission to find this lady with the signs of the khandro, and some days later they came back with two contenders for the post. Tulshuk Lingpa rejected the first one for not having the requisite markings but the second had the marks, exactly as he said. Her name was Chimi Wangmo, and she officially became my father's khandro and second wife.'

'Had they met before?' I asked.

'Certainly,' Kunsang replied. 'She and her entire family had been disciples of Tulshuk Lingpa for a long time. They had known each other of course but he didn't know she was the khandro.'

'How did your mother feel when your father took another wife?'

'Angry,' Kunsang said, 'When a second wife comes, won't there be a problem? Sure—of course!'

'How did *you* feel when your father took another wife?'

'I was not happy,' he replied. 'But then my father's disciples came to me and to my mother too. They told us that it was written in the scriptures that to open Beyul he needed a khandro. This was supposed to happen. It had to be. They told us not to get upset.'

Another time, Kunsang told me, 'I don't know whether my father had many girlfriends but a lot of women fell for him. He was good-looking.'

I met Tulshuk Lingpa's second wife, Khandro Chimi Wangmo, who lives in a house across a dangerous ravine from Simoling Gompa. I went there with her and Tulshuk Lingpa's grandson, Gyurme, who was accompanying me on my trip to Lahaul and acting as my interpreter. As we negotiated the treacherous slope

Gyurme, grandson of Tulshuk Lingpa.

to his grandmother's house, Gyurme told me that it would be impolite to ask her anything personal whatsoever. When we arrived at the house, she came in from the fields where she was busy planting potatoes to speak with me. She was reticent and anxious to return to her potato fields. It was clear she didn't want to speak of earlier times.

Khandro Chimi Wangmo posing with a stuffed snow leopard that had recently broken into her cowshed, seriously injured a cow, was half-killed by the cow's kick, and was then finished off with a bullet.

ဆ   က

When I asked Rigzin Dokhampa, the researcher at the Namgyal Institute of Tibetology outside Gangtok, about the role of the khandro he told me the following story:

There was a terton in Tibet. One day he went with his khandro to a rugged mountain area in order to find ter. Tertons are like that. You cannot find the logic. They wake up one morning, and they know today is the day. Maybe they have a dream; maybe they receive a vision. But they know today is the day they'll find a text hidden by Padmasambhava a thousand years back in a particular rock face of a twisted mountain they've never seen. They'll tell their disciples; they'll warn them, 'Whatever I say, don't contradict me. Say OK, OK. I may ask for the impossible.

But do not doubt. Whatever I do, do not doubt it.' To find ter isn't as easy as knowing where it is, going there and taking it out of a cleft in the rock, as if it were a manuscript that was hidden there. To take out ter is to reach into another dimension and bring a piece back.

So this terton went with his khandro beyond any trail, into the tangled mountains where neither of them had been before. They climbed narrow cliffs and razor-like fissures until they reached a place where the huge stone mountain they had ascended ended abruptly in a sheer cliff of a size and magnitude that was hardly imaginable. Far below, a river cascaded over a series of raw waterfalls. On the other side rose a cliff every bit as sheer as their own but higher, dwarfing them and blocking the sun. A cold wind blew up the chasm.

The terton stood on the edge of the abyss. He held out his hand and pointed across to a fold in the rock on the cliff face opposite. 'The ter is there,' he said.

The question, of course, was how to get there. It was as impossible to descend to the river as it would be to climb the other side.

Even tertons can experience doubt.

The khandro sensed the seed of doubt in the terton's mind even before it surfaced. She ran up behind him, yelling out 'Get the ter!' and pushed him off the cliff.

There was a huge vulture flying below them. The terton landed on it. It brought him to the other side, and he took out the ter.

ॐ   ॐ

Tulshuk Lingpa used to perform a special form of divination, called the *trata melong*, in which he stuck a convex brass mirror into a bowl of rice, performed a ritual, then invited people to look into the mirror to see if in the dull shine of the burnished brass they saw any images, which he would then interpret. The ability to see in the mirror is known as *tamik*, which literally means picture eye. Those with tamik have the ability to see images that predict the future, unravel mysteries of the past, and communicate messages from the spirits. Though it was not unknown for older people to have this mysterious ability, it was usually children who could see, especially girls. In them, it seems, the intuitive channels were still open and the active imagination stronger.

Rigzin Dokhampa recalled how Tulshuk Lingpa used to perform the trata melong ritual at Tashiding. 'Not only girls can see in the mirror,' he said. 'I was a child when Tulshuk Lingpa was in Tashiding, maybe fifteen, sixteen. He used to go to one of the temples at the Tashiding Monastery with the local children to perform this ritual. I would be there, my brother would be there—and maybe thirty other children, both young monks and lay children also. He did this many times. It was something we children could participate in, and we'd all be very excited. He would do the ritual, push the mirror into the plate of rice and have each of the kids look into the mirror one after the other. Then he'd ask us what we saw. Some could see; others couldn't. It was a special ability.

'One time when my turn came, I looked into the mirror and after some moments the mirror disappeared and in its place there was a beautiful large mountain with many streams of water flowing down it. I saw huge stupas on the mountain and long prayer flags. On top of the mountain snow was falling. On the right side, there was a wide trail rising with the slope of the mountain, which was washed away in places. I told Tulshuk Lingpa what I saw, and he said the stupa and prayer flags were good signs. But the parts of the trail washed away—that he said was not so good. Other children saw yaks, sheep, mountains—like that.'

৪১   ৫৪

Of everyone who ever looked into Tulshuk Lingpa's melong, or mirror, khandro Chimi Wangmo's younger sister, Yeshe, was by far the most gifted. Though Yeshe could neither read nor write, she had tamik. She was often employed by Tulshuk Lingpa to look into the mirror, even before they went to Sikkim. Though a teenager and married at the age of sixteen, she was also destined to become Tulshuk Lingpa's khandro, and her fate was closely wrapped up with his.

One morning when Tulshuk Lingpa was living in Pangao, a rich Indian merchant braved the treacherous slope to his cave to plead for his help. He was in a panic particular to a rich man who has just lost everything.

'Help me, please!' he implored. 'My safe was just stolen with everything in it—everything I have—and the police can't find a single clue. Please, Master, perform a mo so I can find it.' Mo is a

Yeshe.

form of divination lamas routinely perform using their mala, or rosary, or else a pair of dice.

'No,' Tulshuk Lingpa said, 'I won't perform the mo; for this we must perform the trata melong. We must use the mirror, and for that we need Yeshe.' Yeshe was in Manali at the time, about two hours up the valley. Somebody got her, and in the afternoon Tulshuk Lingpa propped the brass mirror in a plate of rice, performed his ritual, and instructed Yeshe to look very carefully into the mirror and to notice every detail.

What she saw was that the thieves couldn't move the safe very far. So they put it down, got some help—around eight people— and then they could carry it. They brought it to a stream.

Tulshuk Lingpa then said to her, 'You must look very carefully to see which stream it is. We have to go there.'

The image changed, and the sun was setting. The thieves started to panic, asking themselves what to do with the safe. So they covered it with stones and with branches.

From her description, the merchant knew which stream it was. It was just below his house. They went to the spot, and everything was exactly as she saw it.

I first heard this story from Kunsang. Frankly, I didn't believe it. Later others independently recalled the story with an uncanny accuracy in detail.

CHAPTER NINE

The Discovery

When the Chinese invaded Tibet and started ransacking their way through Kham, smashing monasteries and throwing monks in jail, there was a secret convocation there of high lamas and tertons. Foreseeing the ripening of the end times which would culminate in their having nowhere to turn for sanctuary, their thoughts naturally turned to their south, and to the hidden beyul in Sikkim.

The Tibetan name for the Kingdom of Sikkim—which stretched in fertile valleys south of the Tibetan Plateau—was Demojong, which means the Valley of Rice. The beyul hidden within Sikkim was known as the *Great* Valley of Rice, or Demo*shong*. This Great Valley of Rice hidden within the outer kingdom was—despite obvious logical inconsistencies—supposed to be three times the size of the outer kingdom. This would be rather like a shoebox hidden inside a matchbox—and remaining undiscovered for over a thousand years.

The last one to make the attempt to open the Hidden Land was Dorje Dechen Lingpa sometime in the 1920s. Though many lamas in Sikkim know the story of his attempt to open the Hidden Land, it was difficult to find details since no one was alive who remembered it. For that I needed a historian, so I went to the Namgyal Institute of Tibetology outside Gangtok and had extensive discussions with their senior researcher, Rigzin Dokhampa, who was a great practitioner of the Tibetan Buddhist dharma as well as a scholar. He was also a disciple of Tulshuk Lingpa, which I found out the first time I met him. I was in the Institute's museum and had a question about one of the sculptures. The security guard guided me into Rigzin's office. Rigzin offered me a seat and I asked my question. Before leaving, I asked him if by chance he had ever heard of Tulshuk Lingpa and his journey to Beyul. 'Of course,' he exclaimed. 'I am from Tashiding, and both my brother and I were his disciples. We learned thangka painting from him.'

Rigzin told me that Dorje Dechen Lingpa was an incarnation of Lhatsun Chenpo, whom you could call the patron saint of Sikkim. When Dorje Dechen Lingpa received indications and instructions in ter about the opening of Demoshong, the beyul in Sikkim, he wrote to Chogyal Tashi Namgyal—the king of Sikkim—saying that he was the incarnation of Lhatsun Chenpo and that Padmasambhava had given the prediction that he would find the Hidden Land. He wanted the king to grant him permission to come to see him in Gangtok. The king consulted with Taring Rinpoche, a high lama who was giving oral teachings at the time at Pensong Gom-

pa. Taring Rinpoche was himself reputed to be the incarnation of Lhatsun Chenpo and happened to be the king's brother. He told the king that since *he* was the incarnation of Lhatsun Chenpo, the writer of the letter must be a fraud, and therefore Dorje Dechen Lingpa was not invited to the kingdom.

Dorje Dechen Lingpa was not so easily put off. He was, after all, heading for a kingdom both larger and greater than the Chogyal's Valley of Rice. So with about twenty monks from the Domang Gompa, he set off on foot, crossing the Tibetan Plateau and the

Rigzin Dokhampa (1943—2005), senior researcher at the Namgyal Institute of Tibetology, Sikkim.

high, snow-swept passes of the Himalayan range and went down to the Kingdom of Sikkim in order to open the way to the Hidden Land.

Their first stop in Sikkim was the Doling Gompa, a small Nyingma monastery set in a forest not far from the town of Ravangla, across the wide valley from Tashiding. They stayed there for a few weeks and Dorje Dechen Lingpa took out quite a bit of ter—statues and scriptures. He went briefly to the Tashiding Gompa, whose name translates to Auspicious Centre and is considered to be at the heart centre of Sikkim. It was prophesied that the lama who would open Beyul Demoshong would come to Tashiding. Since he didn't have permission to be in the kingdom, he kept his visit there low-key and didn't stay long.

They went to Rinchenpong Gompa in West Sikkim, not far from the Nepal border, and from there to Risum Gompa. Since they were going high into the snow mountains, they had many horses and mules with them as pack animals. Risum lies deep in the mountains, the last place before the snow, and quite near the Western Gate to Demoshong. Like the Biblical Heavenly Kingdom, there are four gates to the Hidden Land.

At this crucial juncture there occurred, as Rigzin Dokhampa described it, a very bad omen. Dorje Dechen Lingpa and his twenty followers were staying at the home of the headman of Risum, Penchu Tekadar, who was the owner of the gompa and had built it. One night there were terrific thunderstorms with heavy hail and lightning. Dorje Dechen Lingpa's followers were used to sleeping in tents. That night he told them to sleep in the monastery itself, which they all did except for one. The lama in question was a practitioner of Chod, a practice that is performed in dangerous places such as cremation grounds and graveyards with fresh graves. He insisted—against his master's wishes—on staying outside to practice.

That night there was a terrific storm that pelted the ground and covered it with huge pellets of hail and illuminated the sky with violent flashes of lightning. In the morning they found that not only did the lightning shatter rocks and splinter trees, it also killed the lama practising chod and over half of their mules and horses. This was a bad omen indeed, and Dorje Dechen Lingpa was ready to give in to the omen and give up his quest to open Beyul Demoshong. But the wife of the headman stepped in, offering him as many horses and mules, food and other provisions he needed to continue his journey. He accepted her offer and ascended the snowy slopes.

Bad omens are rarely followed by favourable ones, and indeed there were further bad omens (which will be described later), and in the end he had to give up. He returned to Tibet and died before reaching his home monastery at Domang. Before he died, he announced that when he returned he would take not one but three incarnations. According to Rigzin, that is exactly what happened.

'One of the incarnations,' he told me, 'is Jigdal Namgyal, our last king's youngest brother. He lives in Gangtok below the higher secondary school. Another—I don't remember his name—was born from the wife of Penchu Tekadar, the headman of Risum, the one who offered Dorje Dechen Lingpa the mules and provisions so he could continue. The third was also born in Sikkim. He is known as the Yangthang Rinpoche. In his seventies, he lives mostly in Yoksum.

'Both the son of Tekadar and the Yangthang Rinpoche went to the Domang Gompa in Tibet to be trained. At that time they were quite young, in their mid-twenties. Both of them showed such great intelligence that they became famous. In our monastic system of learning we memorize scriptures in the morning. An extremely intelligent person can memorize twenty or perhaps twenty-five pages in a morning. When I was a student, I could memorize fifteen. Yangthang Rinpoche and Penchu Tekadar's son memorized one volume each every morning: more than 100 pages. So the people became very excited.

'During this time, Tibet's troubles with the Chinese began. When it became increasingly dangerous in Kham, they escaped to the capital Lhasa where news kept reaching them of the increasingly dire conditions in Kham, of the resistance and the wholesale slaughter. Tekadar's son said to Yangthang Rinpoche, "We are lamas and have escaped from the troubles. That is not right. We must share in the suffering and help as we can." Penchu Tekadar's son returned to Kham, where he was killed.

Yangthang Rinpoche remained in Lhasa, which was soon occupied by the Chinese. He was later put in a Chinese prison for twenty years.'

Ever since Dorje Dechen Lingpa failed to open Beyul Demoshong in the 1920s, the lamas and tertons of Kham wondered who would be the next one to attempt the opening. Though they considered Dorje Dechen Lingpa the right lama to open the way (the ter, after all, was revealed to him), they faulted the times, saying the time wasn't right for the opening of the beyul. The 1920s were relatively peaceful in Tibet, and the need for a place of refuge wasn't so great. But with the Chinese invasion of 1951 and the subsequent brutality, what would be more important than a place of refuge? Therefore the high lamas and tertons of Kham gathered secretly in order to perform the divination necessary to help them discover the next one to open Beyul Demoshong. Special pujas were performed, and visions were received: visions of Khandro Yeshe Tsogyal who told them the five attributes by which the one to open Beyul Demoshong could be known. They wrote a pecha with the description, rather like a literary 'Wanted' poster, and hundreds of hand-lettered copies of this pecha were made. They were distributed to lamas throughout Kham.

Many Tibetans, especially from Kham, started fleeing south to India. It wasn't yet time for the all-out exodus with the Dalai Lama in 1959 but things were getting rough, especially for the lamas who found themselves targets of Mao's anti-religious zealots. Many were braving the high passes for an uncertain life in India. To survive, newly arrived Tibetan refugees took to begging or worked as day labourers and road workers. Though Tibet and India shared a border, the mountains separating them were the highest in the world and life in the two countries couldn't have been more different. How difficult it must have been for a people who measured wealth by the size of their herds on the high empty plateau to suddenly find themselves cast among the Indian masses, scraping for survival.

Zurmang Gelong was one of the lamas who were at the convocation in Kham. He fled over the high passes to India with only a copy of the pecha and the clothes on his back. It was written in the pecha that the lama who would open Beyul Demoshong would originally be from Kham but would be found living in an area known as Tod, or 'upper Tibet', comprising a large area of the western Himalayas: Lahaul, Spiti, Kinnaur, Zanskar and Ladakh. Having experienced the Chinese invasion first hand, Zurmang knew above all else that it was necessary to find the lama to open Beyul.

He travelled to the western Himalayas with the wish and prayer of finding the lama who would open that place of shelter for all Tibetans. But along the way, the quest for survival came to dominate his existence and he found himself, like the hero of mythology, forgetting his quest from the sheer exhaustion of working on a road crew cracking rocks for the construction of the new road up the Kullu Valley. He lived below the road along the banks of the Beas River in a camp of makeshift lean-tos of sticks and river stone occupied by about a hundred of his colleagues, a mix of displaced Indian families, rootless wanderers and Tibetan refugees like himself.

Above their camp were huge cliffs, and he started hearing about a lama who lived in a cave up there. At first he heard he was a crazy and drunken lama. He was too tired after a day of cracking stones with a heavy hammer to climb the cliffs for such a lama. Besides, Zurmang was from Kham. No local lama could compare with a Khampa lama, he thought to himself, so he didn't pay much attention to the news. But he kept hearing of this lama who lived in a cave, so he finally asked, 'Who is this lama?' When he heard that he was from Kham, he became interested. He grabbed the pecha and climbed to Tulshuk Lingpa's cave.

Since Kunsang was there when this Khampa lama wearing a road labourer's clothes and a pecha under his arm arrived at the cave, we have a first-hand account of what happened.

'He was dirty,' Kunsang told me, 'and his clothes were covered in rock dust. The moment he opened his mouth, my father picked up on his distinctive Khampa dialect. So their conversation began commonly enough, my father started asking him the normal questions: Where are you from? What monastery did you study at—that sort of thing.

'When the pleasantries were over, the lama started steering the conversation towards—of all things—Beyul Demoshong. I was surprised since it had always been my father who had been speaking of Beyul, saying he was going to lead the way; but now he was silent, as if he didn't know a thing, and just let this lama talk. I could tell there was something up. With my father, there always was. I've always been thankful he let me—as his only son—partake in so many *interesting* situations. He was crazy—sure! But there was always another angle—a perspective from which it all made sense, in the end.

'Then my father, in an almost casual way, let it slip that he had been visited by Khandro Yeshe Tsogyal. You should have seen the Khampa lama's eyes widen. He looked at my father in a new way. I could tell he was weighing something, on the verge of both rejoicing and disbelief. The pecha he was carrying described the five attributes by which the lama who would open Beyul Demoshong could be recognized. Not only would he be discovered in the western Himalayas where we were but he was to be originally from Kham. There were four other attributes: he was to be tall, have long braided hair, have eyes like a tiger and be a *myonpa*—which translates to madman or crazy person.

'As he looked at my father, you could practically see him ticking off the attributes one by one. When he got to the last he hesitated, until he considered my father's name, the fissure in the cliff face where we were all sitting, and the fact that he lived there with his wife, daughter and son.

'Zurmang Gelong decided to get closer to the point, so he asked my father whether he'd ever heard of Dorje Dechen Lingpa.

'"Of course," my father replied, "I knew him as a child. He's the one who coronated me and gave me my name."

'It was with a trembling hand that Zurmang Gelong unwrapped the pecha from its cloth cover. He described the meeting of tertons and read a few lines of the pecha's description of Beyul.

'My father reached into a cleft in the rock wall and took down a pecha written in his own hand, which he had written after his encounter with Khandro Yeshe Tsogyal. He unwrapped it and read the same lines, word for word, dictated to him by Yeshe Tsogyal during his vision of her.

'Zurmang Gelong pressed the pecha to his forehead with tears streaming down his cheeks. "When you go to Beyul," he implored my father, "you must take me with you. I've been praying for this for so long. It has been my dream."'

ℰ   ℜ

Increasingly, people flocked to Tulshuk Lingpa to hear him speak of Beyul.

Kunsang remembers his father saying, 'One day I must go to Shangri-La. Whoever wants to come with me, come but only if you have no doubts. If you have doubts, please don't go. Stay here!' Kunsang remembers him saying this especially when some jinda provided him with a big bottle of something nice to drink. Tulshuk Lingpa got a reputation from this, as you can well imagine. Some thought him mad; others pressed him, continually. 'When will we go, Master? When?' It was especially the people from Simoling, those with the greatest faith in the one who had delivered them from disfigurement and death at the hand of the female cannibal demoness, who wanted to go with him. Even his closest disciples pressed him continuously. But for years, he held them off.

'The time is not right,' he would tell them. 'We must do more pujas; we must be purified and ready. Not one doubt can enter our minds. Then we shall be ready.'

'When my father spoke of Beyul,' Kunsang told me, 'he spoke in the language of the scriptures, which in Tibetan is not comprehensible to the common people. So they used to come to me, and ask what he was saying.'

Kunsang burst out laughing.

'At the time I was just a kid, a teenager. They'd gather around me, eyes full of wonder, and because I was Tulshuk Lingpa's only son they'd ask me how we were supposed to eat in the Hidden Land, how we'd get clothing and what the weather would be like. I told them that to get to that place we'd have to cross over some high altitudes but once we got there it would be quite hot in some places—and cold in others.

'Then they'd tell me, "It is uncertain how long your father will live once we reach Shangri-La but after he dies, you will take over. You will certainly take out ter in the Hidden Land!" They didn't understand that you didn't die in the Hidden Land, and I didn't correct them.

'They'd ask me how we'd enter the Hidden Land, and I used to tell them that Beyul cannot be seen with the naked eye. There would be a huge stone with a stream flowing over it, and you would jump into the waterfall and come out the other side. Others thought Tulshuk Lingpa would get to Beyul first, and then throw down a rope. Later my father's two closest disciples, Namdrol and Mipham, told me that what I had been saying wasn't true. They said there was no waterfall. "The way to Beyul," they told me, "is really difficult: all snow and ice." It's true. My father said his route would be the most difficult. I spoke of the waterfall because I had heard of another beyul called Pemako, some hundreds of miles east of Sikkim where the Tsang Po River descends through the Himalayas in a series of hidden waterfalls to become the Brahmaputra.'

'What did you expect to happen once you entered Beyul,' I asked Kunsang.

He made the thumbs up. 'Happy,' he said.

People often told me that Tulshuk Lingpa held the key to Beyul, and it wasn't always clear that they didn't mean it literally. The key grew in some people's imaginations until it was the size of a crowbar that they expected Tulshuk Lingpa to thrust through a chink in the world around us in order to open a crack into another.

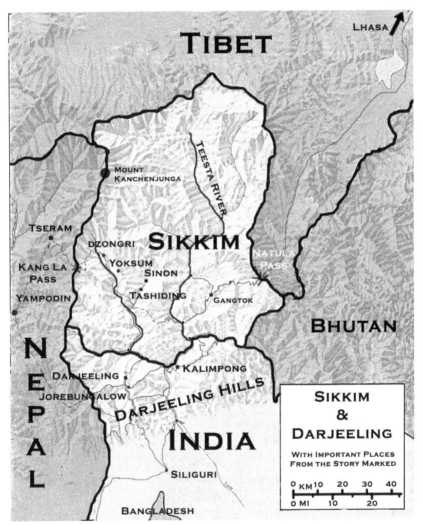

Sikkim and Darjeeling, showing important places from the story.

CHAPTER TEN

The Reconnaissance

In 1959, the Chinese culminated their brutal attack on Tibet by taking control of the once-forbidden city, the capital Lhasa. Pleading with his people not to respond with violence to the violence and brutality the Chinese meted out (estimates are that over a million were murdered by the Chinese before their takeover was complete), the Dalai Lama fled south over the Himalayas and found asylum in India.

When word of this reached Tulshuk Lingpa, he knew the Tibetan dharma and people were in graver danger than they had ever been in before, and that therefore the time was drawing close for the opening of Beyul Demoshong. Together with his consort and a few of his closest disciples, he made a journey to Sikkim in order to get a feel for the landscape and—as we shall see—to encounter various deities and guardian spirits.

We have unusual insight into the inner realizations and visions Tulshuk Lingpa experienced during this trip in the form of a pecha, or scripture, in which he wrote about it. The text, which he describes as a 'song of the road', is titled *The Creeper-Plant of the Mind* and it was given to me by Kunsang. It is here, in his own words, that we get a glimpse of the extent to which Tulshuk Lingpa was subject to visionary states, from which he gained his knowledge and experience of the beyul.

> The time has reached the highly degenerate state of the final five hundred years, in which the armies of the barbarians destroy the peace and happiness of humanity, when the teachings of the Buddha are destroyed from their very

foundation, reducing the happiness and prosperity of the world to the size of a sun ray on a mountain pass.

Listen to this story of how I went to Demojong [Sikkim], rendered into a song.

If you sincerely follow what I teach, you will certainly be happy. Whatever I do, I do it not for my own interest. Nourishing the desire for the good and welfare of the many, I am little concerned with what others do—or with whether they praise or insult me.

Tulshuk Lingpa gives the exact day he set out with his small band of disciples:

In the evening of the twenty-first day of the eleventh month of the Iron Male Mouse year [Sunday, 8 January 1961], the year that was said to be harmonious with the four elements, I left my home in Pangao and went to the capital, Kulluta.

Kulluta is the local Buddhist name for the town of Kullu, the administrative centre of the district, a rather large town about thirty miles south of Pangao.

One evening when I was in a mixed state of sleep and the true nature of mind, the deity Dorje Lekpa (a *dharmapala*) appeared before me in the guise of a monk. He smiled at me and addressed me thus:

'Oh! Great and noble man! Though the negative forces burning with wrath might curse you, no harm can be caused to you by these evil spirits and demons. This is because of your pure heart and the strength of your noble aspirations. Since all things are empty and non-existent, you will live long and accumulate more merit, and your acts of benevolence will increase. However, you must be cautious not to associate with foolish people. Together with the retinue of your firm-hearted and devout followers, do your utmost to fight the forces that cause spiritual obstructions. Be sure to make offerings and to chant and pray as much as possible.

Since you have accumulated much merit, you may go anywhere you like without fear. I will provide all the help you
need to ward off impediments.' As soon as he uttered these
words, I woke up from my dream-like state.

For Tulshuk Lingpa, the landscape he passed through was only
nominally of the early part of the sixth decade of the twentieth
century. From Kullu, he and his retinue passed through Mandi
which he refers to as 'the palace of the Zahor king', the Zahor
king being the father of Padmasambhava's consort in the eighth
century who tried to burn him alive. They travelled 1200 miles
by train east across the north Indian Plains, then reentered the
Himalayas and went north towards Sikkim, stopping off just
south of the kingdom at Kalimpong (which he calls Kalinka in
the text) to see Dudjom Rinpoche, Tulshuk Lingpa's root guru.

Chokshi, the young man responsible for bringing Tulshuk
Lingpa to Simoling, was with Tulshuk Lingpa on this journey.
He told me that they left secretly, and no one they met on their
journey would have suspected the mission they were on—to lay
the foundation for a journey to another world—or even that Tulshuk Lingpa was a lama. He wore regular clothes—only rarely
would he wear robes—and his hair was long. When asked, they
said they were on a pilgrimage.

Dudjom Rinpoche lived just outside the town of Kalimpong in
the village of Madhuban. Chokshi described to me how Kalimpong was full of Tibetan refugees. Disoriented, frightened and
traumatized by the brutality that prevailed a few days' march
away over the Jelepla, the main pass to Tibet on the Lhasa trade
route, they were pouring into Kalimpong and other towns across
the Indian Himalayas, living reminders of the importance of finding the beyul.

As they headed up the hill to Madhuban, then a small village on the edge of which Dudjom lived in a large British colonial
house, they had a conversation that Chokshi told me went something like this:

'Please, Master, we are going to meet a great lama. You are
also a great lama. You cannot meet him wearing the old shirt and
pants you've travelled in. Please, change into your robes.'

'The clothes one wears don't matter,' Tulshuk Lingpa responded. 'It is what's inside that matters. Besides, it is always better not to show on the outside what one is inside.'

'But Master, please, we are your disciples!'

Tulshuk Lingpa gave in to their entreaties, not because he was convinced they were correct but out of a sense of compassion. In the forest surrounding the village—Madhuban translates to Honey Forest—he took off his street clothes and put on his white robe.

Chokshi told me they spent three days with Dudjom Rinpoche, and that Tulshuk Lingpa disclosed to his master the reason for their journey, to investigate the vision he had had of Khandro Yeshe Tsogyal and the other signs he'd received along the way. Dudjom Rinpoche was himself a high terton, as well as a mature and learned lama.

Of his encounter with his guru, Tulshuk Lingpa wrote these lines: 'He received me with a smiling countenance and addressed me thus, "Proceed. All the precious literary treasures and the prophecies of the Hidden Land of Demoshong are in conformity with your coming to this place."'

Chokshi recalled that Dudjom also warned Tulshuk Lingpa to keep his mission secret and to take with him only people of unusual clarity and purity, and above all else to proceed slowly. He sensed in his young disciple an impatience that could prove troublesome. Time must mature before an opening can occur.

'Those you take with you,' Dudjom warned him, 'will determine your success or failure. They will each have to leave everything behind, not only physically but in their inmost thoughts as well.'

From Madhuban they travelled a few hours to Jorbungalow, a small town near Darjeeling, and to the monastery of arguably the greatest Tibetan yogi practitioner of his day: Chatral Rinpoche. When Chatral Rinpoche heard Tulshuk Lingpa's story, he gathered Tulshuk Lingpa's disciples around him and read from a terma that was hidden by Padmasambhava and discovered long ago. It described Beyul in great detail.

Then Chatral Rinpoche gave them some practical advice. 'When you are in the high mountains to find the gate to Beyul, don't make a fire at night. It will attract animals and spirits.

Here, use this,' and he gave them a human thighbone horn. 'Blow this at night,' he told them. 'It will scare away the animals and keep the spirits from bothering you, too.'

On the third day they were there, Tenzing Norgay came to see Chatral Rinpoche. It was Tenzing Norgay who, a few years earlier, together with the New Zealander Edmund Hillary, was the first to scale the highest peak in the world, Mount Everest. It was a feat that made him both world-famous and, though he was born in Nepal, his adopted home Darjeeling's favourite son. He came to Chatral Rinpoche because one of his two wives was very ill. The doctors were unable to heal her and he wanted the great lama, of whom Tenzing Norgay was both a disciple and a sponsor, to help her. When he presented his case to Chatral, the lama laughed: 'You are very lucky you came today. If you would have come tomorrow, the man who could help your wife would be gone.'

He then introduced the great mountain climber to Tulshuk Lingpa, telling him that this was the lama with the greatest abilities to heal and that he should take him to his wife. So Tenzing Norgay took Tulshuk Lingpa and his small retinue to his house in Darjeeling, where they performed pujas and administered Tibetan herbs. Tenzing Norgay's wife quickly recovered, which earned Tulshuk Lingpa both a new disciple and a sponsor. 'Whenever you are in Darjeeling,' he told Tulshuk Lingpa, 'you must stay in my house,' which Tulshuk Lingpa did. Tulshuk Lingpa kept secret from Tenzing Norgay the real reason for their journey, that they were investigating the way to Beyul. Dudjom's warnings were fresh in his mind, and Tenzing Norgay was a gregarious, famous fellow who would not have kept the secret.

From Darjeeling, they went north to Sikkim to begin their investigations. Before Sikkim became a state of India in 1975, it was a separate country: a kingdom that traditionally had been closely aligned with Tibet. So when Tulshuk Lingpa and his followers travelled from Darjeeling down through the tea estates to the Rangeet River, which formed the border between India and Sikkim, they had to pass through an immigration checkpoint on the other side of the bridge. Since Tulshuk Lingpa was Tibetan and had passed into India on the sly, he didn't have proper papers. Therefore a bit of careful negotiation was called for, which Tulshuk Lingpa accomplished in his typical tulshuk manner—with a bottle of liquor. This left him and the officials not only drunk but also friends. This would prove useful in the future.

In Tulshuk Lingpa's account of this journey, he tells us that they arrived in the town of Singtam on the first day of the twelfth month, or 17 January. In Singtam, he writes, 'Amid a tremendous confusion, I saw a hoard of gods and demons showing their likes and dislikes towards me. However, I took no interest in their doings.'

They proceeded further and, 'I inquired from people the name of the place and the history of its beginning. However, since I could not understand the local language, I resorted to sorcery, and went straight to the much-famed holy and secret cave of the dakinis situated there.'

That evening Tulshuk Lingpa conducted an 'internal fire offering'. Then, he tells us,

> I fell into a light sleep in which the world of appearance turned into the shape of a triangle, in the centre of which a red-faced young woman, both smiling and wrathful, carrying a vajra knife and a cup made of a human skull, addressed me thus:
>
> > Proceed, proceed to the Hidden Land,
> > Do not, do not split from the friends you like,
> > Do not, do not listen to fools without faith,
> > Do not, do not forget the prophecies of Padmasambhava,
> > Attain realization, realization for the good of all beings,
> > Torment, torment the gods and spirits into keeping their sacred oaths.
> > Make them, make them develop an altruistic attitude towards others.
> > Generate, generate pure thoughts.
> > It is possible, possible that the door of the sacred place will open again.
>
> Having said that, she touched my lips to the nipples of her two breasts three times and declared that I had then fully obtained the blessings, initiations and transmissions

of the three Buddha bodies of the khandro. Then, showering me with absolute love, she vanished into space. I woke up from my dream in perfect joy.

From the cave of the dakinis, they proceeded to the holy centre of the kingdom, the Tashiding Monastery. Set on top of a mountain at the end of a ridge, which falls off to where two rivers merge, Tashiding has a 360-degree view of the surrounding mountains and earns its name well, for Tashiding means Auspicious Centre. Tashiding is the 'centre' of Sikkim the way the heart is the 'centre' of one's being.

It is said that Padmasambhava himself blessed the place.

In those days one had to walk to Tashiding, skirting cliffs and fording rivers on footbridges through a spectacular landscape. Tulshuk Lingpa describes his meditation upon their arrival:

I had all round a feeling of total peace and happiness. This sense of utter happiness transformed itself into great compassion and the spontaneous manifestation of happiness. Towards the beings of the six realms and those of the present time, I developed an irresistible feeling of compassion. In such a mood—through my deep contemplation—whatever sights and sounds I experienced were turned into the body, speech and mind of Chenresig, the Buddha of Compassion. After getting up from this meditation, I offered prayers and benedictions in order to expand and maintain the clear light of sleep.

That evening I was visited by various khandros, one of whom made many extraordinary forecasts; another gave me books containing secret oral instructions as well as secret predictions and percepts.

Two days later, in the morning, Tulshuk Lingpa explored the area to 'find out whether the place possessed any auspicious signs and marks'.

I offered prayers to the divine master of the place, and made an extensive examination of the whole area. Several signs and marks indicated auspicious and happy tidings. Being happy and cheerful, I offered the following words of praise, 'Oh! Most wonderful is this place, Demojong, wonderful is the way of its formation. It is something like the blossoming of the broad leaf of the blue lotus.'

There are five large caves of Guru Padmasambhava. The white and red rivers flowing together towards the south are a sign of the obtaining of Buddhahood by some living in the southern areas. The rainbow and the cloud rising up majestically are the signs of welcome by the astral guides and messengers. The turquoise-coloured hills and valleys are decorated with auspicious trees and plants. On the precious rocky mountains flowers and fruits hang their heads low, filled with nectar-like water; their sweet scents are carried by the winds. With the sacrificial clouds appearing as domes standing over things offered during a ceremony and the endless congregation of strong-hearted dakinis, I cannot help but praise this place, the wonder of which knows no bounds. Thus, having offered my sincere compliments from the core of my heart I made an extensive tour of the place, and saw many kinds of spectacles.

That evening a khandro named Langpoi Gochen, appeared in my dream and gave me instructions that helped me eliminate negative emotions and mental dullness. Then she revealed to me many literary treasures of Demojong, after which innumerable gods and spirits gathered in the sky, attempting to impress me with their wrathful demeanour and their intention to cause me injury and threaten my life.

And while they were thus discussing among themselves, a voice claiming to be that of Manjushree, the Buddha of learning, declared, 'This man is the messenger of Padmasambhava: hence no harm should be caused to him. Whichever door of this secret country opens, whether in the east or the west, it is in the interest and good of all beings. Hence everyone should work towards that objective and help.'

Then a hoard of local deities, the protectors of Mount Kanchenjunga, numbering a hundred, gathered. The chief among them said, 'Do not open the door of the sacred place at this time. First you must carefully examine the situation. These days, people show fake belief only. And there are now none who, without deceit, show any faith from their heart.

'Oh man, it will simply be a cause of fatigue for you.

'The number of people who sincerely believe what you say may be compared to the number of stars in the day; while the heretics, who insult and entice others, are like the thickened stars of night. Hence, it will be difficult to find a way to achieve success. People who cherish bad things for others and do not carry out the spiritual commitments will, in the end, cut short your own life. Would it not be better for you to move about in secret with a few of your true and ardent followers?'

In reply to this I said thus, 'Guru Padmasambhava advised me, "By opening the door of the Secret Country, thou shalt bring about the happiness, prosperity and glory of three thousand blessed followers." Hence, I shall accept and carry out these hard works with all sincerity. As for you, give up your envy and harshness. Why not rather extend your help in order to make the Hidden Land a friendly country?'

Having said this, I meditated upon the fact that gods and spirits are nothing but the creations of one's own mind; and while thinking thus, the so-called spirits disappeared without a trace.

When this dream-like state vanished, there came from out of the sky a sweet sound—Hung . . . Hung . . . Hung— that continued for a long time, after which it turned into a voice, which said, 'Go west, to Padmasambhava's cave of meditation, which is known as Nub Dechen Phug. There, meditate upon the wrathful demoness Drowo Loe until there is no difference between you and the demoness; then offer lavish presents to the gods and spirits.'

So I went to the cave called Nub Dechen Phug, and through my meditation I assumed myself as the deity. Then I made lavish offerings of nectar-like *serkyem*, a sacrificial drink. I offered *torma* [offerings] to the eight classes of worldly demons.

Then I left that place. In three days, I arrived at a cave called Milam Phugmo (Dream Cave). There I came across the tantric deity Heruka dressed like a hermit with rising hair, wearing ornaments of human bones, carrying a staff topped with human skulls. 'Come,' he said. 'Let us go sightseeing.'

And so we did.

Within a few moments we arrived at the top of Mount Kanchenjunga and saw Beyul Demoshong, a country that had hitherto remained entirely hidden. The sky was filled with the rays of rainbows and clouds where the khandros who hadn't taken human form were passing their time singing and dancing. From the hills and rivers oozed the fragrant smells of medicinal plants. All around, the natural scenery contained unfathomable wonders.

Then the hermit, making some gestures with his fingers, addressed me thus in a very sweet voice: 'Alas! In the east of this Hidden Land the five summits of the snowy mountains assume the air of a lion. Beneath are precious lakes containing milklike nectar, and a number of hidden-treasure caves containing precious stones and crystals. In the south, where rainbows and clouds have covered the black forests, you will find abundant resources of silk and food. In the west, where there are forests of medicinal plants, there are also mines containing gold, silver, iron and copper—as well as other materials for household purposes. In the north, where hail and rain fall over the snowy mountains, there are miraculous treasure caves of arms and weapons. There are also wonderful mines that preserve religious treasures, such as images and writings of the Buddha. In all four directions, in the centre, as well as in the bordering areas, there are numberless treasures of household goods to fulfil all one's needs. In the valleys, hills and forests one comes across uncountable varieties of medicine and food, as well as the elementary materials for silk and clothes and different kinds of paints, as well as grains for the preparation of tasty food and drink. Other inexhaustible earthly goods and pleasures are to be found there, which will satisfy one's senses. Besides the eastern and the western paths, there are no other paths leading to this place. The instruments, names of places and other important keys—like a road guide for the opening of the doors of this place—lie in the five great caves and at Tashiding. If you do not fall prey to the cajoling of the gods and demons who do not keep their promises, and who are immodest in character and who desire evil for others—if you thus escape from the evil effects of the demons, undoubtedly you will come to own this sacred place. Do not forget what I have just told you: take it seriously in your heart.' He repeated this last line three times, and I woke up from my sleep.

Thereafter, we went to the cave called Dechen, where we discovered many signs of undesirable fighting and epidemic and disintegration taking place in India and Tibet and other areas, which I will not dwell upon in writing.

I remained for two days in that cave of Padmasambhava and made a thorough investigation of the place. At that time a ferocious demon came straight at me and started bullying me in various ways. I could not immediately say whether the incident was real or took place in a dream-like state. I took recourse to meditation, and by meditating on emptiness brought the evil under control. Later I saw visible signs of the fact that I had brought the spirit under my control.

One morning at dawn, I dreamt of a high stone platform upon which was seated Lord Padmasambhava himself. He was smiling, and his round eyes were directed towards the great expanse of the sky. With a loving heart, he made me the following prediction:

'Alas! Alas! Now the most degenerate time has come. Before long, the land of Demojong [Sikkim] will be visited by the threat of outsiders. Therefore the time has come for the opening of the hidden country. In spite of this, human beings have become more heretical; few are the people who are faithful and cherish positive thinking. The red storm of impediment caused by evil spirits that do not act according to what they promise are on the rise. An evil spirit has entered into the heart of every individual being. However, a few, due to their good deeds, will keep a close association with you and will even come to see my face.

'Moreover, if they meditate on Padmasambhava and his consorts, break not their sacred vows, and continue to act according to my predictions, they will certainly be able to achieve supreme consummation of Buddhahood in this life.

'Those who doubt and cannot believe the predictions of mine, the so-named Padmasambhava, and remain attached to their relatives and the friends of this life and this world will not be able to fulfil their aspirations. How, then, could they enjoy the fortune of visiting the hidden sacred land?

'Those who do not believe me and other incarnate beings, those who have the wrong view of our activities, use abusive language against us, and instead believe in the tricks of the hypocrites—and are therefore unable to act according to the holy teachings—will fall down into hell. Therefore, it is important that you associate only with people who abide by the holy vows.

'While opening the great door of the Hidden Land you must make religious offerings as much as possible. Make circumambulations of the four caves. Worship the lords of the land by burning incense and by performing religious ceremonies for the prevention of internal dissention. It is important that you should make fire offerings in the name of the khandros. That will help subvert the gods, spirits and demons. All will come to your help, and your impediments will disappear—both inwardly and outwardly. And you will be able to take many of the fortunate ones to the sacred land.

'Give up your hesitations. All of you: offer your prayers. The holy vow you make is infallible. Moreover act according to the guidebook to the land of Demoshong and the secret advice of the khandros. Don't confound your ways and means to achieve your religious goals. Be tactful. Preserve your natural disposition towards the correct view and establish the life force of meditation. By the bold endeavour of your conduct, not concerned with hope and fear, lose not courage to do good for yourself and others. Do not forget what I teach.'

Saying this, Padmasambhava vanished into an unknown place, and there appeared unthinkable numbers of mysterious signs, which I perceived either directly or through unconscious feelings.

Tulshuk Lingpa concludes *The Creeper-Plant of the Mind* with some general considerations:

In making a journey to Beyul Demoshong, all doubt and hesitation must totally vanish. O you multitude of people who are possessed of your past good deeds and fortunes, if you desire to visit the rugged country, the Hidden Land of Padmasambhava, give up your distrust, which is like a poison; develop in your heart a sense of faith and pure thought. Avoid the company of people that commit sinful acts in these degenerate times. Join the company of the faithful followers of the dharma. Do not attach yourself to worldly things. Come! Join me in my tour of Demoshong. May it be the cause of peace and happiness for all beings.

CHAPTER ELEVEN

Géshipa

There was a prophecy written in a pecha, or scripture, that when the time came to open Beyul Demoshong, the lama who would open the way would first announce himself at the Tashiding Gompa. Though none of the lamas of that monastery—nor anyone else for that matter—could tell me which pecha it was written in, let alone show it to me, it is a well-known part of Sikkimese lore. It is a belief that has changed the course of many a person's life. For when Tulshuk Lingpa and his followers arrived at Tashiding, though they arrived unannounced, there were people living there who had left their homes as far away as in Bhutan in order to be there when the prophesied lama arrived.

One such man was Géshipa. Now in his mid-eighties, he left his native Bhutan when he was thirty-six years old expressly to go to the Tashiding Gompa in Sikkim and await the arrival of the lama prophesied to open the door to the hidden realm. While others had been waiting in Tashiding for years, and even generations, Géshipa was an accomplished and well-known diviner, steeped in the prophecies. When he heard of the Chinese invasion of Tibet, the destruction of the monasteries, the incredible carnage and the exile of the Dalai Lama he knew that all these negative signs pointed in a single direction: towards the ripening of the time for the opening of Beyul Demoshong. He arrived there only a few months before Tulshuk Lingpa first walked up the hill from the village.

Both of Géshipa's parents were dead by the time he reached his first birthday. When he was a child his grandfather, who was a great yogi, died while in meditation. They left him in the full lotus posture and, as is the case with many accomplished Tibetan lamas, his body did not decay.

At first the young boy did not understand what it meant for someone to be dead. His uncle explained it to him by reminding him of a dog that had recently died in the neighbourhood. Géshipa had smelt it and seen its body rot and attract flies and maggots. When he understood what death meant, he didn't believe his grandfather was dead, so lifelike his body remained. Far from smelling of decay, there was a scent in the air of flowers in the vicinity of his grandfather's body. His uncle explained that it was his grandfather's spiritual attainment that prevented his body from decaying. Because the boy had grown up seeing his grandfather deep in meditation and not moving for days at a time, he still couldn't connect the state his grandfather was in with death. To make this connection clear, his uncle put the boy's hand to his own mouth and asked him what he felt. He felt the warmth of his own breath. Then his uncle took his hand and held it before his grandfather's mouth.

'What do you feel?' his uncle asked him.

'Nothing,' he was obliged to reply. 'It is cold.'

It was then the boy realized something of the mysteries his grandfather explored while he was alive—sitting in meditation as if he were dead—and now that he was dead appearing still to be alive, preserving his body from the fate of the dog after death.

It was then the boy decided that he would dedicate his life to exploring similar mysteries.

He became the apprentice of a high lama who was a great diviner and soothsayer and the rainmaker for the king of Bhutan. As part of his training, he underwent the first of many meditation retreats, which lasted three years, three months and three days. Though most lamas undergo this meditation retreat, they usually do so in their late teens or early twenties. Géshipa was only in his early teens.

With hardly any food to eat his diet consisted mainly of nettles, which he gathered himself and cooked over a wood fire. He ate so many nettles that his skin turned green, just like the famous Tibetan poet yogi Milarepa.

He had inherited his grandfather's scriptures and it was during this retreat, nearly starving to death and freezing, that he read in them about the Hidden Land. He read that in the Hidden Land you never have to worry about having enough to eat.

'Plant a seed in the morning,' he read, 'and you can harvest by the evening.' You never had to worry about having enough clothing. No matter how cold it was, you'd always be warm.

Hungry, cold and alone in his cave, these words left an indelible mark on his mind. He decided that he would devote himself to finding this hidden land. Now in his mid-eighties and having never returned to Bhutan, Géshipa lives north of Tashiding in Yoksum, the last village before the high mountains and the 'Western Gate' to the Hidden Land.

The Yabla family, the wealthy landholding family in the village who were major sponsors of Tulshuk Lingpa, put him up in a wood-slat room above their cowshed where he lives to this day, and where I met him many times.

Géshipa is perhaps the happiest man I've ever met. Combining the innocence of a child with the wisdom of a sage, his belief is so direct that it is infectious. It was in his presence, more than in anyone else's, that I felt the lived reality of possibility that the quest for Beyul represents.

The first time I ventured to Yoksum to meet Géshipa I had the grown son of the Yabla family, who was well educated and spoke English perfectly, translate for me. When I communicated my reason for being there, that I wanted to speak of Tulshuk Lingpa and Beyul, Géshipa was reticent.

'These are secret things,' he said. 'Tantra. I can tell you nothing.'

I tried to get him to mollify his stance. But my interpreter had to be somewhere and left Géshipa and me to our own devices without a language in common. Though Géshipa had lived in Sikkim for over forty years his Nepali—the lingua franca of Sikkim—was still rudimentary. He lived in a world that appeared only to intersect with ours, and it was a world one couldn't help feeling immediately drawn into. By merely looking at him, one knew he held the keys to great mysteries—for not only did he look every bit the part of the Eastern sage, he lived with the simplicity of one.

When I was on my way to Yoksum and mentioned his name, people told me he was famous throughout Sikkim for performing divinations and controlling the weather. He was an accomplished rainmaker. It seemed whenever there was a drought, people would come to him, as they would if there was need for a dry day in monsoon. Shortly before I visited him, a newly constructed monastery nearby was to be inaugurated with a three-day ritual to which some high lamas were being helicoptered in, including a representative of the Dalai Lama. It was the middle of monsoon. Monsoon in Sikkim is severe, often raining incessantly for days at a time, and only rarely is there a twenty-four hour period without rain. The lamas of this new monastery came to Géshipa, who performed rituals he had learned as a child when he was apprenticed to the king of Bhutan's rainmaker. Those three days were dry. It is a matter of record.

On another occasion, Géshipa related to me a story from his time as an apprentice rainmaker when three representatives of the Bhutanese king arrived at his teacher's retreat in eastern Bhutan with a letter from the king. The rains had failed and crops were beginning to wither in the fields across the kingdom. The letter—which had been sealed with the king's own seal— instructed his teacher to make it rain, which he did with his usual alacrity. It rained so hard that within three or four days everybody in the kingdom had forgotten the drought and there was now a grave danger of floods. The king sent his representatives again, this time without the pleasantry of a letter but with instructions for him to stop the rain immediately. They had with them a heavy rope and instructions from the king to use it if within a day of their arrival the rain did not stop. They were to tie him up and douse him in water with only his nose above the surface until he stopped it.

When we found ourselves alone that first time with hardly a language between us, Géshipa pulled a kerosene cooker out from under his bed. He poured water from a plastic bottle into a pot, pumped and primed the cooker and started boiling tea. He was squatting on his haunches mixing in the tea and sugar, and though we tried we couldn't converse. So I undusted one of the few Nepali expressions I had at my disposal. *'Kay garnu,'* I said. What to do?

Géshipa found it so funny that of all the possible things I might know in Nepali I knew that expression, at once so common and so expressive of the simple wisdom of accepting what is and finding happiness in the present. This was something Géshipa seemed a master at—just plainly being happy at the passage of time—and he started rocking with laughter, squatting over the pot of boiling tea, saying, *'Kay garnu, kay garnu!'* Then he said, 'Englayshee?' He wanted to know the English equivalent.

'Kay garnu: Nepali,' I said. 'English: What to do.'

'WaDoDo,' he attempted, and I repeated it until he got it right.

Then he took out an ancient and battered address book and wrote phonetically in Tibetan script first *Kay garnu*, and then 'What to do', the whole time repeating it and laughing like a tickled Buddha. This seemed to have great importance for him; he wrote it in a few other places as well, so he couldn't possibly lose the English for *Kay garnu*.

The next time I visited Géshipa was about nine months later. Wangchuk had taken well to his role as an interpreter between his father and me during our long interviews in Darjeeling. Now we had taken our collaboration on the road, tracking down people and places in Sikkim connected with his grandfather's story.

Speaking both Nepali and Tibetan fluently, Wangchuk was acting as my interpreter and wonderful companion as well as undergoing his own journey of discovery about his grandfather, about whom he had grown up hearing stories but with none of the details we were uncovering.

When we walked up the dirt trail from Yoksum and climbed the old wooden stairs above the cowshed and entered Géshipa's room with *khatas*—the ceremonial scarves one presents to lamas—as well as a bag of fruits and biscuits to present to him, Géshipa stared at me, obviously recognizing me but trying to figure out from where.

So I raised my index finger to the heavens, twisted it and said, 'What to do?'

Géshipa almost fell out of his robe. 'What to do?' he repeated. 'What to do?' He was howling now with laughter. 'He's calling you Mr What-To-Do,' Wangchuk said as he handed Géshipa the fruit and biscuits and they started speaking Tibetan. I didn't pay them much heed as I took my seat on the bed opposite Géshipa's. Then I noticed Géshipa was writing in that same battered address book and Wangchuk was helping him sound something out.

Géshipa turned to me. He held the page close to his eyes so he could focus. Cautiously he mouthed out the words, 'Bout do die. What to do? A bout to die—what to do?' and he burst out laughing, even more intensely than before. He poked his finger to his chest: 'About to die.'

Then he said something to Wangchuk in Tibetan, which Wangchuk then interpreted: 'He's saying that he's very old now, and that he's about to die.'

'What to do?' Géshipa repeated with the levity of Zorba when the towers came crashing.

Wangchuk had a girlfriend in Delhi, with whom he was always trying to communicate using his mobile phone. But in Sikkim the towers are far apart and the mountains high; even though he was forever pulling his mobile phone out of his pocket and trying to get a signal, he couldn't get a signal strong enough to place a call. While we were sitting in Géshipa's room conducting our interview with him, he quietly took out his mobile phone. He turned it on and, even in the dim interior of that room towards sunset, I could see the surprise on Wangchuk's face.

'Look,' he said, 'a perfect signal!'

It was true. He quickly called Delhi. When he got his girlfriend on the other end, he stepped out of the door of Géshipa's room on to the old wooden staircase for some privacy but the signal faded the moment he crossed the threshold of Géshipa's room. The only place during that entire trip where his mobile phone worked was inside the room of that wizard.

The third time I went to Yoksum to visit Géshipa, I went with both Kunsang and Wangchuk. Kunsang and Géshipa hadn't met in over forty years. When we arrived this time, the rickety wooden staircase leading to Géshipa's room above the cows was full of black dogs—thirteen to be exact—who started barking and howling at us and blocking our way. Since their barking was accompanied by wagging tails, they seemed harmless enough; we pushed by them and into Géshipa's room.

After Kunsang and Géshipa exchanged greetings and comments on how the other looked—such as was natural for the first meeting in over forty years (Géshipa was in his late forties and Kunsang eighteen when last they met)—I asked Géshipa why there were so many black dogs guarding his door.

'It is because of the *dip shing*,' he replied.

I asked my faithful interpreter Wangchuk what dip shing was. He didn't know, so he asked his father.

Kunsang knew well.

'Dip shing isn't known to all lamas,' he said. 'It is known only to tertons. It is a potion for becoming invisible. I remember my father teaching Géshipa, Namdrol and Mipham about it. But you need some ingredients that are very difficult to obtain. Géshipa has been working on this for decades.'

Géshipa just started speaking, and it was all Wangchuk could do to keep up with the translation.

'The black dogs are a long story,' Géshipa began. 'I lived in Tashiding until about two years ago. Ever since the time Tulshuk Lingpa was here I've been collecting the ingredients. Some of the ingredients are easy to find, like the afterbirth of a black cat. Namdrol had that. He dried it, and had it with him all the time in a little pouch tied to a fold of his robe. He had it with him when we went to open Beyul.

'The hardest ingredient to get is top secret, and I cannot talk about it.' He then proceeded to speak of it with Kunsang but in such low tones that Wangchuk couldn't catch what he was saying.

After some moments of this top-secret association, Géshipa sprang up on his bed with surprising agility for someone his age, and took a scripture wrapped in cloth and sealed to its dusty shelf with an intricate lace of cobwebs. He sat back down, unwrapped it, searched for the right page and started reading softly to Kunsang about this secret ingredient, which Wangchuk thought might be of human origin.

Then Géshipa continued in a louder voice and Wangchuk resumed interpreting: 'The second-most difficult ingredient to find

Géshipa with Kunsang.

gives this potion its name. It is also the most important: the crows' nest. You need the twigs from a crows' nest but only from a very special crows' nest.'

Wangchuk whispered in my ear that dip shing literally means invisibility stick in Tibetan, the stick in question being the kind with which a crows' nest is constructed.

'There was a boy in the neighbourhood,' Géshipa continued, 'who was always climbing trees. I took him with me and we walked from Tashiding up to Ravangla. This was years ago. We went into the huge, ancient forest on the mountain above the town and we walked until we heard crows in the distance. We followed the sound until we saw the crows. Then we followed them until we were on the backside of the mountain and after three or four days we found where they made their nests high up in the trees. I had brought the boy because he climbed like a monkey. I sent him up with a rope to get a nest. The rope was for him to tie himself to the trunk before he climbed out on to the branch. But he refused to use the rope. The more I insisted, the higher he climbed out of my reach and started swinging from branch to branch laughing at me.

'He scampered up to the crows' nest, disturbing the crows who let out a raucous chorus of impotent protest. I yelled up to him to make sure the crows were completely black. Sometimes crows can have purple tails or wings, you see, and these won't do. He assured me of their black colour. So I told him to take the nest from the tree and bring it down.

'The nest was practically as big as the boy, made out of hundreds of sticks. I started examining it but the boy said we should hide it, so no one could see what we were doing. Though there was no one else there, he was right. These are secret things. Tantra. So we put the nest in a sack.

'We slept in the forest again that night, and in the morning we walked down to the river. It isn't just any stick from a black crows' nest that will work in the potion of invisibility. You have to test it.

'So we went to the river's edge. It was really a mountain stream, bounding down the mountain but the flow was swift and it would do. I broke off a piece of the nest, a stick about three inches long, and I dropped it into the flow. The boy had no idea why I was doing this but what he saw sure made him stare with wide eyes. For the stick hit the surface of the swiftly moving flow and moved *upstream*! This was exactly what it had to do if the nest had powers. The boy broke off another piece of the nest and tried it himself.

'"Stop!" I shouted. "We were lucky to find such a nest. Others have spent years looking. Don't waste it!"

'But the boy kept breaking off pieces of the nest, throwing them into the stream and watching them float against the stream's current—eyes full of wonder—until I grabbed the nest, threw it back in the sack and started back up the slope towards Tashiding.

'When we got to Tashiding, I put the nest into the metal chest under my bed with the other ingredients. As you can see, it isn't easy collecting the ingredients for the dip shing—though once I had the crows' nest, the black cat's afterbirth was easy.'

'Sure,' I quipped to Wangchuk under my breath, 'You just have to find a black cat, get it pregnant—and wait.'

Géshipa, though not understanding what I'd said to Wangchuk, laughed along. Then he continued, 'The dip shing takes years. But it is worth it. In the end, you apply just a little bit like a black paste on the forehead between the eyes—and like that, you're invisible.'

'One can make a potion to become invisible,' I said, 'but it's another thing if it really works.'

'Working,' Kunsang said curtly in English, as if to put a complete stop to any doubt. 'You need piece of crow nest. Black-cat-born-time.'

'He means the afterbirth of a black cat,' Wangchuk interpreted.

'Two things, these ones,' Kunsang continued, 'and third is black cat shit. Fourth one, very useful but top secret. I know but cannot say. I putting little inside my bag, then tying bag to one shoe. Doing mantra, then my bag is—I-am-losing. Everybody notice bag gone; they no see, I no see.'

'Tied to shoe?' I asked Wangchuk. 'What the hell is he talking about?' I was beginning to feel as if I'd entered the land of topsy-turvy. Wangchuk had grown up the son of his father, grandson of perhaps the craziest treasure revealer Tibet had ever produced,

and could understand the language of wizardry. Yet he came
down solidly on the side of his generation. Sceptical, rational and
modern in outlook, Wangchuk was not only a good interpreter
but a bridger of worlds. He respected, though not necessarily
followed, the ways of his ancestors.

'Tied to shoe,' Wangchuk explained, 'so you don't lose the bag
when it goes invisible.'

'Yes, yes!' Kunsang concurred, 'Only string seeing. If not tied,
losing bag. Crows' nest *very* powerful.'

'Let me get this straight,' I said. 'You need a piece of a black
crows' nest and a twig that goes upstream when put in water.
That twig. And then you need black cat afterbirth.'

'Oh, this one very important!' Kunsang exclaimed. 'Third one,
shit of black cat.'

He then said something to Géshipa in Tibetan about black cat
shit, and Géshipa started telling the story of how he secured his
supply.

Wangchuk interpreted:

'Since I did not own a black cat, I went into the village looking.
I am not so young, so it wasn't easy. Seeing a black cat behind
someone's house, I chased after it and caught it with my own
hands. I caught it, put it in a sack and brought it home. I tied its
leg to a string to wait for it to shit. But in the morning, the string
was broken and the cat was gone. It had climbed a tree nearby and
was meowing. The string had gotten wrapped around a branch. It
was stuck there. So I sat under the tree, waiting. I knew it would
have to shit sooner or later, and sure enough after a few hours I
saw it drop. I scooped it up and got the boy to climb the tree and
free the cat. Black cat not important—black cat shit important!'

'So that's the third,' I said to Kunsang. 'The fourth, what's
the fourth?' I was trying to trick Kunsang into divulging the
secret ingredient.

'Fourth one is—' Kunsang said, catching himself. 'Fourth one
I forget. Géshipa show me in book. But I don't know. He know; he
know.' 'You just said you know,' I shot back. 'You said, "I know
but I cannot tell." Now you say you don't know.'

'I don't know, really. He know. I forget but he show in book.
Difficult to find. Very difficult!'

'Can a person also go invisible?'

'Sure thing! Then nobody will see you. *Kema, kema*: incredible! I don't do this kind of work. Fourth thing, very difficult to find. Géshipa found it.'

'Why would you want to go invisible?' I asked.

'Sometimes necessary.'

'Why? To hide from the police? What did you do?'

Laughter.

'Have you gone invisible before?'

'No.'

'Do you know people who have?'

'No. Only stories.'

'The fourth ingredient is from human beings?'

'No, no, no—I forget.'

'You don't want to say?'

'Géshipa had the secret ingredient,' Kunsang said. 'I remember years ago, Géshipa telling me, "If one day I go to the Hidden Valley, I'll bring one small leather bag with everything in it—snake meat, frog meat, all dried. Black cat, too, all dry. Black dog meat, dry. I'll make everything dry and take it with me." But what to do? He had everything. He even had elephant liver, cut in little pieces. But all stolen.'

'Stolen?'

'Yes,' Kunsang said. 'Stolen.'

'What happened? Wangchuk, ask Géshipa what happened.'

'It had taken years to collect,' Géshipa said, 'and I had almost all the ingredients. I was living at the Tashiding Monastery in those days. As I got each ingredient, I put it into the locked metal box under my bed. Then, one day I went to put something else into the box and the box was gone. It hadn't gone invisible; it was stolen, along with one hundred and fifty rupees. So I had to start all over again. That's why there are so many black dogs at my door.'

I couldn't divine the connection. It had been my first and, I thought, quite innocent question. So I asked again, almost in desperation, 'But why all the black dogs?'

Géshipa got up from where he had been sitting cross-legged on his bed to squat on his haunches before his kerosene cooker and start a fire for tea. He poured water into a pot, opened a can of tea and threw in a huge handful. Taking a flat rock off the top of another rusted old can, he reached his hand in and threw handfuls of large-grained sugar into the water as well, oblivious of the ants that had been feeding on it.

Géshipa spoke so matter-of-factly of fantastic things that one could easily imagine their reality. There was gentleness in him, an innocence that was alien to any sort of guile. He lived with the simplicity of a man for whom the material world around him was of so little concern because the scope of his creative imagination was so immense. His eyes were at once innocent and deep. They sparkled as if they wanted to communicate what no words could— the accumulated wonder of their eighty-six years of looking on a world that was just plainly more fantastic than the world most of us look upon.

When he had poured tea for the four of us, he sat back down.

'The black dogs?' he said. 'They are quite necessary. For dip shing you need black dog meat. It started like this: one day I was walking through the village when I saw a black dog that had just died on the side of the road. That's how it is with this dip shing; sometimes you have to wait for such an opportunity. One of the ingredients is the meat of an entirely black dog. Since I am Buddhist, I cannot look for a black dog and kill it. Therefore I have to wait. I took the dog—it was a big dog—and I held its front legs and I swung it over my shoulder and brought it home on my back. There I cut off strips of meat and dried them.'

Kunsang turned towards me, bursting with laughter: 'The meat of a black dog and the stick from a crows' nest—flowing upstream. Incredible, incredible; insane, insane.'

'If you got the meat,' I asked Géshipa, hesitatingly, 'why the thirteen black dogs at the gate?'

'Oh, them?' he said, as if it were obvious. 'They're for the shit, not the meat. They're not for becoming invisible. They have nothing to do with dip shing; they're for making rain. There are other methods for making rain but using black dog shit is the most effective. You have to dry the black dog shit and grind it. Then you have to mix it with tsampa and make round balls out of it. You mix tsampa and water and form it into a vajra. First you touch the tip of the vajra to the shit. Then you dip it in a natural spring. That's how you stop rain. You also have to throw shit into the fire at the same time.'

Though I couldn't quite believe I was having this conversation, I asked him, 'How much shit do you need? Does it have to be the combined shit of thirteen black dogs?'

'No,' Géshipa said in a measured way as if he were a theologian discussing a fine point of doctrine. 'It actually has to be a black dog with a white sun and moon on its chest, over the heart.'

'Then what are the other dogs for, to keep it company?'

'It is like this,' Géshipa said, 'I told Yab Maila—the owner of the big house, my jinda who owns this cowshed—I told him that I needed a very specific black dog. So one day he saw a black dog and he offered the owner 2000 rupees. The owner liked the dog but 2000 rupees is 2000 rupees. So he sold the dog to my jinda and my jinda gave it to me. But the dog wasn't right. He doesn't understand about the white marks. He thinks the more dogs the better, so a few days later he came home with another dog, this one he had purchased in Gezing for 2500! But again it wasn't right. It wasn't until he came with the thirteenth dog that he got one with the proper markings, a little white moon and star over its chest. Then I told him to stop. But I think he's still keeping his eyes out for more.'

Kunsang gave me a wink. He got up, and excusing himself he braved the gauntlet of black dogs to find a bush on which to pee. He was gone quite a while.

'I just saw Yab Maila, the owner of this land, Géshipa's sponsor,' he said when he returned. 'He was also a big sponsor of my father's. We hadn't met in over forty years! It seems Géshipa has been speaking seriously about making another attempt at Beyul. Yab Maila made me promise I'd convince Géshipa not to. He's too old and has a heart condition. Yab Maila said Géshipa's mind is like a child's. The old man might be crazy but the young man is the one going around finding him black dogs, and paying for them!'

Kunsang looked at me with wide-eyed mirth.

'Is all of this true,' I asked Kunsang, 'or is this crazy?'

His reply was simple and to the point, 'It is truly crazy!'

As Kunsang, Wangchuk and I were walking back to the village in a merry mood, a black dog was lying in front of someone's house.

'Oh, look,' I said, 'I think it has a white spot!' At that moment the dog jumped to its feet, the hair on its spine bristling. It lowered its head and growled.

'Don't touch my shit,' Kunsang growled back like a ventriloquist, without moving his lips. '*Don't touch my shit*!

'Smart dog,' he said, 'maybe the incarnation of some lama. I don't know. Some crazy bad lama!'

Kunsang (L) and Wangchuk, Yoksum, Sikkim.

CHAPTER TWELVE

The Auspicious Centre

Tashiding Gompa, the Kanchenjunga range in the background.

Tashiding Gompa is a forty-five minute walk up a wooded mountain path from the village of Tashiding. On the auspicious day that Tulshuk Lingpa and his khandro and followers were first climbing that path, Géshipa was coming down from the gompa on his way to the village. He says that when he turned a corner and saw this lama wearing a white robe with long braids wrapped around his head, his khandro at his side and his attendants following, he had a sudden intuition. Remember, Géshipa had left his native Bhutan for Tashiding precisely because he had divined the time was coming for the lama who would open Beyul to arrive there.

Géshipa stopped and waited for Tulshuk Lingpa to reach him; then Géshipa pressed his palms and inclined his head.

'Where are you from?' was the first thing he asked Tulshuk Lingpa.

'I am from Kham,' came the reply.

Géshipa could not help himself reaching down to touch the lama's feet. He knew the prophecy that the one to open Beyul would be from Kham, and that's why he had asked the question. When he stood back up, Géshipa had tears rolling down his cheeks.

'We have been waiting so long,' Géshipa said and brought him up to the monastery.

Among the lamas of Tashiding, many of whom lived with their families in houses surrounding the monastery, word quickly spread—in a secret sort of way—that Tulshuk Lingpa had arrived.

Tashiding Gompa is a collection of temple buildings, behind which lies an area of stupas. There is a kora, a well-worn path circling the temple complex and stupas, by which the faithful circumambulate the holy site intoning the holy mantras, cycling through the 108 beads of their rosary-like malas.

Along the kora, towards the back behind the stupas, one finds the rock face by which the monastery actually derives its name. The full name of the monastery is Drakar Tashiding. Drakar means white rock. Tashiding means Auspicious Centre. So the name of the monastery translates to White Rock of the Auspicious Centre. The rock face does in fact have a light-coloured area roughly rectangular in shape and the size of a small door, and it is this section of the rock face that lends its name to the monastery. Since the most ancient times, there has been a belief prevalent in Sikkim that this white area of the rock is actually a door to Demoshong. There was even a small cavity in the rock inside of which was a loose stone. The opening of the cavity was such that though one could fit one's hand into the cavity and move the stone, you couldn't get the stone out. This was the 'key' to the door.

One of the lamas of Tashiding told me the story of a lama from the Pemayangtse Gompa, situated on a neighbouring mountain, who came to Tashiding to perform some prayers. He stayed at Tashiding for some time and used to do many koras every day, morning and evening. With each kora, he'd pass that white rock door. As he passed it he got to thinking about how his ancestors used to speak of Demoshong, what it would look like and how one would know when it was time for it to be opened. It would happen in the Great Age of the Seven Fires and One Water, *kalpa medun chuchik*. A kalpa is a great age. Medun chuchik means seven fires, one water. That means that whatever heat one sun generates today, whatever heat we receive, will be multiplied seven times. Everything will burn, all crops will wither and nothing will survive. After that there will be rain. That will be the time for the opening of Demoshong.

So this monk was doing his koras morning and evening. With every round as he passed by the white stone door he deepened his meditation about Demoshong. One time around, he stopped in front of the white stone door and started praying. According to the lama who told me the story, this lama from Pemayangtse started praying to the rock and suddenly found himself transported to the land behind the door. He met seven dakinis and they gave him a plant called sakusha. Sakusha is the Sikkimese name of the plant; the lama recounting this story couldn't tell me the English name. But he assured me it grew in Demoshong and nowhere near Tashiding. The dakinis gave him the plant, made him promise not to tell anyone about the Hidden Land and to take the plant to Pemayangtse Gompa.

Then, quite suddenly, he found himself transported out of the Hidden Land and he was standing once again in front of that stone door, holding in his hand the sakusha plant. Without telling anyone what had happened, he grabbed his bag and started down the mountain towards the Rangeet River at Legship in order to cross the river and climb to Pemayangtse. When he reached the river he was hot and sweaty. He took off his clothes and left them on the river bank. He took the plant with him right to the water's edge and left it on a river stone there, and he bathed himself in the river. While he was washing the river rose and swept the branch away.

ℝ   ℞

When they brought Tulshuk Lingpa to the Drakar stone that first day, he stood silently before the rock face and examined it closely. 'This stone has ter in it,' he proclaimed, 'but I am not the one to take it out. It isn't time.'

He took a small stone and scratched into the stone above the door the following tantric formula: Ha A Sha Sa Ma. People asked him what it meant. 'One day a terton will come who will understand,' he said. 'He will be the one to open this door.'

Géshipa and the other lamas of Tashiding, though pulsing with excitement that the lama had arrived who would fulfil their highest dream by opening the door to the secret place, kept this knowledge to themselves. To everyone else it was simply that a great lama had arrived, and the occasion was marked by a festive atmosphere. People flocked to get his blessings.

One of the most powerful families in the area was known as the Yabla family of Yoksum. They were—and are—the big landholders of Yoksum. In fact it was the Yabla family that was to give Géshipa his place above the cows a few years before I met him there. There were six brothers in the Yoksum Yabla family. They were important people then, and they are important people now. They own hotels and the biggest beer brewery in Sikkim. Five of them were destined to become close disciples of Tulshuk Lingpa. The only one who didn't believe in Tulshuk Lingpa and Beyul was the youngest brother, known as the *kansa*. The course of his life was to bring him to another magical land, controversial in its own right for its irreality. Famous now throughout India for having made it to that promised land, he is a major Bollywood star, well known for playing the dark villain under the stage name of Danny Denzongpa.

The first of the brothers to have contact with Tulshuk Lingpa was the eldest, Yab Maila, the tax collector for the king. He came bearing gifts of fruit, cloth and bottles of liquor. He was greatly impressed by Tulshuk Lingpa, and that night, back in Yoksum, he had a very auspicious dream concerning Tulshuk Lingpa and the Hidden Land. Yab Maila's father had been there when Dorje Dechen Lingpa had come to Sikkim to open the way, so he knew the stories. He guessed correctly that Tulshuk Lingpa was there because of Beyul. So he returned to Tashiding, a walk of many hours—there were no motorable roads at that time—and Tulshuk Lingpa admitted to him privately that he was there because of Beyul. Yab Maila became Tulshuk Lingpa's jinda, or sponsor. 'When you go to Beyul,' he pleaded with Tulshuk Lingpa, 'be sure to take me with you. But you should leave Tashiding now,' he warned. 'There are too many people here. You must keep your reason for being here secret. Why don't you come with me to Yoksum? You can stay at my house.'

Tulshuk Lingpa, together with his khandro and disciples from Simoling, walked up the valley to Yoksum, the last village before the wooded slopes rise to the snows and the glaciers of Mount Kanchenjunga. Before he left, Tulshuk Lingpa called Géshipa aside. Géshipa was not his name until that time. He was known as Gomchela, which means Great Meditator. Tulshuk Lingpa said, 'I name you Géshipa.' Géshipa means Four Hundred in Tibetan. 'I name you Géshipa because you will come with me to Beyul, and you will take out 400 books of ter there. Four is the number of gates to Beyul. You will know them well.'

In Sikkim, there are four major caves sacred to Padmasambhava, caves where Padmasambhava hid ter for future generations. Before Tulshuk Lingpa took his leave of Géshipa he told him to meet him on a particular day at one of the sacred caves, the one named Lho Khandro Sangphug. It is the southern cave, on the banks of the Rangeet River not far from the border with India.

As Tulshuk Lingpa and Yab Maila were walking up to Yoksum, Tenzing Norgay was coming down leading a group of climbers. Following his successful ascent of Mount Everest, Tenzing Norgay was much in demand as a leader of climbing groups. As they drew close, Yab Maila warned Tulshuk Lingpa not to tell Tenzing Norgay anything about the Hidden Land. 'This must be kept secret,' he warned. 'Tenzing Norgay is too famous. If he knows, the word will be out and even the king will come to know of it. Above all else, we must keep this from the king; therefore—' and he put his finger to his lips. To the end Tenzing Norgay, though he remained Tulshuk Lingpa's jinda, never knew the real reason for his coming to Sikkim.

After spending some time in Yoksum, Tulshuk Lingpa returned briefly to Tashiding. Then he announced that he would be leaving for Simoling. Both those who knew his real reason for coming to Sikkim and those who didn't were afraid if he left, he'd never come back. They begged him to stay. 'We'll give you a place to live,' they told him. 'We'll provide you with food, clothing—whatever you need. You won't have to worry about a thing. Just stay.'

Tulshuk Lingpa met Géshipa at the Lho Khandro Sangphug cave on the appointed day. The name Lho Khandro Sangphug means Southern Cave of the Dakini's Secret Vagina. We do not know what secret things they had to do there. After that, Tulshuk Lingpa's investigations were complete, and he returned to Simoling.

The caretaker of the Tashiding Monastery, the man with the keys. When we first met, he explained to me through pantomime that he lost his eye by falling into a cooking fire while a young child.

CHAPTER THIRTEEN

The Return

One day—it was close to a year after Tulshuk Lingpa returned to Simoling from Sikkim—he said, 'Those who are interested in going to Paradise, to the Hidden Valley of Immortality—now's the time. We go. We go tomorrow!' It took him close to a month to actually leave but Simoling and Pangao and the surrounding areas were abuzz with the news. There were debates among villagers and within families, between those who believed in Tulshuk Lingpa and those who thought he was a drunken, crazy lama. Those who were going needed time to rid themselves of their possessions, selling off enough to finance the journey and giving away the rest. Kunsang told me that in the beginning there were about seventy families that wanted to go but in the end only half that number went.

Tulshuk Lingpa made it clear that only those with true and unflinching faith should even think of coming with him. Opening the way to a hidden land is a tremendous act—calling as it does upon tremendous physical, spiritual and imaginative powers. He knew that the fate of the entire enterprise would hinge upon the fate of each individual who came with him. One's faith had to be total, and the test of this was given even before leaving. Only those who would gladly give up everything—every attachment to both people and material goods and even the notion of return—were fit for such a journey. If you wanted to plant your crops as an insurance policy against a failed attempt, if you wanted to only loan your house out and not sell it or give it away in order to have something to return to, your faith was thereby shown not to be great enough. Your lack of faith would present an obstacle sufficient to block everyone's way.

For those who left for Sikkim, over 150 people, such faith was not a problem. I've spoken with many of them, and they gladly rose to the opportunity by selling off those possessions that were easily sold to raise funds for the journey and giving away the rest, including their houses. What good would the price of a house do them when all they needed was the money to travel to Sikkim and for the food necessary to reach the gate, high in the snow mountains of Sikkim? As Tinley's mother-in-law had told me, all tickets to the Hidden Land were one-way.

When asked what they should bring, Tulshuk Lingpa told his followers that they'd need food and bedding only until they reached Beyul: once they arrived, they wouldn't need such things. He told them to take some seeds, though. That way they could grow their own crops there.

Tulshuk Lingpa left with his khandro and some of his closest disciples. The rest came in a couple of batches some months later. After Tulshuk Lingpa had left, and the others were readying themselves to go, the police came to Simoling making inquiries. They said to the lamas who remained at the monastery, 'We have heard that this village will be emptying out and you'll all be following your lama to the Hidden Land. Is this true?' 'No,' they lied, 'this is not true. We are going to meet our head lama in Sikkim but it is only for a pilgrimage. We know nothing of the Hidden Land.' The police left, only to return some days later. They started asking people in the village too. This time the lamas heard of it and confronted the police, 'Why are you coming around here again, asking foolish questions. We told you before: we aren't going to the Hidden Land.' The police left and never returned to ask questions in Simoling.

At the time, Kunsang was with his mother in the cave in Pangao. One police inspector and three constables risked slipping into the Beas River at the bottom of the cliff to come to the cave in order to make their inquiries. 'Is it true that your husband has gone to Sikkim and many more from here plan on leaving soon in order to go to Shangri-La?'

Kunsang's mother lied. 'No. This is not true. We are only going for pilgrimage.' They didn't believe her. So she tried to win them over by making some food for them. Officers of the law always like such things. While she was cooking for them, Kunsang ran up to the village and got one of the big landholders, a big man, with influence. He came to the cave and gave the police hell for giving trouble to the wife of their lama. The policemen left and didn't bother them again.

Shortly before Kunsang, his mother and sister Kamala left for Sikkim, Kunsang remembered that his father had said that a stone within the cave had ter in it, which he would one day take out. Since his father had gone to Sikkim and would never return, and since they'd all be soon following, he thought that being the son and grandson of tertons meant maybe he could take it out. So one day when their mother was away Kunsang and Kamala dug out the stone his father had mentioned, which was in a little alcove in the cave that served as the family altar. Under that stone, there were two other stones. Kunsang knocked his knuckle on one of them, and it resounded with a hollow sound. He lifted the stone, and a large black snake raised its head and flicked its tongue at him. He recoiled and ran away. 'It definitely wasn't the right time,' Kunsang told me. 'And I wasn't the right person.'

As the time drew near for the family to leave for Sikkim, Kunsang became melancholic and, he admitted to me, quite sad to say goodbye to everybody who was staying behind and to everything he had ever known.

'I had never been away from home before,' he explained. 'Sikkim was on the other side of India and Shambhala very much further. I knew we'd never return. I was excited but also afraid.

'Then people told me, "You have nothing to worry about. 100 per cent! Your father is going to be King of Shambhala, and you're going to be prince!"

'Then I was very happy, me, *Prince of Shambhala!*'

When Kunsang told me this story, he howled with laughter, 'Me, Prince of Shambhala—*Prince* of Shambhala!'

Kunsang's attitude towards his father and his going to the Hidden Land was deeply reverential, that of an absolute believer in both his father's spiritual accomplishments and in the reality of Beyul. Yet when a point of absurdity about some detail of the story or even of the entire enterprise itself occurred to him, he never shied away from expressing it. His was a knife-edge understanding—expressing the reality of Beyul as an unquestionable truth in one breath and punching holes of absurdity spiced with tremendous humour into it with the next. Behind his irreverence was always a deep feeling for the truth that can be contained by neither facts nor logic and can be found only in contradiction. Such was his father's legacy.

He proudly said on many occasions, 'My father, he was the *crazzziest* lama who ever lived.' I often had the feeling his father taught him not only dharma but also his own particular brand of craziness and through him, more than through any other source, I had a window into Tulshuk Lingpa's character.

When Tulshuk Lingpa arrived back in Sikkim, he lived at Tashiding and made it his base. With his followers from Simoling and Kullu following and setting up camp on the hillsides next to the monastery, there was little hiding his true mission. People from Sikkim, Darjeeling and Bhutan heard the news and started moving to Tashiding, swelling the original population of perhaps seventy-five in the monastery and the houses surrounding it to over 400 people. Many of the lamas at Tashiding who are there to this day moved there because they wanted to be there when the prophesied terton came to open Beyul. Others moved there when they heard Tulshuk Lingpa had arrived.

ഇ   ൶

In the course of writing this book, I went with Kunsang and his son Wangchuk to Tashiding. Kunsang hadn't been to Tashiding in forty-three years. I had been to Tashiding on my own and with Wangchuk the year before. Having seen how reverentially the lamas of Tashiding treated Wangchuk when they heard he was Tulshuk Lingpa's grandson, I knew it would be a great occasion for them when Kunsang—Tulshuk Lingpa's spiritual heir—arrived unannounced.

'Just think,' I said to Kunsang as we sat resting on a rock on the side of the steep path to the monastery. 'The Prince of Shambhala is coming, and they don't even know! How can this be? This just isn't right.'

I stood up and motioned Kunsang to lead the procession up to the monastery, for Wangchuk to follow, and I took up the rear. Making my hands into a pretend trumpet, I puffed out my cheeks and made the sound of a fanfare by pressing air through my lips.

'Bumb-be-de bummm, be-de-dummmm! The Prince of Shambhala is arriving! Bumb-be-de-bummmm!'

'The Prince of Shambhala,' I announced, making a flourish to Kunsang. 'The Crown Prince,' I continued, motioning to Wangchuk. Then I pointed my finger to myself, 'And their scribe!'

That is how we arrived at Tashiding, like three raving lunatics, hysterical with laughter, 'Bumb-be-de-bummmm! The Prince of Shambhala, the Crown Prince, and their scribe are arriving!'

Word quickly spread of our arrival, and soon all the lamas and many of the older people who were there in the early sixties were gathered around Kunsang who started telling stories. Then we all got up and went to the *drakar*, the stone door to Shambhala. Ever watchful and hopeful that the terton will arrive to open the way, perhaps they thought Kunsang was their man and this was the time. But Kunsang, with whatever powers he inherited from his ancestors and with whatever wisdom he gleaned from his life experience growing up in the extraordinary way he did, is always quick to say he is not a terton.

Instead of opening the door, he and the lamas of Tashiding examined the stone noting how the door used to be of a lighter colour, which was interpreted as indicative of the darkness of our times. They searched for Tibetan letters imbedded in the stone, an *Om Ah Hung*—the opening syllables of the mantra of Padmasambhava—which used to be above the door. They discovered that the letters had migrated across the stone face. Pointing them out to each other, they were each more hopeful than the next in locating these migrating letters in the magic rock, door to another realm. I don't read Tibetan, though I can recognize Tibetan letters. I recognized no letters in the cracks they pointed out in the rock face. Perhaps my powers of imagination weren't great enough.

Then, to see who might open the way, the ancient robed lamas of Tashiding took turns playing a sort of spiritual pin the tail on the donkey. Each lama would take five paces away from the stone face, turn and stare straight at the 'key' to the door—the fist-sized hole in the rock within which was a loose stone. Holding his right arm out before him with index finger extended and taking his bearings, he then covered his eyes with his left hand and took stumbling steps towards the wall until his finger touched the rock. Tradition has it that if your blind finger finds its way into the hole, the door will open. When my turn came to see if I might be the one to open the door and let all these venerable lamas—who had been waiting so long—through, I came up wide of the mark. Opening my eyes, I felt inside the keyhole but the stone inside wouldn't move. One of the old lamas told me, with an edge of anger in his voice, how a Bengali tourist had heard of the secret of the keyhole and its miraculously loose stone imbedded in a stone wall. When no one was watching he took out his penknife and tried to pry the stone out, in the process jamming it forever.

Followers of religious leaders are notorious for lowering their teachers' understanding to the level of their own while exalting their teacher's attainments beyond all measure. Therefore we needn't judge the terton's level by that of his followers. Lamas earnestly stumbling blind with their index fingers stretched before them and stubbing them against a stone wall don't necessarily reflect the terton's understanding of just what a crack in the world might be and the methods he'd employ to open it.

Where did Tulshuk Lingpa draw the line between fact and fancy, or between metaphor and literal truth? Just what did he have to fulfil before he could attempt an opening? We know he had to do certain things before an opening could be made. He had business, for instance, in two of the major caves in Sikkim visited by Padmasambhava.

One of them was the northern cave, known as Lhari Nyingpuk, which translates to the Heart Cave on the Gods' Hill. Tulshuk Lingpa left Tashiding at one point to go there with five of his close disciples including Géshipa, Namdrol and Mipham. When Kunsang, Wangchuk and I were in Yoksum, Géshipa described what happened.

They got to the cave—a few days' march from Tashiding— and Tulshuk Lingpa performed a puja after which he picked up a stick, scratched a circle in the floor of the cave and told his disciples to dig. They didn't have any tools but used stones and their bare hands. As the hole grew, Tulshuk Lingpa was staring into it. Then he suddenly told them to stop. 'Enough,' he said. 'Fill it back in.' When they had, he told them he had seen ter in the ground but it wasn't the time to take it out. 'I saw a stone dorje,' he told them. None of them had. 'It is one of a pair,' he continued. 'The other one is in Demoshong. I only had to confirm it. It is not for me to take this one out.'

We know there are four gates to Demoshong, one in each of the cardinal directions. There are also four caves, which are allied to the four gates. Tulshuk Lingpa also went to another of the caves—the western cave—called Nub Dechen Phug, which translates to the Western Cave of Great Bliss.

Again he went with five or six of his closest disciples, among them Géshipa, Namdrol and Mipham. This time his disciples were ready for anything, and they brought tools just in case. Tulshuk Lingpa did a puja, indicated a place outside the cave in the ground just before the entrance and told his disciples to dig there. Proud of themselves for the foresight of bringing digging implements, they started digging. At three or four feet down their shovels and picks all glanced off a huge flat rock covered in a strange brown material.

'Turn the rock over,' Tulshuk Lingpa commanded, 'and I will take out a tremendous ter.'

'But Master,' Namdrol protested, 'it is too big to turn over. We don't have the tools. We'll hurt our backs.'

Tulshuk Lingpa became furious. When a terton is taking out ter, you should never contradict him. He is stepping through a crack in the logic that holds the world together; therefore you should not hold him to your own paltry standard of what is and is not possible.

Tulshuk Lingpa reached into the belt beneath his robes and pulled out his purba, the magic purba he had taken out of the cave in Tibet with Dorje Dechen Lingpa. He held it before him, point up. Then spinning it in his hand, he jumped into the hole with a flourish, stood on the flat rock and touched it with the tip. Though he had only touched the tip of the purba to the rock, the rock cracked and a piece broke off. Tulshuk Lingpa reached into the crack and took out a small piece of tightly rolled yellowed paper.

Jumping out of the hole, he told the others to fill it in and he walked away.

Back at Tashiding, he unfolded the meaning in the few scratches written on the tightly rolled paper. He dictated it to one of his disciples who wrote it down. Usually he would have had Namdrol be his scribe but he was still angry at Namdrol for having introduced doubt at the decisive moment. The resulting book, of only three pages, was only a minor ter: a prayer to make the deities happy on the way to Demoshong. The ter he could have taken out, if they could have miraculously turned the large stone, would have been a guide to all the ter in Demoshong. Some of his disciples tried to convince Tulshuk Lingpa to go back to the cave with the right tools to turn the rock so he could get the ter he had gone there for but he said the time for that was past.

Most of Tulshuk Lingpa's disciples from Himachal Pradesh were from Simoling. By most accounts, over half the village went to Sikkim, selling enough of their possessions to make the journey and giving away the rest. There were also two families from a village down the valley called Koksar, which is just north of the Rohtang Pass, including the khandro, her sister Yeshe and their mother. People in that village tried to dissuade those who wanted to go, saying Tulshuk Lingpa was crazy and would lead them to ruin. The two families who were followers of Tulshuk Lingpa made their preparations for leaving in secret and left in the middle of the night without telling anyone. They walked over the Rohtang Pass to Manali, where they got a bus to the Plains.

As the waves of people from Himachal Pradesh arrived in Tashiding, the atmosphere became electric. Word spread throughout Sikkim and the Darjeeling Hills that the long-prophesied lama had arrived, and everybody had to make a decision. People's faith was so great that many were divesting themselves of their material goods—land and homes included—without ever meeting Tulshuk Lingpa, just on the word that he was the one. Fields were lying fallow. Many more were staying at home but had provisions ready so when they heard the time had come, they could leave everything and head directly for Mount Kanchenjunga and pass through the gate while it was still open. I spoke with people who had gone north into the high mountains to hide tsampa, corn and other provisions in caves so when they heard the way was open, they could go as quickly as possible without having to first buy food and then carry it into the high mountains. It looked as if half the Kingdom of Sikkim would have left for the Hidden Land once Tulshuk Lingpa had made the opening.

Tulshuk Lingpa's followers who gathered at Tashiding were from all over the Tibetan world—Lahaul, Bhutan, Sikkim, Nepal and the Darjeeling Hills. They spoke a polyglot of languages. With each group from their own distinct region, speaking their own language, they tended to form groups and live together in encampments slightly set apart. Everybody was suspicious of the Lahaulis, since they were the ones who came with Tulshuk Lingpa and were his oldest and closest disciples, some having known him for over twenty years. Often they would speak with Tulshuk Lingpa in a language the others couldn't understand. The others always feared that when the time came, Tulshuk Lingpa would take with him only his older disciples and sponsors—the ones from Lahaul whom, one old woman from Bhutan told me (with more than a hint of jealousy even after all these years), he treated like his own children. While it is true and quite natural that his closest disciples tended to be Lahaulis, there was no reason to think he would have left the others behind. Yet such is human nature, even for those attempting to leave this world for a world beyond war and ethnic troubles.

₨   •   ₧

Kunsang told me that when people came to see his father they would often bring offerings of food. After everyone left, Tulshuk Lingpa would instruct them to throw the food out. They were afraid of being poisoned. Chang, homemade beer, was especially suspect.

I too in my travels around Sikkim was often warned to be careful of being poisoned. At first, I thought people were warning me because hygienic conditions can sometimes be less than optimal. But the poisoning I was being warned against and about which Kunsang was speaking was not accidental but deliberate—and deadly.

The first time I heard of this was while walking in North Sikkim, relying on the kindness of strangers to put me up for the night. One night I told my host my intentions of walking to a small town I will call X (so not to bring insult to an entire town), and he gave me a stern warning.

'If you go to X,' he told me, 'bring your own water and food. Don't accept anything there, not even a cold drink or tea.'

I asked him why.

'Food poisoning,' he said.

'Bad hygiene in X?'

'They poison people there.'

'On purpose?'

'Yes,' he said. 'Black magic. Human sacrifice. There are people there who worship a dark goddess who demands human sacrifice. They believe by killing you they will gain the wealth you would have accumulated over the course of your life. They also believe they will acquire your luck. Look, you are a Westerner. Just by the fact that you can travel so far means you are both extremely lucky and wealthy, at least by local standards. Therefore you would be a perfect target. So be careful!'

The next day I walked down the Teesta River Valley, through little villages in a vast mountain landscape. The other side of the river, where deep forests rose to spectacular heights, was Dzongu. It was a reserve for the indigenous Lepcha people restricted to foreigners. I enjoyed my walk immensely, passing through the tiny mountain villages, stopping now and again on a flat stone overlooking the deep to have a snack and take off my shoes and relax. My host's warnings had made me change my plans. Instead of spending the night in X, I'd get a jeep from there back to Gangtok.

A few kilometres before X, I met a man who invited me to his house for tea. He was a farmer, mainly of cardamom, but also had a nursery and pigs and was quite wealthy. His house was large, rambling and quite new. We sat in his living room, and he asked me where I was headed. I told him to X and then on to Gangtok. 'When you are in X,' he said gravely, 'don't take any food. Poison.'

I acted as if I didn't know anything about it: 'They have bad hygiene there?'

'No,' he said in a hushed tone, 'they will poison you. Black magic. Human sacrifice. They believe by killing someone they will gain wealth. Don't take even tea there.'

'What poison do they use?'

'It is called *kapat*,' he said.

He told me the symptoms of poisoning by kapat. 'First your throat will begin to hurt and it will go dry. Your eyes will grow pale; your lips will become papery and dry. Your fingernails will become yellow; your teeth will turn blue and form cracks; your joints will ache. Then you will feel dizziness and your heart will feel pain. It will kill you from within five minutes to six months, depending on the dosage.'

'Where do they get it?'

'In the market. But if anyone sees someone buying it, they will go through the village yelling out "So-and-so bought kapat!" So no one will eat at his house.'

'Do you think it really works? Do people gain wealth through this human sacrifice?'

'Yes,' he said, 'I have seen it. People do grow rich, for a while. Then things turn bad for them, and they become very poor. They become like beggars. They become outcasts of society because people know what they've done.'

As he was telling me this, his wife brought me tea. I suddenly felt myself in an episode of *The Twilight Zone.* I could just hear the viewing audience all yelling out, 'Don't drink the tea! How do you think a simple farmer lives in such a rich house?'

'How would I know if someone was trying to poison me?' I asked. 'For instance, how do I know what's in this tea?' I asked it jokingly, though with a tinge of concern.

'You can look at me and tell I wouldn't hurt you, can't you?'

I drank the tea. They also gave me a delicious lunch. And I've lived to tell the tale. I do look at my fingernails from time to time but they haven't turned yellow—yet.

I walked into X. It was just another dingy little bazaar town that looked like a Hollywood stage for a Western movie. While waiting there for about an hour for a jeep heading to Gangtok, I drank my own water and ate the crackers I had brought with me.

Poisoning was not always deliberate and inflicted on others. There was one disciple of Tulshuk Lingpa who poisoned himself. His name was Gyorpa, and by all accounts he was a bit crazy. He had been a student of Mandrel, one of Tulshuk Lingpa's closest disciples and an expert in Tibetan medicine and herbal remedies. One day Gyorpa became ill with a high fever, and he decided to treat himself. He indiscriminately picked all sorts of herbs, ground them up into a powder, mixed them in water and drank them. Naturally, his condition only worsened. So he started climbing trees, breaking off branches and grinding up their bark and eating that. He developed continuous diarrhoea, a tremendous headache, and his fever shot up and kept climbing until he was dead.

The old woman at Tashiding who told me about his death ended her story by saying, 'I guess that will teach you not to eat ground-up trees.'

CHAPTER FOURTEEN

Lepcha Tales

Beyul means Hidden Land. Both its existence and its opening are cloaked in mystery and are meant to be kept secret. Tulshuk Lingpa's teachers, Chatral Rinpoche and Dudjom Rinpoche, warned him to keep quiet and take only a few disciples. They cautioned that Beyul could not be opened by brute force. Yet events seemed to take on a life of their own. Tulshuk Lingpa had taken centre stage at the central monastery in Sikkim and the numbers of his followers were growing daily, all of whom were intent on vanishing from this world and all its problems to enter a land that was known to exist on the slopes of Mount Kanchenjunga ever since people first started living in the land that became known as Sikkim.

The original inhabitants of Sikkim were the Lepchas, an ancient group of people who since the earliest times spoke of a valley hidden on the slopes of their sacred mountain Kanchenjunga. In order to understand the Lepchas' knowledge of the Hidden Land I went to Sonam Lepcha, one of the culture holders of the Lepcha community, a musician and keeper of their most ancient lore.

'We call this land—the land of the Lepcha, what others call the Darjeeling Hills and Sikkim—*Mayel Lyang*,' he told me. 'Mayel means hidden. Lyang means land. We also call it *Mayel Maluk Lyang*. Maluk means to rise up. The Lepcha god hid a treasure, and one day it will be found. So *Mayel Maluk Lyang* means "The land in which the Hidden Treasure will Rise". We Lepchas, we call ourselves *Matanchi Rongkup*, which means Mother's Beloved Ones.

'Though we call our land Mayel Lyang, Mayel Lyang is really the name of a valley high on the slopes of Mount Kanchenjunga.

'It is called Mayel Lyang because the valley is hidden. The first god and the first goddess created the first Lepchas from the pure snows of the high mountains. This is where we came from. Westerners have written their books and they argue amongst themselves, saying we migrated from the east, the north, the west or the south. None of them can agree. This is because they are all wrong. We migrated from nowhere. We come from the high slopes of Mount Kanchenjunga. Our language is older than theirs. The Lepcha language is older than Hebrew. It is older than Sanskrit, Tibetan and even your English. Lepcha is the original language of the world. It was the language spoken in the Garden of Eden! In 1987 our written language was 5675 years old. Researchers don't go from place to place; they don't visit the villages. They just read the books written by other researchers and they write new books. The lies get passed on. They think Mayel Lyang is a mythical valley.

'If you write of this, people might think it's only a story, and that Mayel Lyang exists only in the imagination of a few crazy old people. But I will tell you a story that proves this place is real, that it isn't mythical but only hidden.

Sonam Lepcha.

'Some time back, there was an old man named Tee-koong Nanak. One day he went hunting blue sheep, which roam wild on the high slopes. He crossed Ponang Hill and started climbing. A cloud came low on the mountain and there was a storm. The storm passed but night had fallen. He saw a village. There were seven stone houses in that village. Blue sheep, usually so skittish and afraid of man, were sleeping in front of one of the houses. When he reached that house, an old couple came out and told him he could stay for the night. Though the house was in the high snow mountains, in its garden there were cucumber, pumpkins and other vegetables. He was quite dizzy, probably from the altitude. They served him food in a golden bowl with a golden lid. He couldn't recognize what it was they gave him but it was extremely tasty. At night, when he was ready to sleep, the old couple who had served him seemed to have grown even older. He slept. He felt neither hot nor cold.

'In the morning when he awoke no one was there. He called out but there was no answer. So he opened the door to the room where the old couple had gone to sleep. On the bed were two babies: one, a boy and the other, a girl. Since there was no one else there, he could not leave the babies alone. As the day progressed, the babies grew older. At midday they were middle-aged, and at night they were again the old couple he had met the night before. They served him food in the same golden bowl. The golden bowl was full of food and it was hot. When they turned their backs he took the golden bowl, shoved it under his jacket and ran out the door. As he was running away the old couple shouted after him, "You have to eat that food here." But he didn't listen to them. He ran away along a trail but whenever he turned back he couldn't see the trail he had just run along. The jungle was so thick and the slope so steep that it seemed impossible he had just passed through it. A cloud came low and he could see nothing. He came to the Rangyong River. There was a small hill just beside the river. He stopped there and took out the bowl but it wasn't made of gold. It was nothing but leaves stitched together, and the food inside was nothing but rotting leaves. But it was still warm.

'The hill where he stopped was called Kazimpon. The hunter was from Lingtem Village. This is in the Dzongu district. The man's name was Nanak. The place he went to was Mayel Lyang. Now no one knows where that is.'

'What does it mean,' I asked him, 'that people in Mayel Lyang change from being babies to old people every day, only to become babies again?'

'It means they are immortal,' he said.

'I went to Dzongu,' he continued, 'to a remote village called Sakyong. This is where Nanak set out to hunt the blue sheep. An old person there told me this story. Then he took me to Kazimpon Hill, where Nanak discovered that his golden bowl had turned to leaves. There is a hot spring just at the base of the hill.'

Mount Kanchenjunga straddles the Sikkim-Nepal border, on both sides of which there are stories about a herder who stumbled into the Hidden Valley. The tales vary slightly with the tellers but it typically goes like this:

A herder of sheep goes into the high snow slopes of Mount Kanchenjunga looking for one of his animals who has gone astray. He follows its tracks in the snow until the tracks disappear in a green valley of tremendous beauty. He comes to a house and they ask him why he came there. He tells them he was looking for his sheep, and asks them if they've seen it. Like a man who drops a coin into a gutter only to find a bar of gold, they tell him he needn't worry about the sheep. It is nothing. They tell him he has made it to the Hidden Valley.

In another version, a herder of sheep is grazing his animals on the high slopes of Mount Kanchenjunga and every day one of his sheep comes back with fresh seeds and greenery stuck to its coat from plants that grow nowhere near such high altitudes. He decides to follow the animal to see where it goes. Thus he happens upon the Hidden Valley.

The inhabitants of the valley give him food and a place to sleep and the next day they give him a pumpkin. They show him the way out of the valley, warning him not to tell anyone where he's been. They also warn him not to break the pumpkin open until he reaches home. But on the way their warning eats into him. He is overcome by impatience and curiosity, and breaks the pumpkin open. Half the pumpkin is filled with gold coins and the other half, with seeds. If he had waited until he made it home, it would have been entirely filled with gold coins.

In another version, the herder is watching his hosts in the Hidden Valley cook. He sees them put a grain of rice into the boiling pot but when they open the lid, the pot is full. There is enough rice for everybody. Everything in the valley is very beautiful, and he finds that he has become very intelligent and his mind has become clear.

He is so happy in the valley that he wants to bring his wife and children there. He tells his hosts that he wants to leave, without telling them why. When he's leaving they give him a few grains of the special rice, and tell him not to let anyone know about the Hidden Land. He can use the rice for others to eat—one grain will even feed a thousand people—but he is not to let anyone know.

Climbing out of the green valley, he finds himself back in the snow. He knows he'll have a hard time finding the valley, so at a strategic point he takes off his jacket and pins it under a stone so he will know where the way to the valley begins. Then he continues down to where he had been herding his sheep. All of his sheep are still there except for the one he went looking for when he stumbled upon the Hidden Valley. He herds them together and drives them down out of the high pastures to go and get his family. In the late afternoon he comes to a little hut where there are seven other herders, all spending the night. He stops with them for the night but they've looked through the hut and there is nothing to eat. Thinking of his magic grains of rice, he offers to cook. They laugh at him, 'What will you cook when there is nothing *to* cook?'

They make a wood fire and put over it a pot of water to boil. While they're distracted for a moment by a rustling in the bushes, he puts one of the magic grains in the pot. They sit around the boiling pot for close to an hour, at which time he opens the lid and it is full of rice. The herders are amazed. How did this happen?

'I put rice in the pot,' he says.

But the others don't believe him.

'We were sitting here the entire time; we never saw you put rice in the pot.'

They eat the rice, which has a most delicate flavour, and they won't leave him alone. All night they badger him about how he made the rice, until finally in the wee hours of the morning he confesses everything: how he had made it to the Hidden Valley and gotten the magic rice.

At sunrise they insist he show them the way to the valley. They force him. So he leads them up above their grazing lands into the snow, and though he knows he is close he cannot find the way. Then he sees the jacket he left to mark the entrance to the

Hidden Valley. Though it is pinned under the same stone, it is high on a rock face the size of a mountain—impossible even for a mountain goat to reach, let alone a human being.

Close-up of Darjeeling and Sikkim and the way to Beyul Demoshong.

CHAPTER FIFTEEN

Monarchical Machinations

With Tulshuk Lingpa and his swelling group of followers occupying the central monastery in the kingdom, sooner or later the king was bound to find out. The first communication between the two of them was actually initiated by Tulshuk Lingpa. To increase auspiciousness and remove obstacles in the way of opening the gate to Demoshong, Tulshuk Lingpa decided it was important to build five stupas of different colours: one at each of the four major caves sacred to Padmasambhava, and one at Tashiding. The one at the eastern cave was to be yellow; the western one, green; the northern, red; and the southern one, blue. The fifth stupa, at the auspicious centre Tashiding itself, was to be white.

When Yab Maila—the elder brother of the big house in Yoksum—heard of Tulshuk Lingpa's plan he warned the lama that if he went ahead and built the stupas, he'd get in trouble with the king. 'We'll have to ask the king's permission first,' he said. So Yab Maila went to the king (as the king's regional tax collector he had easy access to the palace and the king) and asked for his permission, which the king refused. 'If I have to build these stupas,' the king said, 'I'll consult our own Sikkimese high lamas, and after such consultation I'll build the stupas myself.'

When Tulshuk Lingpa got the news, he said, 'The king's ignorance on these matters will only cause him obstacles; if these stupas were built, Sikkim would be a better and stronger kingdom.'

Many to this day believe if the king had allowed Tulshuk Lingpa to build the stupas, Sikkim wouldn't have been taken over by India and would have remained an independent kingdom.

ℬ   ℭ

Tulshuk Lingpa's days were spent performing rituals and preparing for the journey to Beyul. Then one day he announced it was time to go to Mount Kanchenjunga.

Kunsang remembers it well. 'When my father announced that it was time to go, there was tremendous commotion and of course nobody wanted to be left behind. "The work we are about to do," my father said, "is very delicate. I cannot take everybody. If we have important news to relay, I will send someone back to tell it."

'The Lahaul people said, and they said it in their own language, "Rinpoche, we think only Lahaul people should go with you."

'But Tulshuk Lingpa said, "No, I'm taking some people from Lahaul, some from Bhutan and some from Sikkim."

'And so it was that Tulshuk Lingpa chose twelve of his closest disciples, mostly strong young men both from Himachal Pradesh and Sikkim, local guys like Atang Lama who knew the mountains well. He also said I should come.

'But my father was crazy! As we were preparing to leave, we asked him what we should bring. "Nothing," he said. "Only the clothes on your backs and a little tsampa." When we protested about the distance we'd have to travel and the cold nights on the high snow slopes, he told us with confidence—which couldn't help but rub off on us—not to worry. "We will have no troubles where we're going," he told us.

'Though my father was serious about the work before him, he was laughing and joking with those he'd leave behind. They were excited too, even though they weren't coming, even though they were secretly afraid that Tulshuk Lingpa and the rest of us—the Lucky Twelve—would all just disappear without a trace. They feared the gate to Beyul would open, the guardians would admit us and then close without a trace.

'Just before we left, while my father was busy with something else, the lamas of Tashiding and Sinon pulled aside those of us who were chosen and gave us stern advice. "Be very careful with Tulshuk Lingpa," they told us. "No matter what he says, no matter how crazy, just listen to him and never say no. Never contradict him; it could cause a bad omen. No matter what, just obey him. Guard him properly. Most important of all: don't let him get lost."

'As we left Tashiding, my father was at the head. I can still see him to this day. He was wearing a white robe and a silk shirt. His hair was braided into two ponytails, which reached the small of his back. Clouds of sang, the pine bough incense, engulfed us all. For the first hundred yards down the hill our route was marked by buckets of water with flowers floating in them as a sign of auspiciousness, as is the custom. All of Tashiding accompanied us down the hill to the edge of the village, at which point Tulshuk Lingpa sent them back to the monastery. He didn't want to draw the attention that hundreds of people passing through the centre of the village would attract. They presented him with innumerable khatas, silk ceremonial scarves, for his safe journey.

'"Go back to the monastery and wait there," he told them. "The next time we'll see each other might just be in Beyul Demoshong! The guardian spirits of the Hidden Land will be putting khatas around *your* necks in welcome!"'

They walked that day to Yoksum, the last village before the trail rises through the deep pine forest's timberline, where it opens out into slopes of steep rock, deep snow, vast glaciers and peaks piercing the heavens.

'When we arrived in Yoksum,' Kunsang recalled, 'things were immediately out of hand. News of our coming had preceded us. The entire population was lining the way into the village, bowing and placing khatas around our necks. As we walked to Yab Maila's house, where we were to spend the night, we passed through clouds of incense. Yab Maila's house was packed with people, each more anxious than the next not to be left behind when Tulshuk Lingpa opened the way to the Hidden Valley.'

Yab Maila was a shrewd man. When he had approached the palace about Tulshuk Lingpa's five stupas, he hadn't done so as a devotee or sponsor of the lama but as a representative of the palace relaying a request from the district in which he was in charge of collecting taxes. The manner in which the palace turned the idea down made clear to him that opposition to Tulshuk Lingpa lurked in the palace, though at first he didn't fully understand why. When his younger brother Yab Jantaray—who happened to be the head of palace security—met Tulshuk Lingpa and became his follower, he too kept his involvement with Tulshuk Lingpa secret. One couldn't hope for a more trusted member of the palace to act as spy; as head of palace security, he was perfectly placed to know the palace's thinking concerning Tulshuk Lingpa and his trip to Beyul. Since he was fully expecting to depart shortly from the kingdom of His Majesty the King for a kingdom far greater and not so far away, it appears he had no problem keeping his brothers informed as to what was brewing at the palace concerning Tulshuk Lingpa and his trip to Beyul.

Sikkimese lamas, especially those in the hierarchy around the king, felt that if Mayel Lyang were to be opened it was to be done by one of their own lamas and not a Tibetan.

The security people also had their concerns. This was early autumn, 1962, and the Chinese invasion of Tibet was a fresh and ongoing concern in everybody's mind. The Chinese, who had long considered Sikkim part of their territory, were on the verge of betraying the brotherly relations with India by invading regions of the Himalayas under Indian control—a move that would plunge the two countries into the 1962 Indo-Chinese War, which began on 20 October. It was in this atmosphere that the security people started floating theories that Tulshuk Lingpa was really a Chinese spy looking for a new route to Tibet by which the Chinese could invade the kingdom.

With this background it was no wonder that when Yab Maila saw the crowds converging on his house with Tulshuk Lingpa at their lead, he began to panic. Though it was mainly villagers streaming into his house, there were some he didn't recognize. They could have been spies from the palace. He managed to pull Tulshuk Lingpa aside and warn him.

Tulshuk Lingpa took the situation, which was out of his control, and in his typically tulshuk manner turned it around. He sat cross-legged on the throne that had been set up for him in the main room. So many people were packed into the room that not another could have possibly fit, a fact which was attested to by the number of people pressed against each other at the doors to the room. The buzz in the room was palpable as anticipation grew of the words Tulshuk Lingpa would utter concerning his imminent opening of Beyul.

But instead of speaking of Beyul, Tulshuk Lingpa started giving a very long-winded and exhaustive lecture on arcane points

of Buddhist doctrine that had the exact effect he desired as the
electric excitement in the room began to dissipate and the eyes
of his audience began to glaze over. The press of people at the
door began to let up as some of those sitting inside grew tired
and left. After two hours, there was room for people to stretch
their legs. After three hours, some were even dozing in the back
and after four the room was almost empty. In the end everyone
but those who were travelling with Tulshuk Lingpa had left, including any that might have been spies. Everyone thought it
must have been only a rumour that Tulshuk Lingpa was going to
open the Hidden Valley, which their ancestors had been talking
about for countless generations. Otherwise, how could he be giving such a boring talk on the eve of his departure describing the
thirty-seven bodhisattva vows and the ten stages the bodhisattva
goes through on his way to Buddhahood, including the levels of
indefinite transformation and expanding reality?

Yab Maila gave Tulshuk Lingpa and his disciples a huge din-
ner. Then he gave them sugar, salt and tea to add to their rations
of tsampa. He also gave them quilts, and ropes with which to
strap them to their backs.

Yab Maila used the opportunity of Tulshuk Lingpa's going to
the outhouse to try to give the disciples more provisions but everybody protested. 'If we take more, Tulshuk Lingpa will scold
us!' Then Yab Maila spoke confidentially to the disciples. 'You are
twelve people,' he said, 'You hold all the responsibility. Look after
Tulshuk Lingpa carefully. Don't let him get lost. He might try to
wander off. He could hurt himself. So you must watch him closely. But remember, no matter what, don't contradict him.'

When Tulshuk Lingpa returned, Yab Maila suggested that
since so many people in the village wanted to go with them—and
especially since some of them could be spies—they should leave
before sunrise.

Tulshuk Lingpa and his twelve disciples sneaked out stealthily
by the light of the moon to begin their journey into the high,
celestial mountains.

By noon, they were met by a nomad by the name of Tashi who
had heard of their coming and had come down to greet them below the nomad encampment of Dzongri. He brought them up to

Dzongri and to a cave, which he had already prepared for them. He gave them a meal with butter and curd—the best of what a nomad herder could offer.

In the morning the herder came up to Kunsang, the youngest in the group, and showed him his sling. It was a simple device made of two lengths of cord with a cradle for a small stone in the middle. One swung the device, released one of the two cords, and sent the stone flying.

'Why are you showing me this?' he asked the nomad.

'We use the sling when our animals get lost,' the nomad explained. 'When they get lost, they also get scared. When they see the stone fly and hear it smashing to the ground, they come.

'You are heading high into the mountains,' he continued, 'and your father is quite crazy. He will take you to faraway places at the edge of which no one goes. You may lose your sense of direction, which is easy in the high mountains, especially when the slope you're on pierces the clouds. Keep this sling with you, and if you get lost send a stone high in the air and the others will know where you are. If you are in a cloud and they cannot see it, when it falls to the ground it will make a sound. After it falls to the ground start whistling, and then the others will find you.' He taught Kunsang how to use the sling.

When it was time for them to leave, the nomad offered to come with them. 'I am familiar with all the ways,' he told Tulshuk Lingpa. 'With me you won't get lost.'

'No,' Tulshuk Lingpa said. 'You don't have to show me the way. Though I've never been there, I know it already. It is better you stay here and tend to your flock.'

As they were leaving, the nomad gave them each some cloves of garlic to suck on if the high altitude started to affect them. He gave them this advice: 'Don't get separated from each other; you might get lost. We nomads are acquainted with this area but even we have the fear of getting lost. Sometimes when our animals wander off we cannot find them for two or three days, so vast are the slopes of Kanchenjunga.'

They started to climb up the mountain beyond Dzongri. When the herder's encampment was out of view, Tulshuk Lingpa stopped and looked over the vast terrain of sharp mountains piercing the deep blue-black sky of high altitude. Plumes of snow waved from the mountain peaks like flags. There was nothing to indicate that human beings had ever trod there before.

'From this point on,' Tulshuk Lingpa said, 'we will have no more contact with the outside world. We'll encounter no more human beings. From now on we will only have contact with the guardian spirits of Demoshong.'

As Kunsang said of that moment, 'We were happy—happy, and a little afraid.'

For the twelve, it was a defining moment of their journey. Inside each, excitement was vying with fear. As they climbed higher, some of them got headaches due to the altitude. So they untied the garlic they had tucked into their belts and sucked on it.

After some time, they stopped for a meal of tea and tsampa. Huge boulders towered over them, and numerous caves honey-combed the landscape. They were tired from the climb and rested a while. Then they continued higher. The slope became steep-er, the boulders even larger and the caves were more numerous. Tulshuk Lingpa went inside one cave and said the caverns and passages from that cave led to Nepal. After an hour or two of climbing, Tulshuk Lingpa stopped. They didn't know why, wheth-er he was tired or had some other business. They were always looking out for his unusual behaviour.

'You all think we are going to Beyul,' he said, 'but Beyul is not so near; it is very far from here. So don't think we'll reach Beyul so soon. It is very far.

'I will stay here,' he told them. 'While I am here, I want you to split into four groups and go out in the four directions. Spread out and see what you can find. You will go in four directions and you will see four different things. Notice anything unusual, and then report back here to me. If you find anything, bring it to me.'

At the beginning they didn't split up. It was too steep and there was only one way to go. They recalled the warnings they'd received before leaving Tashiding, and they were afraid of leav-ing Tulshuk Lingpa alone, fearful that he would wander off and get lost. So they took a few steps, turned to make sure Tulshuk Lingpa hadn't moved, then took a few more. Thus they went until the rock Tulshuk Lingpa was sitting on was engulfed by a cloud.

They reached a flattish area where they could go in different directions and fulfil Tulshuk Lingpa's request.

As they were forming groups, Namdrol saw the sling in Kunsang's belt. 'What is this thing?' he asked. 'You didn't have it before. Where did you get it?'

Kunsang told how the nomad had given it to him to use if he got lost.

Namdrol said, 'Oh, this is a very good thing. I will take it from you.'

'No,' Kunsang said, 'I won't give it to you.'

Namdrol was a grown man; Kunsang was in his late teens.

'You are only a boy,' Namdrol said. 'You don't have the strength to throw this thing. It is useless in your hands.' He snatched it from Kunsang and fastened it under his belt.

The landscape they found themselves in was so vast that they were afraid they might really get lost. So they picked up two stones each to hit against each other to make a noise.

Namdrol said, 'Now we will split into groups. If you get lost, start knocking these stones together and we will find you. If that doesn't work, whistle. If that doesn't work, I will use the sling.'

They formed groups, went in separate directions and did get lost. Kunsang was in a group of three. After maybe an hour of climbing, he stepped behind a huge rock to pee. When he was through the other two had left him behind. They simply disappeared.

He called out but there was no reply. He knocked the stones together but to no avail. He was alone. Then he heard whistling ahead of him from a side valley he was certain no one of their group had gone up, so he thought it must be nomads. He walked a short way up the valley. Since he could see nothing but rocky slopes rising to snow and a glacier at the head of the valley, he could tell no one was there. He suddenly realized it must be spirits trying to lead him astray.

Kunsang wasn't the first to hear such whistling at high altitudes that issued from no human lips. Sven Hedin, who travelled through Tibet in the early part of the twentieth century and wrote about it in his book *My Life as an Explorer*, quoted a Chinese traveller of a thousand years earlier, 'You hear almost always shrill whistlings, or loud shouts; and when you try to discover whence they come, you are terrified at finding nothing. It very often happens that men get lost, for that place is the abode of evil spirits.'

Stumbling back down the valley, Kunsang's thinking became confused. He lost all notion of the direction from which he had come. Then he noticed the amazing stones lying on the ground: flat stones, round stones, white stones, stones shaped like snakes of different colours, stones of shapes he'd never seen. He recalled that his father had told them to report back on what they discovered and, if they found anything significant, to bring it to him. Kunsang had never seen such beautiful stones in his whole life, such beautiful shapes and colours. He thought of home in Pangao and Simoling, so far away. He was certain with stones like those lying around in such abundance, Beyul must be close. He picked up some of the stones and started filling his pockets.

He had already lost all sense of direction. When the sun passed behind an icy mountain towering over him and plunged him suddenly in the cool shade of evening, he realized he had lost sense of time as well.

He was visited again by fear. He banged two stones together. But there was no reply. He was feeling tired and alone, more alone than he'd ever felt before. He started crying. He was lost without an idea of where to go. He wished he had a compass. He thought if he had a compass he'd be all right.

He started back in the direction from which he thought he might have come, knocking his stones together the entire time. He realized he was completely lost. He was getting cold.

Then he saw a stone thrown by Namdrol's sling arcing through the sky. He walked towards it and then he saw others descending from other directions, converging on the same place. They had also been lost. Everyone was banging stones together and replying to the other's knocks until they all converged on Namdrol. Everybody was there, and they were very happy. Night was advancing, so they started back to find Tulshuk Lingpa. They were afraid that maybe Tulshuk Lingpa had gotten lost. They thought that maybe when they got there he would be gone—gone to Beyul.

But when they reached the place where they had left Tulshuk Lingpa, he was sitting on the same rock as where they'd left him.

Soon it was night. They started making a fire for tea. But Tulshuk Lingpa said, 'It is dark now. Remember Chatral Rinpoche warned us not to make fires at night or we'd risk attracting snow leopards or, even worse, spirits.' Tulshuk Lingpa pulled out the human thighbone horn Chatral had given them, and he blew into it.

They dispersed to various caves, wrapped themselves in the quilts given to them by Yab Maila and went to sleep.

The next morning they awoke early because of the cold and made a fire and started boiling tea and preparing tsampa. They saw that Tulshuk Lingpa was some distance off, writing.

When the tea and tsampa were ready, they offered some to Tulshuk Lingpa but he wasn't interested. He was busy writing something down. He didn't ask what they had seen in the four directions; he also didn't say what he saw. He was busy writing, and they left him alone.

Kunsang remembers how they sat some distance off, drinking tea and eating tsampa and watching Tulshuk Lingpa in the distance, writing. Namdrol and Mipham were discussing how it must have been that when he sent them to the four directions, he was sending them far away because he knew he was going to be visited by a dakini who would give him a ter. When a dakini comes to a lama, no one must see them.

When Tulshuk Lingpa had finished writing he came over to them. 'The work is done, the work is done—the work is done!' he said. 'When Khandro Yeshe Tsogyal came to me years ago in Lahaul, she said we would meet again. She appeared to me yesterday while you were all away. She told me where we have to go.

'Come on,' Tulshuk said. 'Let's go.'

They doused the fire and packed their things. Now that they were getting close to the gate, they were all afraid.

They followed Tulshuk Lingpa up a steep valley that had snow at its highest reaches. They climbed through the snow until they reached the top of the Kang La, a pass that forms the border with Nepal at over 16,000 feet.

Tulshuk Lingpa pointed down the Nepal side to a tiny patch of relatively flat ground covered in green in an otherwise precipitous landscape. At its centre a single nomad tent was pitched next to a cascading mountain stream that issued directly from a glacier.

'There,' he said. 'That's where Khandro Yeshe Tsogyal told me we must go. It is from there we will depart for Beyul. She even told me the name of the place: Tseram.'

Atang Lama, who was from Tashiding and Sinon, became weak in his knees. He knew those mountains well. He knew the name of the encampment on the Nepal side.

The excitement they all felt was tinged with the fear that arises when bravado nears its test. With wildly beating hearts, those who knew how to negotiate steep slopes were already scoping out the route to Tseram when Tulshuk Lingpa—as if to prove his tulshuk nature on the eve of such a discovery—suddenly announced, 'Now we will return to Tashiding. The time isn't right for the opening. The work we have come to these high mountains for is complete at this time. We have other work to do. Let us now return.'

Shocked as they were, they were all secretly relieved in a way that can probably only be experienced by someone in their position, by someone about to leave everything, forever.

When they passed through Dzongri, they met the nomad. Kunsang took the sling from Namdrol and returned it to him. 'I told the nomad that his sling was very useful,' Kunsang told me. 'I said, "If it weren't for your sling we would all still be lost on the mountain." The nomad laughed. "I knew this was going to happen," the nomad said, "I knew you were being led by a *myonpa*, a crazy person. That's why I gave it to you." We all got a good laugh.'

They waited until night fell in the forests above Yoksum before descending to Yab Maila's house. Though he had been sticking close to home awaiting word of the opening, ready to climb to the snowline and beyond, Yab Maila was not surprised to see them return. Such are the ways of the tertons: even when they leave, never to return, they return two days later. What to do?

They slipped out of Yoksum early the next morning. When they passed through the village of Tashiding late that afternoon on their way to the Tashiding monastery, they created quite a stir. Nothing could dissuade believers in Tulshuk Lingpa from their faith in him. But there were others who thought all along that Tulshuk Lingpa was a mad lama; and for them, to see him and The Twelve returning after so short a time from their journey to forever only made them firmer in their convictions. It set their tongues wagging as they watched the intrepid mountaineers and their lama pass; it also set the rumour mill turning. Word of their return reached the monastery before they did, and it didn't take much longer for the news to reach Gangtok and the palace.

The situation demanded a public appearance of the master, and that night Tulshuk Lingpa sat in the Tashiding Monastery surrounded by his many disciples and curious detractors. No doubt, there were also some spies working for the king among them. The atmosphere was electric.

For Kunsang, this trip to the snow mountains was a tremendous experience.

'Being alone on that mountain,' he confided in me, 'frightened me to the core. Yet even if I were lost, never to be found, somehow I knew it wouldn't be the end. Maybe it was because I was just a kid. But remember, we were on the verge of another world. My father had sent us out to report on whatever we found. When I found those strange rocks lying around me, I was sure it was an important discovery. I knew it meant I was close. That's why I filled my pockets with them. Yet here we were back in Tashiding. My father was sitting before his disciples ready, I was assuming, to report on what had happened and he had never once asked any of us what we had found or what happened to us when he sent us away. Those rocks were still weighing in my pockets. So I pulled them out of my pocket and showed them to him.

'When my father saw what I was pulling out of my pockets to show him so earnestly, he burst out laughing. "It wasn't for these stones that we went up there!" he boomed.

'Then it struck me that when my father sent us in four directions it was the same as when he gave his speech in Yoksum and made all the people go away or fall asleep. He had done the same to us, and I was struck by the humour of my father's tulshuk ways. By sending us to the four directions, it might be—it must be—that when he sent us far away, he knew a dakini would come. He must have known Khandro Yeshe Tsogyal was coming. He sent us in all directions just to get rid of us, so he could be alone with the dakini. No one else was supposed to see her. We were sent far, very far away—for nothing! It was just the same as in Yoksum.

'My father held up the scripture he had received on the mountain, the ter that had been revealed to him by Khandro Yeshe Tsogyal, and he read aloud from it. It contained prayers and rituals specifically to appease the dharmapala and *mahapala*, the male and female guardians of the gates of Beyul.'

Dharmapala and mahapala are the Sanskrit names for spirits that in Tibetan are known as the shipdak and sadag. The shipdak are the local mountain deities. They show the way. The sadag are the spirit owners or lords of the land. Sa means soil and dag means owner. There are different shipdak and sadag for each of the four gates to Beyul Demoshong. Unless you appease these spirits, the way will not open.

As Kunsang explained it, these spirits would first appear as wrathful and they would jealously guard the gate. But that gate would be the 'outer gate'. After you passed through the outer gate, you'd come to the 'inner gate' and the same spirits would appear again, not as wrathful guards but to welcome you and to provide you with food, clothes and everything you need for your everlasting comfort. It was a necessary step towards opening Beyul for Tulshuk Lingpa to receive this ter from Khandro Yeshe Tsogyal.

'That is why we went up the mountain,' Tulshuk Lingpa announced, 'and to see Tseram—for now I know Tseram is very close to the Western Gate.'

While this explanation satisfied Tulshuk Lingpa's followers, to his detractors it was just an excuse, and a certain tension surfaced that had hitherto been latent. There had always been those who believed in Tulshuk Lingpa and his journey to Beyul— and those who didn't. This had on occasion split families and entire villages into those who were going and those who weren't. Now that he had set off for the high mountains on a mission that everyone assumed would culminate in the opening of Beyul, only to return a few days later, those who opposed him grew more vocal. The rumours that had circulated at the palace began to run the rounds of the villages: that Tulshuk Lingpa was a Chinese spy, a fraud, a charlatan, a drunkard and a madman.

Tulshuk Lingpa, while not unaware of the rumours and controversy that began to swirl around him, didn't pay much heed to such matters. He wasn't concerned with appeasing those in the human realm who would do him harm. His struggles were squarely with the hidden realm of spirits. He was busy appeasing the guardian deities of Kanchenjunga and the spirit gatekeepers of Beyul, purifying himself and his followers through meditation and performing pujas.

Since the opening was taking longer than they had expected, some of Tulshuk Lingpa's devoted disciples, while they weren't losing faith in him, were beginning to run out of money. This was especially the case with those who had come from Himachal Pradesh. When they had sold their possessions and given away the rest, they had only brought enough to get to Sikkim and to make the expedition into the high mountains. They had never figured on having to maintain themselves there month after month. Even those from Sikkim, Darjeeling and Bhutan had given away their worldly goods and hadn't planted their crops. Funds were running low even for Tulshuk Lingpa's main sponsors, who had been quite wealthy. They tried to pressure him to open the gate quickly. But he was not to be pushed. The proper rituals had to be performed. Certain months were propitious for the opening of Beyul, namely the fourth through the ninth Tibetan months, and timing was everything. Some of his disciples started going above Yoksum into the deep forests and collecting sang, the pine bough incense, and bringing it to Darjeeling to sell. The talk at the palace that Yab Jantaray overheard became harsher. There were some at the palace who wanted to arrest Tulshuk Lingpa, even throw him in jail. He informed his older brother, Yab Maila, who told Tulshuk Lingpa.

CHAPTER SIXTEEN

A Historical Digression

Royal opposition to Tulshuk Lingpa was to become a major factor in what happened next. It also proved to be one of the most difficult aspects of the entire story to research and to come to understand.

One would have thought lamas sitting on hidden knowledge and directions to a hidden land concealing half the world's wealth would be reticent, unwilling to speak to a foreigner poking around and asking questions. But this couldn't be further from the truth. Everyone involved with Tulshuk Lingpa and his quest for Beyul Demoshong were open and more than willing to tell me what they knew. Some of the more learned lamas made it clear that there were certain 'tantric' aspects of the story that couldn't be divulged to the uninitiated. But it was just as clear that while the land to which they all aspired was hidden, they had nothing to hide.

It quickly became apparent that this was not the case with those connected with the Sikkimese royal family. When I asked them about the royal opposition to Tulshuk Lingpa, I hit a wall of silence behind which it was clear secrets lurked.

Over time, my understanding of the royal opposition changed. At the beginning of my inquiry, before I even realized there was such a wall of silence, I had two main theories. Both of them were probably naive: one based on the king having no faith in Tulshuk Lingpa and perhaps even thinking him mad, and the other based on the king believing Tulshuk Lingpa truly had the key to the Hidden Land to which *his* kingdom was but a gateway.

The first theory held that if the king did not think Tulshuk Lingpa was the lama to open the Hidden Land, doubted the

Hidden Land existed or even thought him mad, his opposition would be based on a paternal concern for the simple folks under his charge. Though the landscape of Sikkim is dominated by the snow-clad Mount Kanchenjunga, few Sikkimese have experience with altitude and glaciers. Those following Tulshuk Lingpa were bound to be ill equipped for high altitudes, suffer frostbite and risk death. Already, they hadn't planted their fields; they had given up their homes and possessions. By all accounts the king was concerned for his subjects' welfare and, like a father, would have wanted to protect them. What king wouldn't want to protect his subjects from a mad lama who was going to lead them, like the Pied Piper of Hamelin, into a cave on the side of a mountain never to return?

This reference to ancient legend might not be that far off the mark. As Robert Browning wrote of the moment when the piper led the children astray in his poem *The Pied Piper of Hamelin*:

When, lo, as they reached the mountain-side,
A wondrous portal opened wide,
As if a cavern was suddenly hollowed;
And the Piper advanced and the children followed,
And when all were in to the very last,
The door in the mountain-side shut fast.

If on the other hand the king believed Tulshuk Lingpa held

Pied Piper,
Marktkirche in Hamelin, Germany.

the key, he would have also known that the few hundred of his subjects who had given up all to go to Tashiding and follow him were but the vanguard of an exodus that would sweep his kingdom once word spread that the way had opened. I spoke with many older people in Sikkim who had known about Tulshuk Lingpa and had only been waiting to hear that the way was open. They were hedging their bets by not giving away their houses and possessions and by continuing to plant their fields. Yet once they heard the way had opened, they were ready to bolt for the door. Some were even hiding food in caves along the route so they wouldn't have to carry it when they left Sikkim for the beyul encumbered by their grandparents and children. One never knew when the gate would shut. Many old people across Sikkim told me with a twinkle in their eye that they were just waiting for the news. There was even something slightly subversive about it—knowing that by leaving the Kingdom of Sikkim for a kingdom far greater, they were going against the king.

It would be an unprecedented exodus, one which would leave the king in the rather uncomfortable position of having to explain to an incredulous world how he became a king without subjects. There is bound to be inherent discomfort within the heart of a king when he tries to justify to himself his ruling an entire kingdom based not on merit but on heredity. How much greater would be this discomfort for a king whose subjects all leave for a kingdom they considered infinitely greater.

As I dug deeper, other possible reasons for the royal opposition surfaced. Could it simply have been that Tulshuk Lingpa was Tibetan? It was not hard to discern a mutual distrust and antipathy between some of the lamas of Sikkim and the lamas of Tibet. While the Kingdom of Sikkim was founded by Tibetan lamas and the religion of the country was Tibetan Buddhist in both origin and particulars, it was clear that many Sikkimese lamas felt it important to proclaim their independence and superiority. The Tibetan lamas, on the other hand, felt the Sikkimese lamas were uneducated. They were trained at one or another of the many village monasteries dotted throughout the kingdom, which lacked any of the larger institutions of Buddhist studies such as were found in Tibet.

I spoke with a Tibetan man in his lush private shrine room in the upper reaches of Gangtok whose father had been a secretary to a high Tibetan lama living at the royal palace monastery, and who himself grew up in the royal monastery. He told me outright—with an arrogance that shocked me for the boldness of its delivery—that all Sikkimese lamas were ignorant. 'What could they know?' he asked me. 'Their education takes place in the village.'

The Sikkimese lamas clearly resented the Tibetan lamas with their self-proclaimed 'superior' education. Theirs was the land blessed by Padmasambhava, and it was theirs to rule both in a temporal sense and in terms of the dharma. I was told that the king was no scholar. He depended on his lama advisers when it came to spiritual matters. Since they had a natural feeling of mistrust towards Tibetan lamas, they were sure to feel resentment at a Tibetan lama coming to open *their* Hidden Land, and would have prejudiced the king against him. Their attitude would have been, 'Why do *we* need a Tibetan lama to come and open *our* Hidden Land?'

As I spoke with people and my ideas changed as to why the royals were against Tulshuk Lingpa, I did what I could to get the perspective of those who would have known—those who had con-nections with the royals and the palace. I was far from successful. I followed my leads, and over the course of many visits to Gangtok went from the house of one of those connected with the royal family to another. I spoke to venerable octogenarians whose plush draw-ing rooms sported signed portraits of the royals, those who spoke of Wangchuk Namgyal (the son of the last king, Palden Thondup Namgyal, who was deposed in 1975 when the kingdom ceased to exist and Sikkim was absorbed into India) as 'our present chogyal' (religious king). When I asked what they knew of Tulshuk Ling-pa and the troubles he had at the hands of the government of the then Kingdom of Sikkim, I found myself continually rebuffed. It quickly became obvious that there was more to the story than met the eye, probable skeletons in the palace closets, and that I would get none of it from those who were on the inside.

I found, however, that the citizens of Sikkim outside the elitist circles—the villagers and lamas of Tashiding and Yoksum and the other places where Tulshuk Lingpa had a following—were more than willing to tell me what they thought was behind the royal opposition. While they offered a few interlocking theories that provided quite a few reasons for the opposition, I always felt hampered by those on the inside remaining tight-lipped.

The most common opinion I heard from those connected to Tulshuk Lingpa was that it wasn't the king who was at the centre of the opposition but the queen. Among the common people of Sikkim, this seemed almost universally accepted.

The royal family and most of the Buddhists in Sikkim are Nyingma, the oldest of the four main branches of Tibetan Buddhism. People told me that the queen Maharani Kunzang Dechen, who was at the time very influential in the kingdom's ecclesiastic affairs, was bringing in lamas from one of the other major branches—the Geluks—to perform major state rituals. This would be loosely analogous to Isabella, the queen of Catholic Spain, bringing in Lutheran priests to perform Mass. Some even erroneously told me that the Maharani was a Geluk. The Chogyals of Sikkim traditionally married Tibetan nobility and, while she was the daughter of Tibetan nobility, it was a Nyingma family. Though as Captain Yonda—the captain of the guards under Palden Namgyal, the last chogyal of Sikkim and well known as a staunch royalist to this day—told me, the queen's family were 'strong supporters of the Geluk'.

⁊   ☙

My quest for a wider understanding of the history of Sikkim and the historical background of the Hidden Land found me on a bicycle pedalling past the august stone buildings of Oxford University on a typically cold and rainy autumn afternoon. I was dodging puddles and spray to see a scholar just back from two and a half years of research in Sikkim. His name was Saul Mullard, and he had been searching out documents pertaining to the founding of the kingdom in the homes and private libraries of the elite families of Sikkim. He'd also been travelling to remote, vegetation-covered historical ruins: some dating to the first Tibetans who settled there over 200 years prior to the kingdom's founding in 1646. Being the first serious scholar to search out and study these old documents and make the connections with ancient foundations and fortified walls in the steep jungles, Saul had thought a lot about Sikkim's early history and had a unique understanding.

With my shoes by his door both in deference to their waterlogged state and the long time we'd both spent in the East, we sat by the window in his flat on the third floor of a sprawling

Victorian-style house that had probably once belonged to a single Oxford don and now housed students and visiting scholars. The window next to him was open to the gusting rain and the ancient spires of the university so his cigarette smoke would curl out, and not into my lungs. He listened carefully to my synopsis of the story of Tulshuk Lingpa and his quest for Beyul Demoshong.

When I was through, Saul's comment was swift and pointed, 'You must understand that the Hidden Land is not *external* to this world. I've read the texts, and it doesn't sound like what your lama was saying—that you'd pass through a portal to a land off the map. The Hidden Land is *in* this world. It is like the Kingdom of Shambhala, which is located somewhere behind a ring of mountains. No one's found it but it's there. It would be possible to get there, physically, without going through a "crack in the world". Even more importantly, you'd be able to come back. While Shambhala has never been definitively located, Beyul Demoshong has been found. It has already been opened—over 500 years ago. It was opened by Rigzin Godemchen in 1373. He lived there for eleven years, before going back to Tibet. He even returned to the beyul and died there in 1409.'

Saul paused a moment to light another cigarette.

'And by the way,' he said, 'I've been to the beyul.'

'You've been to Beyul Demoshong?' I was incredulous.

'So have you,' he replied dryly, pausing for effect. 'Beyul Demoshong is congruous with Sikkim, superimposed upon its physical geography. It exists in a kind of parallel dimension. Physically it is Sikkim but it has all these other qualities. Beyul is *in* the physical landscape of Sikkim. You can physically go there—we've both been to Tashiding, so we've both been to the centre of the Hidden Land. But we don't know that we've been there because we don't have the right realization.'

Saul took a long pull from his cigarette and blew the smoke pensively out the window, where it merged with the dense mist that had descended on Oxford.

'Rather than Beyul being in a place outside the coordinates of latitude and longitude, it could be argued that Beyul is actually dependent on a state of mind.'

'Beyul? Dependent on a state of mind?'

'According to the old texts Beyul Demoshong exists on many levels, which accord to different levels of realization. So if you're a normal bloke you can go to Tashiding, to the different caves, and say, "Wow, this was all blessed by Padmasambhava." You are like a tourist following the big signs you see on the side of the road: "Sikkim, the Hidden Paradise". Maybe you'll even snap a few photos. Like the tourist your understanding will be limited, on the surface only. That is the outer level. That's how it is when the tourist enters Beyul Demoshong. He is entering West Sikkim. Though he doesn't know it, he's in the beyul. That's the point: Beyul *is* a physical place, yet without the spiritual attainment you won't even know it.

'On the other hand, if you have the spiritual attainment you'll enter the same place but you are entering Beyul Demoshong, not West Sikkim. '

Saul Mullard, Wolfson College, Oxford.

'So it's a bit like in the Wizard of Oz when Dorothy finds herself back in Kansas?' I asked. 'She sees her neighbours who had all been transformed into other characters in Oz, and says to them, "You were there, and you too."'

'Well, I don't know if I'd go that far,' said Saul.

'Then maybe it would be more like meeting a realized master,' I said. 'Someone might meet him on the road, think he is a bum and give him a coin. Someone else would see him and just know he's the one. So it is dependent on the perceiver's understanding.'

'Something like that,' Saul allowed. 'The Hidden Land of Sikkim is firmly grounded in the geographical features of West Sikkim.'

'This sounds so different from what the people of Sikkim were telling me,' I said. 'From where do you get your concept of the beyul?'

'From the ancient texts, the writings of Sangye Lingpa, Rigzin Godemchen, the whole Northern Ter tradition, and from the documents and legends surrounding the founding of the kingdom of Sikkim, for which the opening of Beyul is key.'

'But none of this seems to tally with the idea of the Hidden Land that Tulshuk Lingpa was heading to,' I said, 'nor the conception I came upon with the many people I spoke with in the region. The ancient texts seem out of sync with the common, present-day understanding of the beyul. Even those living in West Sikkim and Tashiding itself weren't saying they were already living in the Hidden Land. Rather, they told me how they had been ready to give up their existence here in this world in order to go to another. They were clear: it wasn't about transforming awareness and staying home. There was no talk of scales falling from the eyes to reveal Tashiding as the centre of Beyul. They all spoke about the high snow slopes of Mount Kanchenjunga and a cave they'd enter, a gate they'd pass through or a pass they'd cross in order to enter a land from which they'd have no possibility of return. It seems to have little to do with what's written in your scriptures.'

'Precisely,' said Saul. 'What your lama was doing doesn't seem to accord with the scriptural tradition.'

From a scholar's and historian's perspective, that seemed the ultimate condemnation. The implication was clearly that Tulshuk Lingpa was just plain mad.

'So exactly what is this tradition?' I asked. 'What is the historical concept of Beyul?'

'First of all, even before discussing scriptures,' Saul said, straightening himself in his chair, 'you have to picture Beyul from a Tibetan point of view. Imagine: you are up on the high plateau, with little vegetation. Everything is windswept. It's not a very nice place to live. Then you go to Sikkim, and you have these fertile valleys and that's where the idea of the beyul comes in. Look, there are these wonderful places where there is no Tibetan government busy killing other Buddhists because they don't believe in this, that and the other. So this is the place to go.'

'When do you find the first reference to Beyul Demoshong?' I asked.

'Sangye Lingpa was the first to mention it, as far as I know. He lived from 1340 to 1396. He was a great terton, the reincarnation of the second son of the great dharma king of Tibet, Trisong Deutsen, who is credited with inviting Padmasambhava to Tibet in the eighth century. In 1364, Sangye Lingpa discovered his greatest revealed text, the *Lama Gongdu,*which spans thirteen volumes. There we find the first mention of Beyul Demoshong, as well as many other hidden lands.

'The next was Rigzin Godemchen, the founder of the Yangter, or Northern Treasure School. He is the one most closely associated with the terma tradition of Beyul Demoshong. He prepared all the keys. He is credited with actually opening the beyul. He visited other hidden lands as well. A contemporary of Sangye Lingpa, he was one of the greatest lingpas Tibet ever produced. He was born in Tibet in 1337 and died in Beyul Demoshong in 1409. His birth name was Noedup Gyaltsen. Only later did he acquire the name by which he is now known, which translates to the one with vulture feathers. Legend has it that at the age of twelve, three vulture feathers—though I wasn't there and I suspect they were tufts of hair that only *looked* like vulture feathers—sprouted from his head. When he was twenty-five, five more appeared. He seems to have had a particular and peculiar connection with vultures his whole life. When he was in Beyul Demoshong, he took out terma from the central peak of Mount Kanchenjunga. He took out other terma in Beyul as well and sent back some of these terma, as well as sculptures and various other things, to Tibet, suspended from the necks of vultures.

'Tibetan Buddhism is transmitted largely through lines of great teachers and their disciples. These lines seem to be forever branching and ramifying, creating occasion for quarrels. Even though the land both Sangye Lingpa—the guy who first wrote of Beyul Demoshong—and Rigzin Godemchen were concerned with was a land free from strife, it didn't stop controversy from arising. Rigzin Godemchen's first trip to Beyul Demoshong lasted eleven years. When he returned to tell the tale, the followers of Sangye Lingpa were mocking, "You're full of shit, mate." They didn't believe he actually made it to the beyul.

'The Fifth Dalai Lama, known as the "Great Fifth", who lived some three centuries later, said of these two great figures of Nyingma Buddhism in his study of the Yangter tradition—in quite a diplomatic literary style, I must say—that there were "disputes" between the disciples of Rigzin Godemchen and Sangye Lingpa, and this caused "some" hostility. But clearly Rigzin Godemchen is credited with being the first to bring the Tibetan dharma to the people of Sikkim.'

'If he "opened" the Hidden Land,' I asked, 'who did he bring the dharma to?'

'When Rigzin Godemchen came to Beyul Demoshong, the Lepchas were there. These are the aboriginal people of Sikkim, who had been there for who knows how long. There are no records of their migration. He encountered people there of Tibetan stock as well, speaking Tibetan dialects. Even the ancestors of Phuntsok Namgyal, the first chogyal—or dharma king—of Sikkim were already there. I figure they were there by 1270 or so. In fact Sinon, the village just up the hill from Tashiding where Rigzin Godemchen settled, is the very village where the Sikkimese royal family is from. It was in Sinon that Rigzin Godemchen died.

'Wait a minute,' I said. 'Now I'm really confused. I can understand—human nature being what it is—that when Rigzin Godemchen, a Tibetan, arrived in this new land and found only Lepchas living simply off the forest, worshipping the trees and mountains, in history it would be recorded that he'd "discovered" or in this case—"opened"—this land. After all, that is what we're all taught about Christopher Columbus, who "discovered" America—even though America had been populated by the Native Americans for millennia and he encountered them upon arrival. This is what Columbus said: "It appears to me, that the people are ingenious, and would be good servants and I am of opinion that they would very readily become Christians, as they appear to have no religion." It sounds like he could have gotten his inspiration from Rigzin Godemchen over a hundred years before.

'Where was Columbus from,' I asked. 'Milan?'

'Genoa.'

'OK. Say when Columbus arrived in the New World, he found people from a neighbouring city, say from Rome, and he ended up living in a town that had been populated by Romans for 200 years. I'd imagine he would have had a much more difficult time claiming to have "discovered" the place. Just what was Godemchen's conception of who these Tibetans were?'

'The traditional view,' Saul said, 'was that the Tibetans in the beyul were a lost group, and that they had special powers. The Lepchas had been there since time immemorial. They were the true people, the dakinis and *dakas* of Beyul Demoshong. The Lepchas were considered *pawo* and *pamo*, spiritual heroes and heroines.'

'So they weren't considered physical people?' I asked.

'They were considered to be slightly magical. They were people but had incredible spiritual accomplishments. This is what Lhatsun Chenpo says in his works. Everything that grew in Beyul was medicine. The water was medicinal. The pawo and pamo were considered natural healers, probably because of indigenous Lepcha medicine and the knowledge they had of the local flora. This is a knowledge the Lepchas have retained to this day.

'One time I was walking with this Lepcha chap from Sinon,' Saul said, laughing, 'and he took a piece of a plant and stuffed it up his nose. I said, "What's that?" and he said he had a headache coming on. They know a lot about medicine.

'Just imagine what it was like for Rigzin Godemchen when he saw the Lepchas who weren't busy killing each other but were peaceful and quiet, and plucked their medicine from the nearest bush. Now, of course, the Lepchas have been marginalized. Actually, the writing was on the wall from day one. With the founding of the Sikkimese kingdom, the Lepchas that resisted were enslaved. The rest, simply wanting peace, moved off the good land and were eventually pushed into the most difficult and inaccessible mountainsides. That's why the Lepchas, who called themselves the Matanchi Rongkup, or Mother's Beloved Children, became known as the Rong, meaning the Ravine Folk. The first known usage of that term dates to 1735, and that is a quote from something that happened in 1712.

'Just imagine coming to such a very peaceful climate away from all the troubles of Tibetan politics and religious political strife. You end up in this place that is completely peaceful, with all these flowers that no one's ever seen before and all these foods and medicines. It was a beautiful paradise to these Tibetans coming from central Tibet, where there is nothing to eat apart from raw meat. For them, it probably *was* a beyul, a hidden land. No one ever knew it existed. It didn't exist in the geography of ancient Tibet. It was just classed as *monyul*, along with all those places in the south. Since the Tibetan Empire Period, there had been this belief in these wonderful places in the Himalayas, which were so fertile, and then this got approximated into the beyul tradition.

'The Himalayas have always been places where people have run to to get away from persecution. Like Bhutan and Sikkim, many of the Himalayan kingdoms were established by refugees from Tibet. Just imagine arriving from strife-ridden Tibet. You cross a high pass and down into the green valleys, and come to a place like Tashiding—especially Tashiding because the mountains are so striking, dominating the whole region. It's like, "Wow". This is a hill of jewels, with all the flowers growing on it. The vegetation and flowers we see today must be nothing next to what they were.

'I travelled north from Sinon for five hours on foot to go to Palung Ri to find the ruins of the monastery Rigzin Godemchen built in the fourteenth century. I had never seen trees like this in Sikkim. I'm talking about huge trees the width of this room, with moss hanging down. When we went up there, we saw red pandas and wild fowl. I'm quite an avid bird watcher, and I saw five or six species of birds I'd never seen before in Sikkim. I've never seen anything like it. Orchids were growing right out of the ground! Huge trees and thick undergrowth. There wasn't a road—not even a path. At one point we were just holding on to the side of a mountain. There was this tree that had fallen and we were walking on it when it just snapped. We almost fell 100 feet to our deaths. This is what the entire kingdom must have been like.'

'All of this is fine,' I said. 'They came from strife-worn Tibet, found this beautiful natural place to their south and wanted it. They called it a beyul to fit it into their mythical structure, and founded a kingdom probably to justify the subjugation of a people. What is the story behind the actual founding of the Kingdom of Sikkim?'

'Ah,' Saul said, 'this is a particular interest of mine, and the subject of most of my research. The jury is still out on what actually happened but the official story is well known. It was over two centuries after Rigzin Godemchen first opened the beyul that three lamas from Tibet—Nadak Sempa Chenpo, Lhatsun Chenpo and Kathog Kuntu Zangpo—opened three of the gates of the beyul in order to fulfil a prophecy by founding a kingdom based on the Tibetan dharma.

'The story of Nadak Sempa Chenpo was written by his son. Nadak was like, "Remember me?" He was talking to the gate-keepers of the beyul. "Remember in the time of Padmasambhava, when he asked you to guard the way to the beyul until the right guy arrived? Well, here I am!" He ritually cleansed himself, burnt some sang and did some rituals. As it goes with these rituals with local deities, you lure them in. You entice them by offering them chang—the local brew—and then you get them, saying, "Now you've got to do what I say: let me in!" And he got in.

'Lhatsun Chenpo's story is the best. We have this from a book written in 1908 by the king of Sikkim, Chogyal Thutob Namgyal, and his wife the queen. The book is called *The History of Sikkim*. The fact that it was the royals themselves writing the account makes it suspect, as far as reflecting historical truth is concerned, but it contains the clearest, most comprehensive and most-quoted rendition of the "official" founding myth.

'It seems that when the third lama, Kathog, was wandering in the mountains trying to find his way through the gate into the Hidden Land, he came to a ragged wall of impenetrable rocky cliffs. He was forced to retrace his steps. He came to a place called Nyam Gyatsal, which translates to Grove of Joy, a beautiful meadow where Lhatsun Chenpo and his followers happened to be resting after his arduous journey from Tibet. When Kathog told Lhatsun that he'd have to retrace his steps because there was no way to penetrate the cliffs and precipices ahead of them, which looked like the 'gates of heaven', Lhatsun told him that the opening of this gate was allotted to himself, and that Kathog would have to move on and find his own gate.

'Lhatsun and his followers ascended the slopes until they reached the base of the same rocky cliffs and, like Kathog, they could discern no path through them. The difference was that Lhatsun was the one prophesied to open this gate. Lhatsun used his magic siddha powers, and flew over the cliffs to the top of the mountain Kabru. Or perhaps he wandered away from his disciples and disappeared into a low-hanging cloud. At any rate he disappeared and, as days went by with no sign of their master, the disciples concluded he had perished amongst the high, wind-torn cliffs. By the seventh day, they had completed building a stupa of stone in his honour and were preparing to leave when they heard above the blowing of the wind Lhatsun's thighbone trumpet. So they waited on the mountain, praying. After three weeks their master returned as miraculously as he had left, having opened the way to the beyul. They were so moved by their faith in him that they followed him along a path that had been cut in the cliff face and went with him to Beyul Demoshong. They passed through Dzongri on their way to Yoksum. Because of the time Lhatsun Chenpo spent in the high snow and the cold he suffered, his skin is always depicted as blue.'

The day before our discussion I had received a book I had ordered from Oxford's Bodleian Library and its vast seven-storey underground repository of books. The book was titled *Round Kangchenjunga* by Douglas W. Freshfield. First published in 1903, it recounts a journey the author took around that great massif at the turn of the twentieth century. In one remarkable passage he

locates the cliffs from which Lhatsun Chenpo opened the western
gate of the beyul as just above Tseram: the place Tulshuk Lingpa
looked down at from the top of the Kang La Pass and said they'd
have to travel to in order to find the very same gate. Explaining to
Saul the relevance of Tseram for Tulshuk Lingpa's story, I fished
the Xerox I'd made of the passage from my bag and read him the
following passage:

> After a brief halt on the meadow in front of the huts
> of Tseram, we crossed the river ... A woodland path led
> us upward through a forest where the tints of autumnal
> foliage mingled with the dark green of the firs ... and [we]
> found ourselves on a brow overlooking a lovely glade at the
> entrance to the long side-valley up which lay our course to
> the Kang La ... Rocky banks, clothed in Rhododendrons and
> small bushes, enclosed lawns of smooth turf; clear springs
> formed pools in the hollows; the surrounding woods made
> a pleasing background. Late at night, when the dull mists
> at last cleared off, we saw in the moonlight an icy peak,
> one of the south-western spurs of Junnu; at early dawn we
> had a beautiful vision, framed between the slopes of the
> Yalung Valley, of the distant ranges above the Arun. Seen
> through an atmosphere suffused with the first sunbeams,
> their forested ridges lost all local colour and glowed with
> the blues and purples of aërial distance. It was a picture
> which made me long for an artist to make some notes that
> might recall its loveliness.
>
> The charm of this spot did not escape the native travellers
> who preceded us. Local tradition has it that it was visited
> by Lhatsun, the introducer of Buddhism into Sikhim in the
> seventeenth century, and the Saint is said to have given
> it the name of Namga Tshal or the Grove of Joy. Accord-
> ing to the somewhat credulous Babu, 'Lhatsun, when first
> coming to visit these Himalayan regions, spent a few days
> here, struck with the fine scenery and the spaciousness of
> the valley. The fatigues of his long and perilous journey
> from the northern solitudes of Tibet had broken down his
> health, but the few days that he spent here greatly restored

him, not only by the delightful scenery of the place, but more especially by the comforts that he obtained both religious and physical.' So much restored was the Lama that, according to tradition, he flew up through the air to the top of Kabru and spent a fortnight there. Would we might have been privileged to perform similar feats of 'volitation.'

I noticed a glint of wonder in Saul's eyes.

'What do you make of such stories,' I asked, 'and stories of flying monks? Do you think he really flew?'

'Many strange things happen in Tibet,' Saul answered. 'There is a lot that we do not understand—and a lot of these stories are constructed a lot later.'

'At any rate,' I said, 'the three lamas met in Yoksum, right?'

'Yes,' Saul said, 'In fact, Yoksum means "the three great ones" in Lepcha in commemoration of these three lamas meeting there in order to found a new Buddhist kingdom. But Lhatsun stopped the other two from founding the kingdom then and there. "We three are lamas," he's reputed to have said. "We need a layman to rule this country."

'Probably a wise decision,' Saul said chuckling, 'to pick a *local* layman so as not to be perceived as an occupying force. Remember, Buddhism was a foreign religion. This was a religious—or spiritual—as well as a temporal takeover. Remember also, I'm now telling you the official self-justifying myth, the one you'll find—perhaps not in such detail—in any number of tourist brochures.

'Lhatsun pointed out the many prophecies about the "Four Avatars" that would found the new kingdom for the benefit of the dharma. He reportedly quoted one particular prophecy, which was given by Rinchen Lingpa, who died in 1375. It said, "One named Phuntsok from the direction of Gang will appear."

'So Lhatsun deputed a hermit to lead a group to find this place called Gang and find this man called Phuntsok living there in order to bring him back to Yoksum to become king. While Lhatsun and his disciples stayed in the hills above Yoksum meditating, the group he'd sent off had many adventures especially since they apparently had no idea where the place called Gang might be. The story has it that they finally made it to Gangtok, then a small village of no particular importance, which was "the same as the prophesied Gang". This I find suspect for a couple of reasons. First of all, *gang tok* means hilltop, so it could have been anywhere. I have reason to believe that they actually went to Sinon, just up the mountain from Tashiding, which was a Tibetan colony at the time. Anyway, in this place called Gangtok they found Phuntsok Namgyal milking his cows. Phuntsok invited the party into his house and gave them some milk to drink, which the party considered especially auspicious. When they told Phuntsok why they were there, to take him to Yoksum and make him king, imagine how lucky he felt. Milking a cow one minute, and the founder of a royal line the next!

'Actually according to the story Phuntsok was of Tibetan royal stock, having descended from the eighth century Tibetan king Trisong Deutsen. Apparently there were prophecies concerning this as well, though we can assume they were concocted later, after the fact. One prophecy said that if a descendent of Trisong Deutsen be made king of Sikkim, the land would prosper. What you must understand is that usurpers of Tibetan thrones and founders of peripheral Tibetan kingdoms often claimed descent from Trisong Deutsen. It was practically a prerequisite.

'Anyway, these three Tibetan lamas conducted all the necessary rites and installed Phuntsok Namgyal as the first in the line of "righteous" kings—or chogyals—of Sikkim, which was handed down not without its hiccups within the family until the kingdom fell to India in 1975.

'Before the founding of the kingdom, Sikkim was a collection of little kingdoms and spheres of influence which, though none dominated the rest, must have all had their tussles and mini wars. Phuntsok, with the backing of the Tibetans, was able to consolidate a huge area under his control even larger than present-day Sikkim. Yet he knew his hold on power was tenuous. Therefore, he installed his son Tensung as chogyal before his own death to insure the smooth transfer of power.

'Chogyal Tensung had three wives: one Bhutanese, one Tibetan and one Limbu. He died fairly young. Upon his death his fourteen-year-old son Chakdor—the son of the second, Tibetan wife—took the throne. But he was challenged by his half sister Pendi Wangmo—the daughter of the first, Bhutanese wife. Since Pendi was older than Chakdor, she thought the succession should go to her.

'Pendi Wangmo got the backing of the Bhutanese who were only too happy to attack this newly established kingdom, and this sibling rivalry led to the Sikkim—Bhutan War. When the Bhutanese sent assassins to kill Chogyal Chakdor, he fled to Lhasa. While the Bhutanese occupied the Sikkimese palace for eight years, the chogyal lived in Lhasa. He was young and was schooled there—steeped in Tibetan tradition. One story, I don't know how accurate, has it that he became the Dalai Lama's state astrologer. At any rate his association with the Dalai Lama was close, and the Dalai Lama gave him many estates. Finally, with the help of the Tibetans, he drove the Bhutanese out of most of the kingdom and he reoccupied the palace.

'Religion and politics are never very far apart in the Tibetan world. You see, the three Tibetan lamas who opened the beyul in order to found the kingdom were from three different lineages. As everybody who goes to Sikkim knows, Lhatsun Chenpo is practically considered the patron saint of Sikkim. But it hasn't always been so. In the beginning Nadak Sempa Chenpo and the Nadak tradition were the most important, founding the most important monasteries. Lhatsun Chenpo was of secondary importance. Kathog Kuntu Zangpo was always more obscure and, though he founded a Kathog monastery in Yoksum, that lineage never spread in a significant way. Nadak Sempa Chenpo's son wrote his biography and Tashiding, for instance, was allied to his lineage.

'All this changed with the Bhutanese War. Not only were religion and politics mixed together but sex as well. Nadak's grandson had an affair with Pendi Wangmo. She tried not only to run her brother off the throne but also to supplant the entire Mindroling lineage to which he was allied, through the line that came through Lhatsun Chenpo. When Pendi Wangmo's Bhutanese Nadak side was defeated, there was a transfer of politico-religious power from the Nadaks to the Lhatsun Chenpo school. It was then that the figure of Lhatsun Chenpo became important. This is what assured him the position of Sikkim's patron saint. Before that he was too busy flying about the place and meditating in caves with his khandro. He was a great practitioner. He gave wonderful visionary sadhanas and practices.

'The end was not pretty for either Chogyal Chakdor or his half-sister Pendi Wangmo. Some time after the chogyal's return, he went to the hot springs at Ralong. Pendi Wangmo, still thinking of usurping her brother's throne, saw her chance to assassinate her brother. She sent a doctor to Ralong to attend to her brother, who was feeling a bit under the weather. The doctor took the chogyal's pulse and determined the best course of action was a little bloodletting. As per Pendi Wangmo's instructions, he severed a major artery and the chogyal bled to death. The chogyal's attendants brought his body back to the palace under the cover of night, and for a long time they kept it a secret that he was dead. Meals were brought to him as usual, and the word was spread that he was in strict devotional seclusion. Finally they burnt his body at the Pemayangtse Monastery, after which his attendants decided to avenge the murder. They went to Namchi, where Pendi Wangmo was staying and scaled the walls to her room in the middle of the night. You know what khatas are, right? They are the ceremonial silk scarves that are presented to high lamas as a sign of respect. They took one and stuffed it down Pendi Wangmo's throat and killed her.'

Saul looked at his watch.

'Sorry to end on such a macabre note,' he said, 'but I'm afraid I have a lecture to attend.'

Maybe he saw from my face that his dizzying survey of Sikkimese history had left my mind spinning—and my central question unanswered. Just how did all of this relate to the royal opposition to Tulshuk Lingpa? I felt the key was there but I couldn't quite grasp it.

'I just want to stress that religious ideas are often used for political ends,' Saul said. 'This is one of the main lessons of the history of the region, if not the world.'

Saul stood, found a pen and a notebook, put them into his bag and readied himself to leave.

I stood, too.

When we were about to leave, Saul looked me in the eye.

'The earliest reference to Sikkim in Tibetan literature,' he said, 'is as a beyul. Much of the terma literature—the prophecies included—have been translated and transposed in such a way as to justify the foundation of the Namgyal Dynasty. It is at the centre of the royal family's claim to power.'

The rain had stopped, though with the setting sun the fog had thickened. As I unlocked my bicycle, Saul got his out of a little shed. We rode together until the first crossroads, where we parted ways.

'I hope I've been helpful,' he called over his shoulder. Hugging the sidewalk to let a car pass, Saul Mullard disappeared into the fog.

I spent quite some time in Oxford, availing myself of the wonderful libraries. Most days one could find me in the Duke Humphrey's Library, Oxford's oldest reading room dating to the 1480s. In a gap between shelves of leather-bound Latin tomes was a narrow wooden staircase leading to an upper gallery. There at a tiny oak desk where I could look down at the scholars but not be seen and look up at the ceiling's centuries-old alchemical paintings just above my head, I completed the first draft of this book.

During the days after my meeting with Saul I found myself at my desk watching the light of the sun filter through the stained-glass windows, wondering about the ancient prophecies concerning Beyul Demoshong. Could the very notion of the beyul and the prophecies surrounding it have been created by politicians for worldly ends? Had Tulshuk Lingpa twisted these notions to spiritual ends? Or had the politicians and founders of dynasties been the ones to twist spiritual truths to political ends? How did the resolution of this question impact upon the question I had hoped to answer by meeting Saul, of why the royal family was against Tulshuk Lingpa?

Watching the sunlight dancing through the ancient stained glass and letting my mind wander, it suddenly struck me that it didn't matter whether the king thought Tulshuk Lingpa held the key or was a madman, whether there was an issue with his being Tibetan or whether the queen was out to get him because he was a Nyingma lama—all of these might have been factors, or not.

By simply saying the beyul was yet to be opened, Tulshuk Lingpa was striking a blow at the centre of the founding myth of the kingdom. In a tacit way, he was questioning the legitimacy of the Namgyal dynasty itself, which would surely be enough to have him thrown in jail.

CHAPTER SEVENTEEN

Royal Inquiries

One day, perhaps two months after they returned from Mount Kanchenjunga, word reached Tulshuk Lingpa that some representatives of the palace were going around asking questions about him and that he would be interviewed. The investigative team of four was headed by two men: the first was known as Gonde Drungyig, an official within the Ecclesiastical Department, and the second was a learned lama known as the Chagzoe, the treasurer. He was the private secretary of Dzongsar Khyentse Rinpoche, a high lama who was living at the palace monastery. The Chagzoe was also the stepfather of Sogyal Rinpoche, the now-famous lama who wrote the book *The Tibetan Book of Living and Dying* among other works.

Travelling from village to village, asking what the people knew of Tulshuk Lingpa's background and his proposed trip to Beyul Demoshong, they were charged with determining whether Tulshuk Lingpa was a fraud. They were also trying to get a grasp on numbers, to ascertain how many families were planning to go with him to Beyul. Apparently, the palace wanted to know how many of their subjects they would be losing. Yab Maila warned Tulshuk Lingpa that he'd have to tell them something about Beyul, enough to keep them satisfied, if not everything.

When Gonde Drungyig and the Chagzoe entered Tulshuk Lingpa's room, they offered him khatas and gifts. Though they had grave doubts as to his authenticity, allegiance and perhaps even his sanity, they followed courtly protocol and showed him the respect due to a high lama; he showed them the respect due to official representatives of a king.

Tea was brought, and when the pleasantries were complete they got right to the point. 'We've been hearing rumours and they have gone as far as the palace, that you are going to the Hidden Land and planning on taking people from Ravangla, Tashiding, Gezing—from all over Sikkim—with you. It looks like the kingdom might be emptying right out.'

Tulshuk Lingpa was characteristically vague and contradictory when answering their questions. He neither confirmed nor denied anything they said. If this frustrated the investigators, they did not show it. In higher circles of Sikkimese—and mostly any— society, courtly decorum often prevails at the expense of truth. Where open disagreement is a breach of the social fabric there are sure to be intrigues. That is the price paid for maintaining social norms. Tulshuk Lingpa understood this well, maybe even better than his interrogators. He both admitted and concealed everything. He gave them everything and nothing with the deftness of a seasoned diplomat. He even unwrapped the ter he had taken out above Dzongri and read them portions of it. Tulshuk Lingpa presented his khandro to them and had her sit at his right.

By the end of the interview while the investigators felt more secure, they were in fact more confused. They had had a better understanding of Tulshuk Lingpa, his motives and his intentions before they ever laid eyes on him. Tulshuk Lingpa had that ability. Fact and fiction, truth and its opposite were not to be held in the hands and weighed as much as juggled.

As the interview was wrapping up, Gonde Drungyig pulled a surprise. He said the king had instructed him to inform Tulshuk Lingpa that he would have to travel to Gangtok and prove his powers to the king by performing a miracle.

This was the only thing in the entire interview for which Tulshuk Lingpa gave a definitive answer.

'Of course,' he said, 'I'd be glad to go to Gangtok and perform a miracle for the king.'

At this Gonde Drungyig smiled, but it caused a minor ruckus among the disciples who had been sitting in on the interview. One of them filled Gonde Drungyig's teacup, purposefully spilling some in the process as a diversion, while another managed to whisper in Tulshuk Lingpa's ear, 'It is a trap. If you go to Gangtok, they will throw you in jail!'

When Gonde Drungyig's attention was back upon Tulshuk Lingpa, Tulshuk Lingpa said, 'Please inform the king that though I'll be glad to fulfil his wish and be tested, the capital is no place to perform a miracle. I will do it here. I will have to perform divinations to determine the propitious date but it will have to be performed here. I will send a delegation to inform the king of the time and date. I invite him, all his ministers and anyone else who wants to witness the miraculous!'

It was with the greatest courtesy that Gonde Drungyig and the Chagzoe took their leave of Tulshuk Lingpa. While they had been with Tulshuk Lingpa their two assistants had been questioning the lamas of Tashiding and people in the neighbourhood, trying to get a feel for how many were planning to go with Tulshuk

Tulshuk Lingpa and his daughter Phenzom.

Lingpa to the Hidden Land. They saved the senior monks for Gonde Drungyig and the Chagzoe to interview. So instead of leaving then for Gangtok, they started questioning the senior lamas of Tashiding.

The first question they asked them was blunt and to the point, 'Are you all planning on going with Tulshuk Lingpa to Beyul?'

The monks were cautious and lied. 'You do not understand,' they said, 'Tulshuk Lingpa talks about going to Beyul but he doesn't really *mean* it. When we ask him when we will go, he says, "Not now, not now." When we press him, he says, "After some months." After some months, he says, "When the weather clears." When the weather clears, again he says, "After some months." Now we know he is not here because of Beyul. He is a great lama. He is giving dharma teachings and initiations. He has many students of thangka painting. People come to him and he heals them. Why would the king have any problem with that?'

The Chagzoe said, 'But we just spoke with Tulshuk Lingpa and he told us everything. We met the khandro, his second wife. He brought her here to Sikkim for the purpose of opening the gate to Beyul. Tulshuk Lingpa told us everything. He even showed us the ter and read from it.'

The monks continued their lie. They couldn't imagine that Tulshuk Lingpa would have been so frank with the king's representatives. They thought they were being tricked into revealing secrets.

They told the representatives again, 'This Beyul story, it should be of no concern to the king. We are only practising dharma.'

After reporting all this to the king, the king sent the Chagzoe to Kalimpong in order to interview Dudjom Rinpoche. The Chagzoe told the high lama, who was Tulshuk Lingpa's root guru, 'I've just come from Tashiding where I interviewed Tulshuk Lingpa, and he told me everything. Some say he's not serious about actually going to Beyul but he brought his khandro, a sure indication that he has every intention of opening the gate. He told me everything but he wouldn't tell me when he would depart. He is your disciple, so you must know when. So please tell me.'

Dudjom Rinpoche said, diplomatically but to the point, 'Tulshuk Lingpa is a terton, and Beyul does exist. He is the right man to open Beyul. I have no idea about the timing. Only he can know this.'

When the Chagzoe reported this back to the palace a storm began to brew, which turned into a cyclone with Tulshuk Lingpa at its centre. The eye of a cyclone, though the winds circle around it, is always calm and so was Tulshuk Lingpa who skilfully took himself out of the tumult by announcing he was going on a six-month retreat at the Sinon Gompa. A three-hour walk almost directly uphill from the village of Tashiding, set on a slight levelling of a steep mountain slope, Sinon Gompa was—despite its historical importance as described by Saul—a small monastery with only a few wooden houses surrounding it. Set amid forests and sheer rock faces overlooking the village of Tashiding and the monastery on the top of the hill beyond, it was a perfect place for the retreat he suddenly announced. He brought with him his family, including the khandro, and his closest lama disciples. For Tulshuk Lingpa it was a time of great concentration upon the opening of Beyul. With all but his closest disciples back in Tashiding fending for themselves and running out of money he was able to concentrate on his mission, which was to find and open a crack in the world.

But first he had to perform a miracle for the king. So a few weeks after the investigators visited him, Tulshuk Lingpa announced the date of his miracle. He said he would perform the miracle on such-and-such date at eight in the morning on the rock slopes below the Sinon Gompa, and he invited everyone—from the king and his ministers to every villager across the kingdom and beyond—to witness it.

To announce the date to the king and to ask him to be present Tulshuk Lingpa put together a delegation consisting of the head lama of Tashiding Gompa, the head lama of Sinon, as well as Yab Maila, and another disciple by the name of Kunsang Mandal who was the tax collector from Shoshing. To officially stand in his stead, Tulshuk Lingpa sent his son Kunsang. Kunsang recalled that they walked from Tashiding to the closest road, which was a few hours away at the Rangeet River and from there they got a ride to Gangtok.

'When we arrived at the palace,' Kunsang told me, 'we gained easy entrance since the delegation included two of the king's tax collectors, one of whom had a brother who was the head of security.

'It wasn't the king holding court that day but the crown prince, who was sitting on a throne under a huge tent on the palace grounds wearing a robe of beautiful Sikkimese brocade. When we were brought before him the lamas made their offerings to the crown prince, and the crown prince blessed them. Then they presented me to him. I stepped forward, ready to bow to the crown prince, but he stopped me. "That isn't necessary," he said. It was a sign of respect for my father but secretly, in my heart, I was thinking of the Hidden Land and how my father would be king there—how he and I were equals since I, too, was a crown prince.

'We sat on wooden benches across from the throne and the lamas told the crown prince our business, which was to announce the date of the miracle a few days hence.

'The crown prince said he would come there himself.

'As we got up to leave the crown prince ordered lunch for us, since we had come from so far.

'While we were eating, I remember Yab Maila saying, "The crown prince said he will come but he won't. He'll send a few representatives. They say one thing; they do another."

'As we were leaving the palace compound we had to wait for the palace guards dressed in their plumed splendour to pass before us playing drums and trumpets. I felt as if I'd stepped into the pages of a fairy tale. I had never seen anything like it.

'We went to the Green Hotel in the centre of town where we would spend the night. The two tax collectors in the party, Yab Maila and Kunsang Mandal, had business with the finance minister. While there, they told him about Tulshuk Lingpa. The minister told them that if Tulshuk Lingpa did good work for the dharma, the government would be likely to give him a salary.

'When they told the rest of us the story back at the Green Hotel, we all got a good laugh out of it. "What would Tulshuk Lingpa need with a salary?" the head lama of Tashiding said, laughing. "We're going to Beyul!"

'We were still laughing over the absurdity of Tulshuk Lingpa on a salary when there was a knock at the door. It was Gonde Drungyig, the head of the team that had come to Tashiding to investigate and had insisted my father perform a miracle. "I heard you came to the palace today to announce the day of the miracle," he said. "I will be there."'

CHAPTER EIGHTEEN

The Miracle

'It is not down in any map;
true places never are.'
Herman Melville

The day of the miracle arrived. Even before the sun rose, people started converging on Sinon with the excitement of knowing that this would be a day they would always remember. Maybe the miracle would be the opening of the crack itself; maybe today the gate would open to a land beyond cares, an event that even their great-grandparents were awaiting. Lamas were known to fly. Maybe he would create a castle larger than the king's from the billowing clouds and disappear into it. Rumour had it that not only the crown prince but also the king was coming. Even in a land shrouded in mystery to the rest of the world, a land of lamas and demons and gods where the mountains hid unknown valleys, it wasn't often that a wonder-working lama performed a miracle. Today the famous terton would perform his supernatural feat especially for the king.

Rigzin Dokhampa was there on the morning of the miracle. Sitting in his office at the Institute of Tibetology outside Gangtok, he recalled for me what happened. He and his brother Sangye Tenzing were from Tashiding and they were in their teens at the time. They were disciples of Tulshuk Lingpa, studying thangka painting with him. Rigzin told me that shortly before the announced time of eight in the morning neither the king nor the crown prince had arrived. Even their representative was absent.

The small grassy field below the monastery was teeming and into it walked Tulshuk Lingpa, followed by his daughter

Kamala holding a huge tray of sweets. Just as they were coming down into the field, Kamala stumbled on a root and the tray of sweets scattered.

'The omen is very important for us,' Rigzin told me, 'wherever we go, whatever we do, we have to see the omen. That was a very bad omen, coming right when it did, when her father was about to perform a miracle. If Kamala hadn't dropped that tray Tulshuk Lingpa would have been able to take out ter that day, and there would have been a seven-year period of peace. But she dropped it so he couldn't, and that seven-year period didn't occur.'

Moments after Kamala stumbled and scattered the tray Tulshuk Lingpa grabbed on to the shoulder of a lama on his right, and it took two lamas just to hold him up for he suddenly became deathly ill. Hardly able to breathe, he broke out into a cold sweat and his head was spinning. It could have been a heart attack.

This sudden turn of events needed an equally spontaneous response to turn it around. This is where Atse came in. Atse, whose real name is Sonam Kunga, was one of the lamas of Tashiding. He had a peculiar reputation that was easily summed up in a single word: Cracked. For the unique logic that made him who he was had tremendous gaps in it, and it was easy to imagine his shaved head cracked right down the middle. He was fond of barley beer and by midday was usually incoherent. As a lama Atse was a disaster.

In a rare moment of lucidity some years earlier, Atse had memorized the text of the *Shabden Soldep*, the ritual one chants when a high lama becomes ill.

It was eight in the morning.

Atse wasn't yet drunk.

He had been walking around with this text in his head for years. This was his moment.

Atse stepped out of the crowd, stood next to where they had laid Tulshuk Lingpa on the ground, and in a voice at once sonorous and sure of itself he began chanting to bring Tulshuk Lingpa back from the brink of whatever abyss he was falling into. So much concentrated feeling was in his voice, such inner authority, that silence fell on the crowd. It was a solemn moment, with only the sound of his voice and the wind rustling the high grass. By the time he was through, everyone was concentrating so intently on Atse that they didn't notice Tulshuk Lingpa had gotten back on his feet, his recovery having been as sudden and unexpected as the onset of his mysterious illness.

Over forty years later this chant was still swimming around in Atse's brain. When I visited Tashiding with Tulshuk Lingpa's grandson Wangchuk, we were awakened at six one morning by a loud rapping at our door. It was Garpa, another former disciple of Tulshuk Lingpa, holding Atse firmly by the shirt collar. He shoved Atse into the room, told me to get my tape recorder and then commanded Atse to sing. Though Wangchuk and I were both still half asleep, there was Atse standing in the centre of our room, chanting in a deep voice as only a lama can, the entire text of the *Shabden Soldep* ritual. We had seen Atse the previous days, and

Atse.

he was always so drunk he could hardly stand. Garpa had picked this moment because it was the only time of the day Atse was reasonably sober. The moment Atse had completed the chant, Garpa grabbed him again by the shirt collar and led him out of the room before he could open his mouth again and put his foot in it.

At the moment Atse had finished his chanting all those years ago on the grassy field below the Sinon Gompa, Gonde Drungyig—the official of the Ecclesiastical Department who had first informed Tulshuk Lingpa that he had to perform a miracle—arrived on the scene.

The miracle could begin.

Tulshuk Lingpa led the representative, his main sponsors, closest disciples and family down a short path to where large smooth stone shelves jutted out over the empty space of the valley. There wasn't enough room for everyone there so people crowded the slope above, back to the small field where they'd started. The lamas started burning clouds of sang.

'From today onwards,' Tulshuk Lingpa said, 'there is no one, not even a king, who can either stop us or help us. We can appeal only to the dharmapala and mahapala, the guardian spirits of Beyul and the keepers of the gate. From today it starts.'

He took out the pecha he had received as ter above Dzongri, the text he'd received from the dakinis especially to appease the guardian spirits of Beyul and to entice them to open the way. He unwrapped it and held it in his hands. As he began chanting the text, Mipham, Namdrol, Géshipa and the other senior lamas looked at each other. They understood the significance of his reading this text. Each, in his own way, was ready for a tear in the fabric of reality.

Since no one knew what form the renting of reality would take and what miracle was about to occur, some were looking intently at Tulshuk Lingpa. Others were watching the sky, awaiting a sign. Yet others were looking towards Mount Kanchenjunga, because that is where they were to find the secret hidden country. One man told me he was looking down the steep slope to the Tashiding Monastery because it was the holiest place.

When Tulshuk Lingpa finished the text, he was standing in a dramatic pose with his right foot in front of the left. When he lifted his forward foot, there—where no one was expecting the miracle to occur—imbedded in the stone, was the imprint of his foot.

Rigzin recalled for me that he was there and personally saw the rock flowing like water. 'The rock was boiling and red in colour,' he told me. 'My brother saw it also; everybody who was there saw this.' Others described to me smoke rising from the rock, and the collective gasp that went through the crowd at the sight of their lama leaving his footprint in stone.

There is a strong tradition within Tibetan Buddhism, especially in the oldest branch, the Nyingma, of great lamas proving their miraculous powers by leaving their footprints in stone. Padmasambhava's preserved footprints are found wherever tradition says he visited and they are still, after twelve centuries, places of pilgrimage. The great lamas of the past have even left imprints in stone of their hands, elbows and heads. Yet leaving an imprint in stone was a deed of the legendary heroes of the past, and none could recall a lama having performed this deed in anyone's living memory. As an old lady told me, even the Dalai Lama—the spiritual and temporal leader of the Tibetan people—had never performed such a miracle.

Tibetan Buddhism is not the only faith that has a tradition of their holy men leaving footprints in rock. There are two alone on the Temple Mount in Jerusalem. One is in the Al-Aqsa Mosque, Islam's third-most holy site. It is believed by the faithful to be that of Mohamed. The other, in the Christian Chapel of the Ascension, is purportedly that of Jesus's right foot and was left just before he left this world forever and ascended to Heaven. The Christians believe the Al-Aqsa Mosque footprint was left not by Mohamed but by Jesus. They believe the Muslims broke the rock where Jesus ascended to heaven and that it is actually Jesus's matching left footprint, a controversy we certainly won't enter into here.

As word of the miracle spread up the hill to the small field and the monastery a light rain began to fall, a special and auspicious type of rain with widely spaced individual drops—large and filled with sunlight—known in Tibetan as a Rain of Flowers.

The crowd parted to allow Tulshuk Lingpa and his lamas to climb back up to the monastery through clouds of incense, the very

Tulshuk Lingpa's Footprint, Sinon Gompa, West Sikkim.

air resounding with the sound of horns and conch shells. With pressed palms, they bowed and prostrated themselves before this miracle-working lama. Then the hundreds who had gathered in Sinon that day filed by the footprint and paid homage to it.

I have spoken with many people who were present that day for Tulshuk Lingpa's miracle. While some say the rock began to seethe and bubble and a purple smoke arose, others simply say they were just looking at the sky and suddenly it was there. Most agree the footprint deepened with time, and moisture came out of it. People bent down to put their forehead to it and many tried to take up the moisture with a corner of their clothing. Some wanted to lick the footprint but they were stopped by others who thought that would defile it.

About two hours later Tulshuk Lingpa was with his family inside his wood-slat hut at the monastery having a bite to eat after the morning's exertion when there was a loud and aggressive knock at the door. Kunsang opened it to the highest law official of the kingdom: the police commissioner who, with pistol holstered and ready, was backed by ten uniformed policemen with rifles. They burst into the room and started ransacking their things.

'Where is this miracle you have been promising the king?' the police commissioner demanded. 'I must see you perform it.'

Yab Maila pushed through the armed police guarding the door. 'You have missed the miracle; it's already occurred,' he averred. 'It was announced for 8 a.m. It is now after 10. Where were you?'

'I was galloping my horse up the hill from Legship. We are far from the capital and it took longer than I thought. If you are to do a miracle for the king, you must at least wait until the official representative of the king arrives!'

'We waited,' Yab Maila said, 'and he came. We didn't start until Gonde Drungyig arrived. You, sir, I've never met.'

'Gonde Drungyig wasn't deputed by the king to view the miracle. I was.'

Just then Gonde Drungyig pushed into the room.

'It is true,' he said. 'Last time I was sent by the king. But today I came as a private citizen, out of my own interest.'

The police commissioner cleared the things from a low table on to the floor with a sweep of his arm. Out of his jacket he produced a large map of the Kingdom of Sikkim, which he unfolded and laid on the table.

'If you have it in mind to take His Majesty's subjects to the hidden valley of Shangri-La, I demand you show me on the map exactly where on the slopes of Mount Kanchenjunga this hidden valley is. In the name of the king I demand that you show me!'

'If Beyul were on the map, it wouldn't be Beyul,' Tulshuk Lingpa calmly said. 'You won't find it on any map. Beyul exists, but off the map.'

This infuriated the police commissioner.

'What do you mean you won't find it on a map?' he insisted. 'Is it too small to put on the map?'

'No,' Tulshuk Lingpa said, calmly. 'Rather it is too large. Your map of Sikkim couldn't contain it, for the Great Hidden Valley in Sikkim is three times as large as the outer Kingdom of Sikkim. Besides, if it were on the map, everyone would go. What would be the use? No one would need a terton to open it.'

The police commissioner was practically fuming.

'You say you performed a miracle? Show it to me.'

Tulshuk Lingpa led the police commissioner with his ten-strong escort armed with rifles down to the stone outcropping of rock to see the footprint. The police commissioner bent down and

examined the footprint as if it were a crime scene. He scratched
it with his fingernail. 'You have made this by hand. You have
carved it,' he declared. 'Besides, since I wasn't here when this
occurred, how do I know the footprint wasn't already here when
you put your foot on it? Bring me some of the old people of this
village. I demand to know if this footprint was here before.'

Some of the villagers were right there, and some of them were
quite old, 'We have been here since our birth,' they told him, 'and
we have never seen this before. This was a miracle. There *was* no
footprint before.'

The police commissioner had with him a little case with the
tools of his trade. He opened it now and took out a tape measure.
He measured the footprint, and it was quite small. Then he
demanded to measure the lama's foot. There was a murmur of
dissent but Tulshuk Lingpa assented. He measured the lama's
foot, which was considerably larger than the footprint.

'Unless you perform a miracle again right now and in front of
my eyes and put your other foot in stone right next to this one, I
will declare you a fraud and have to take you in. You think you
are going somewhere from where you will never return? That
might just be the case. I'll take you to Gangtok—where there is a
nice little cell waiting for you.'

Yab Maila protested. 'Tulshuk Lingpa performed the miracle
in front of Gonde Drungyig,' he said, 'one of His Majesty's officials.
What right do you have to take him away?'

'You performed this before an official who was here in an
unofficial capacity. While he might have been sent to perform a
preliminary investigation, I was sent by the government to witness
the miracle, not he. Now you must perform a miracle for me.'

The villagers got angry. 'We thought he was the representative
of the palace,' they called out. 'He came early in the morning. You
were so late. We thought he was the official representative so we
proceeded. Performing a miracle is no joke. It cannot be repeated!'

The police commissioner was not in the least sympathetic. He
was not even Sikkimese. He was Punjabi, from way down on the
Indian plains a thousand miles away.

As Rigzin Dokhampa told me, 'What do Punjabis know about
footprints in stone? The Indian police officer didn't understand

that when you put your foot in stone, you don't leave the imprint of the tips of the toes or the back of the heel. The footprint is naturally smaller than the foot that made it. When the police commissioner measured it, he got it wrong. He said Tulshuk Lingpa was a fake; he didn't know.'

The police commissioner announced that he was taking Tulshuk Lingpa to Gangtok. He grabbed hold of Tulshuk Lingpa's arm to drag him to where they had tied their horses but he sorely misjudged the situation.

The man that the crowd had waited generations for, the one who had just performed a miracle to demonstrate his power to the king and who held the key to the promised land of immortality in his hand, was not so easily to be led off to jail by a Punjabi representative of the king, commissioner of police or not.

A melee ensued in which Tulshuk Lingpa and the commissioner of police formed the inner circle. They were surrounded by the ten deputies with their rifles ready but useless against this unruly mob of robed lamas, old ladies shaking their fists, children and barking dogs.

The police commissioner had no choice but to give in. 'I'll leave,' he told the crowd, 'but I will recommend to the king that Tulshuk Lingpa be ordered to Gangtok to perform a miracle at the palace—and that if he fails, he should be thrown in jail.'

One of the lamas shouted out, 'Even if he performs a miracle for the king and all his ministers, you'll still throw him in jail!'

'That's not true,' he retorted. 'If Tulshuk Lingpa performs a miracle, I will personally carry him on my shoulders and parade him around the palace grounds to the accompaniment of trumpets and drums!'

He pointed his finger at Yab Maila and Kunsang Lama, the head of the monastery. 'You two came last time to announce the time for the miracle. You'll come again and tell us when the next miracle will be performed but this time in Gangtok. You will come and announce it personally to me, the police commissioner.'

Neither of them gave the police commissioner the slightest indication that they would do what he said.

Someone yelled out, 'You might want a miracle but you're not going to get it. By that time, we'll be in the Hidden Land!'

With that, the crowd let out a tremendous cheer.

The police commissioner and his armed deputies beat a retreat to their horses. They swung themselves up on to the saddles and thundered down the mountain towards the Rangeet River, where official police jeeps were waiting to take them back to the capital with their red lights flashing.

Even Tulshuk Lingpa, who had earlier not been afraid of going to Gangtok to perform a miracle for the king, realized the danger.

By the evening Tulshuk Lingpa, his family and disciples from Himachal Pradesh all started packing. Since openly fleeing would attract pursuers—and possible problems at the Indian border—Tulshuk Lingpa announced he was leaving the kingdom for a few days to see Chatral Rinpoche at his monastery in Jorbungalow outside Darjeeling and that he was taking with him only his disciples from Himachal Pradesh. Of course they would never return to the kingdom. Tseram, which Tulshuk Lingpa had pointed out from above Dzongri and which was near the Western Gate, was on the Nepal side of Mount Kanchenjunga. From Darjeeling they could easily cross over into Nepal and depart from this world for one so much greater without having to worry about so small a potentate as the king of Sikkim.

Fearing that the police commissioner had sent an order to all the border crossings not to let Tulshuk Lingpa and his followers flee the kingdom, Tulshuk Lingpa made sure they had a few bottles of liquor ready as they approached the Indian border at Jorethang. 'If the border guards give us trouble,' he told his disciples, 'we'll get them drunk. We'll say we are only going overnight to Darjeeling.'

Shortly before they reached the border with India, he stopped at a stream known as the Rhambang Khola. He scooped some water in his hands and drank it. 'This stream,' he declared, 'comes straight from Beyul.'

CHAPTER NINETEEN

The Flight

They crossed into India without incident and arrived safely at Chatral Rinpoche's monastery in Jorbungalow.

During the next days, the disciples who had stayed behind in Sikkim started arriving there as well. No one wanted to let Tulshuk Lingpa out of their sight. The Sikkimese, Bhutanese and others were afraid as they often were that Tulshuk Lingpa would disappear into Beyul with his oldest disciples and biggest sponsors—those who came with him from Himachal Pradesh— and that they'd be left behind.

There were others who had the faith and wanted to go but could not afford it. Though money was superfluous in Beyul, one did have to pay for the journey and to eat until the gate opened and you could enter. With a leader like Tulshuk Lingpa, there was no telling how long that might take. One woman in Tashiding had a particularly touching story. She sold her pig to raise funds for the journey but even after she sold the pig she didn't have enough money to go. She still sounded sad, all those years later. 'I lost my pig,' she said wistfully, 'and my chance to go to the Hidden Land.'

The longer Tulshuk Lingpa stayed in Jorbungalow, the more attention he drew; the more attention he drew, the more people flocked to him expecting to be taken to the Hidden Land. As the crowd of people clamouring to enter Beyul grew, so did the obstacles. Though timing was important, so was the collective karma of the members of the expedition in gaining the goodwill of the guardian deities. Though he didn't feel the time was ripe to move on towards Tseram and would have liked to stay with Chatral Rinpoche longer, what could he do? Wheels had been set in motion that even he could not stop.

So the jindas arranged for three jeeps to take Tulshuk Lingpa, his family and the important people to the Nepal border. The rest followed by whatever means they could.

From the border, they walked north seven days through jungle-covered mountains towards Mount Kanchenjunga until they reached the first place of any size, the town of Yamphodin. With hindsight, one can see that the events that then unfolded were inevitable. Two or three hundred foreigners following a lama who was going to open 'Heaven's door' setting up camp on the outskirts of a small Nepali hill town were sure to catch the attention of the head of the local government, who was bound to involve the police, who would find it their duty to inform the army, who would feel they had no choice but to pass the information on to the king, then residing at his palace in Kathmandu. When the king of Nepal heard of the situation and that many of his subjects

The woman who sold her pig,
Tashiding, West Sikkim.

were leaving their fields and homes in order to follow Tulshuk Lingpa to this hidden land of plenty, which they expected to access from *his* kingdom, he sent in the army.

From the army headquarters in Taplejung came seventy-five combat-ready troops with rifles drawn. They encircled Tulshuk Lingpa's encampment in a most aggressive manner and cordoned them off for two days. During this time their commander interrogated people, starting with Tulshuk Lingpa. Protocol has it that one must always treat a lama, especially a high lama such as Tulshuk Lingpa undoubtedly was, with respect. So the army commander inquired politely from him what his plans were.

'I hear you are going to Heaven,' he said. 'How many people are you planning on taking with you?'

'300.'

'300! That's too many.'

'But there's room for 2000.'

Jinda Wangchuk, who Kunsang said was the cleverest of Tulshuk Lingpa's disciples, whispered in his master's ear that he'd better remember what happened with the king of Sikkim and be cautious.

'Actually, we are not going to Heaven,' Tulshuk Lingpa said, backtracking on what he had just told them. 'We only want to go on a pilgrimage to Tseram to perform a puja. We have to go there every twelve years for a six-month puja, after which we'll have better luck. That is why we are going.'

Tulshuk Lingpa's new version of why they were going to Tseram, a tiny nomad encampment just below the line of glaciers, was completely contradictory to what he had just told them and to the stories that were swirling around this lama all the way to the palace in Kathmandu. But he managed to be entirely convincing. Such was the nature of his charisma.

For two days, while his heavily armed men held the perimeter of the encampment and didn't let anyone in or out, the commander interrogated one after another of Tulshuk Lingpa's disciples and everybody had the same story. 'Hidden Land? What Hidden Land is that?' they'd ask innocently, 'We're just on a pilgrimage.'

Ordinarily, the commander would have dropped it there in exasperation and let them go. Whether they were going to

Heaven or only to Tseram mattered little to him; once they were in the high mountains, they'd all be out of his hair. But this order had come straight from the king himself. Besides, Tseram was at high altitude near the border with Sikkim where foreigners needed permits, which he wasn't authorized to issue.

On the third day, it was clear they were at a standstill. Jinda Wangchuk said to the commander, 'You are always asking questions about and speaking with our leader. Who is your leader? *We* want to speak with *him*.'

A jeep was brought, and Jinda Wangchuk led a delegation of five representatives, disciples of Tulshuk Lingpa chosen for their ability to speak well, and the commander brought them down to the army headquarters in Taplejung so they could speak with his superiors.

There the conversation between the head of the army in Taplejung and Tulshuk Lingpa's representatives went something like this:

'We've heard you are going to Heaven with your lama.'

'That's not true; we are only going to Tseram. We have a six-month puja to perform. We must do it every twelve years.'

'Are you sure you're not going to Heaven?'

'Entirely sure: 100 per cent.'

'I can issue you permits to go to Tseram but only if you promise you're not planning on going to Heaven. Because if I give you permits to go to Tseram, and if I later hear you've gone to Heaven, it's my head on the block. The king will come here personally and chop it off! I'll lose my head, and everyone else around here will lose their jobs. I can grant you permits but you must promise!'

'We promise: we have no plans whatsoever of going to Heaven.'

This was a story Kunsang was particularly fond of repeating at odd moments, when we were speaking of other things. 'It was damn crazy,' he'd suddenly blurt out. 'That time in Taplejung, the army man saying, "If you go to the Hidden Valley, king coming—cut my head!" We said, "No, no no. Only puja. Every twelve years we go to Tseram, doing puja, coming back." "OK, then. I give you permit. But if you go to the Hidden Valley—cut my head. Cut my head!"' Kunsang would tell this story laughing hysterically and swiping his hand across his neck.

The five representatives with Jinda Wangchuk at their head returned to the camp at Yamphodin with a six-month permit for everyone to go to Tseram. They had even extracted a promise that if after six months they hadn't "gone to Heaven", they'd be granted an extension.

Kunsang told me that once the army left them alone they stayed in Yamphodin just long enough to gather supplies. As seemed to be the pattern, his disciples—especially his oldest ones from Himachal Pradesh—were pushing him to go higher immediately and open the gate. It was a long time since they had left their homes. They had crossed India to Sikkim and now to Nepal in order to go with him to Beyul. Their money and supplies were running out. They were growing impatient. Once-proud sponsors were beginning to wonder where their next meal would come from. Word of their whereabouts had reached Sikkim, along with the rumour that he'd be opening the gate at any time. Nobody wanted to be left behind. There was a constant flood of people over the mountains from Sikkim to Yamphodin swelling their numbers, constantly drawing increased attention to them.

Once the authorities found out they had been hoodwinked and that Tulshuk Lingpa *was* taking them to Heaven, the army was sure to reopen the investigation and revoke their permit. Fearing once again that he'd end up in jail and not in Beyul, Tulshuk Lingpa announced that they'd be shifting to Tseram, an isolated place where no one would bother them. Even the nomads, who grazed their animals on the higher slopes of Mount Kanchenjunga and used Tseram as a camp, wouldn't be there since it was winter.

Tseram, a one-day trek from Yamphodin almost straight up-hill, was not far from the glaciers that cap Mount Kanchenjunga. Tulshuk Lingpa, his family and main sponsors occupied the abandoned wood-slat huts in the settlement, while the others lived in makeshift tents and in the caves that dotted the landscape.

In an attempt to keep their numbers from swelling unmanageably, Tulshuk Lingpa sent regular messengers sneaking over the Sikkim border—which was just up a steep rocky slope from Tseram—to tell the people who were still arriving at Tashiding in order to find him to stay there. He conveyed that he'd inform them when the time arrived to open the gate. Those who knew his tulshuk nature and that he could decide to open the way on the spur of the moment continued to climb over the high mountains to Tseram so as not to be left behind. This increased the pressure on him to open the way. Food had to be brought from Yamphodin, and with time even the market at Yamphodin wasn't large enough to supply their needs. They had to go further to Taplejung, which of course was dangerous since the army headquarters was there.

Kunsang described the time in Tseram as a very happy time. 'We would go to the jungle where there were many birds,' he told me. 'I used to talk with the birds. I would whistle and the birds would sing back. Once some people heard me whistling to a bird and asked me what I was doing. "I'm talking with the guardian deities," I told them, and they laughed. We used to talk with our echoes too. Everybody was happy. The birds were happy; we were happy. There were mountain goats with curved horns around Tseram.'

When some people from Yoksum were returning there, Tulshuk Lingpa sent Kunsang with them. He was to personally deliver his father's promise that he would let them know when he was going to open the gate to Beyul. The idea was to convince those in Sikkim to stay there and not further strain the already strained conditions in Tseram. Kunsang was also to come back with supplies.

It was a three-day trek from Tseram up over the pass into Sikkim and down through Dzongri to Yoksum. Since Tulshuk Lingpa had fled Sikkim for Darjeeling under a cloud of suspicion, the arrival in Yoksum of the lama's son Kunsang had to be top secret. As Kunsang told me, 'I was also a bit crazy at that time. If they had caught me, they would have thrown me in jail.' The king had his spies.

When they neared Yoksum, they hid in a forest above the village until night fell. Then they sneaked Kunsang to the big house, the house of Yab Maila and his brothers, one of whom was the head of security for the royal palace and another was collecting taxes for the king. Both of them had been asked by the king to be on the lookout for any suspicious activity. And here they were, hiding Kunsang from the king's men.

They fed Kunsang and hid him in a back room until well after midnight. Then they disguised him and brought him a little out of the village to a cave where no one would ever think of looking. There he hid out while Yab Maila collected supplies of tsampa, corn and other food to be brought through the mountains to Tseram. While Kunsang lived in that cave, his father's disciples who had stayed behind sneaked up to the cave bringing him all manner of food and homemade beer. The fear of being left behind when Tulshuk Lingpa opened the gate had grown to paranoiac dimensions. Many thought Kunsang had come secretly to tell Yab Maila and family that the time had come. As they plied him with goodies, he had to deny repeatedly and vociferously that he was there to tell Yab Maila and family of the opening. They extracted from him promises that they wouldn't be left behind. 'We have all hid provisions in caves along the way to Tseram, so we can meet you for the opening in no time. So remember to tell your father not to forget us. We're ready!'

It took five days for Yab Maila to gather the sacks of provisions to be taken to Tseram without attracting attention and also to organize five discreet nomads who wouldn't attract attention by carrying them to Dzongri and beyond. On the night before leaving they sneaked Kunsang down to Yab Maila's house. There, behind closed doors with curtains drawn, they had a party with trusted disciples of his father and lots of drinking and dancing. It was to celebrate Kunsang's last night in Sikkim before going to Beyul where he was sure to become prince. The occasion was a wild and happy one, though for Kunsang it was tinged with a bit of nostalgia and sadness.

At well after midnight Kunsang's head was spinning from the homemade beer. They sneaked him out of Yoksum to where the five nomads were waiting. With sacks strapped to their backs, and by the light of the moon, they climbed into the high mountains.

After they climbed beyond Dzongri, they hid the sacks of food in a cave where no one would find them. One of the nomads decided Beyul was better than herding sheep and goats, so he pledged his herd to the others and went with Kunsang to Tseram. Later, Tulshuk Lingpa sent people to get the provisions.

ဢ   ಞ

Garpa was living at Tashiding when Tulshuk Lingpa arrived and quickly became his disciple. Garpa still lives in Tashiding. His life work is carved on untold thousands of *mani* stones, the stones sculpted with mantras in Tibetan script. His workshop, a corrugated tin roof held up with wooden poles and backed up by a stone wall, is situated along the kora at the back of the monastery in a quiet corner behind the stupas, where the land drops off to a slope of pine trees. That's where one can find him sitting cross-legged on an old burlap sack raising small puffs of rock dust by pounding the surface of a flat stone with a well-used but sharp chisel, allowing the mantra *Om Mani Padme Hung* to manifest. Garpa also sculpts reliefs of Buddhas and Tibetan deities.

The first time I met him, Garpa's engaging smile assured me that my presence was not an intrusion. He indicated a block of wood beside him for me to sit on. I asked him how long he'd been carving stones at Tashiding. He asked to see my mala, or Tibetan rosary, hanging around my neck. He proceeded to turn the wooden beads between his thumb and forefinger one by one. I thought he was praying. Then he stopped. He handed the mala back to me, careful that I put my finger between the two beads he had reached. 'That many,' he said, and continued chiselling stone. I counted the beads. Garpa had been carving stones at Tashiding for forty-five years, since he fled with the Dalai Lama when the Chinese invaded Tibet in 1959.

Garpa's clothes are simple. His manner is direct, and he is at ease. Though his work requires his fullest concentration—carving stone is clearly his form of meditation—being interrupted seems part of his daily round. Tashiding is a quiet place, and many of those doing the kora are Garpa's neighbours and have been circling the monastery for an hour or two or more every day for decades. Garpa greets them like the old friends that they are and offers them a block of wood to sit on, pauses his work for some moments to exchange news, then continues coaxing Tibetan letters out of stone.

I found it soothing to become a forgotten presence at Garpa's side, the hammer falling on the chisel with the regularity of the beating of a drum, the chisel carving the stone, the letters appearing. Though Garpa's hands are bent with age, he wields his tools with the precision and artistry of a violinist drawing his bow.

Even once you realize that almost half a century of patient work has gone into carving the mani stones at Tashiding, it is difficult to believe they are the product of one man. Tashiding abounds with walls built entirely of his carved stones. He has carved so many mani stones that there are walls constructed of stones stacked together one on top of another so the lettering isn't even visible. Yet even that which is carved in stone is impermanent. While his more recent works are still brightly painted, his earlier works are weathering with time.

Garpa is neither a lama nor a monk. He has a wife and grown daughter who, together with his son-in-law, live with him in a house just outside the monastery grounds.

I asked Garpa how it felt, knowing that his stones would far outlast him.

Garpa.

'How should it feel?' he responded. 'The beauty of the mani is not coming from me. The mani itself has the beauty in it. I only bring it out. This is what I do.'

I asked Garpa whether he has sponsors, people who pay for his work. 'Occasionally,' he said, 'but it doesn't matter whether I have a sponsor or not. My work is carving stone. This is my form of meditation, to get rid of all bad karma.

'I've had two main sponsors in my life,' he told me. 'They were my root gurus, Dilgo Khyentse Rinpoche and Chatral Rinpoche. Chatral Rinpoche is still alive. He is ninety-four years old. Every year he goes to the mouth of the Ganga below Calcutta and releases thousands of fish bound for the market into the sea. I started carving stones in Tibet before I fled the Chinese invasion. When I first arrived at Tashiding, I wasn't very good. Chatral Rinpoche saw my work and invited me to his monastery outside Darjeeling for six or seven months. He taught me how to carve stones correctly. Since then I've also carved stones at his monastery, at the Pemayangtse Monastery here in Sikkim, and in Nepal.'

Garpa told me that one time the Dalai Lama came to Tashiding. He, too, was surprised to hear that all those mani stones were carved by one man, and asked to see the man who had carved them. Garpa was brought before the Dalai Lama and the Dalai Lama looked mirthfully into Garpa's eyes and pulled his beard. He held Garpa's face between his two hands and laughed. He told him to continue his good works, which Garpa intends to do, though he confided in me that in the end he intends to go to Bodh Gaya—the place of Buddhist pilgrimage where the Buddha reached enlightenment. 'If I go to Bodh Gaya,' Garpa said, picking up his chisel, 'I don't think I'll come back. I will go there and meditate.'

When I asked Garpa about his time with Tulshuk Lingpa, he laughed.

'My name is Garpa,' he said. 'In Tibetan, that rhymes with *trapa*, which means messenger. Tulshuk Lingpa gave some of his disciples new names like Géshipa, which is a crazy name meaning Four Hundred. Who ever heard of someone named Four Hundred? Because of my name, he gave me the title of the Messenger of the Hidden Land. I was young and strong. While

Tulshuk Lingpa was living in Tashiding and he went to Yoksum or some other place, he'd always use me as his postman to relay messages. I became a tremendous runner. I could run all the way from Yoksum to Tashiding in a few hours. You wouldn't know it now from looking at me but I developed great endurance.

'When Tulshuk Lingpa fled Sikkim and went to Nepal—to Yamphodin and Tseram—he still had me act as messenger to relay messages to those left behind in Tashiding but now I had to cross a 16,000-foot pass. In total I made the return journey six times, plowing through snow up to my waist.'

ॐ   ॐ

It is impossible to say how long they stayed in Tseram. In fact details of times and dates were all incredibly difficult to pin down, and some proved impossible until the end. As far as I can guess, they were in Tseram a few months when one day Tulshuk Lingpa took out his melong, the convex brass mirror used in the trata melong, the mirror divination. He stuck the mirror into a plate of rice and performed a puja that put Yeshe into a trance.

Yeshe was nineteen at the time. Her older sister was the khandro, and had gone down to Yoksum in order to deliver a child by Tulshuk Lingpa some months before, a girl by the name of Pema Choekyi. Somewhere along the line, Yeshe also became his khandro.

When it came to the subject of Tulshuk Lingpa and his khandros it was difficult to get people to talk. Since it was almost as indiscreet for me to ask about his lovers as it was for those who knew to speak about them, I dared ask but only got knowing smiles and evasive suggestions in response. A few ventured as far as saying with an enigmatic smile that he *was* charismatic and extremely handsome. It is easy to imagine that someone who could inspire hundreds of people to forsake their worldly goods and the very world itself might very well have power over women. In the non-answers I received it became clear that Tulshuk Lingpa was both attractive to women and had his experiences with them, though you can be sure that as with everything else in his life, his experiences with women weren't of the common variety. He was a great mystic, and the women in his life played a role something similar to that of Beatrice who guided Dante through Paradise in the *Divine Comedy*.

I spent quite a bit of time with Yeshe, and she herself told me what many others had—that she was also his khandro, though she had been married three years earlier at the age of sixteen. I suspect the fact that she was his khandro meant she and Tulshuk Lingpa were lovers, though I am not sure. Tantric secrets might be easier to unravel. What she couldn't hide was her deep and abiding love for him. After over forty years, she still saw him in her dreams. She'd see him performing a puja and blessing her.

Yeshe described to me that day in Tseram when Tulshuk Lingpa performed the trata melong, the mirror divination, and had her look into the mirror. She saw three beings reflected in the mirror, and they were hovering off the ground. One was completely white, and two were completely red. They were slowly floating towards her.

Tulshuk Lingpa said the white one was the sadag, the spirit owners of the land, and the two red ones were the shipdak, the guardian deities of the land. That they were floating towards her meant that they were coming from Beyul to greet them. This was an extremely good omen, for without the cooperation of the local

Pema Choekyi, the daughter of Tulshuk Lingpa and Khandro Chimi Wangmo, and her son Gyurme, Lahaul.

deities and the spirits who guarded Beyul it would be impossible to get anywhere near the gate. The beyul were Padmasambhava's most well-guarded secrets, which would be given up only when circumstances necessitated their opening and only to those pure of heart, intention and motivation. Without the cooperation of the deities and without the necessary purity of heart, clouds would descend, snow would fall and winds would rise up and blow you off the mountain. Support of the deities was never simply given, no matter how predisposed they were to you. They had to be constantly appeased and won over by performing numerous pujas.

When Yeshe saw the deities greeting them, Tulshuk Lingpa decided it was finally time to move higher in order to open the Western Gate to Beyul Demoshong.

'The time has come. The time has come. The time has come,' he said.

He chose twenty of his closest disciples to make the opening. They were chosen for their purity of heart, the depth of their practice and the sincerity with which they had given up all ties with the world.

As they were preparing to leave, those who were to stay in Tseram awaiting word that the gate had been opened gave lavish advice to those travelling with Tulshuk Lingpa.

'Just remember that nothing is impossible,' they counselled. 'As you go to open the Gate, the spirits will feel that you are intruding. They will call forth storms and bring down rain, hail and snow. At that time you must keep your minds pure and don't allow yourselves to be infected by doubt. No matter what Tulshuk Lingpa says don't contradict him. Even if he says, "Bring me the moon," don't tell him it is impossible. Try. Keep your minds pure.'

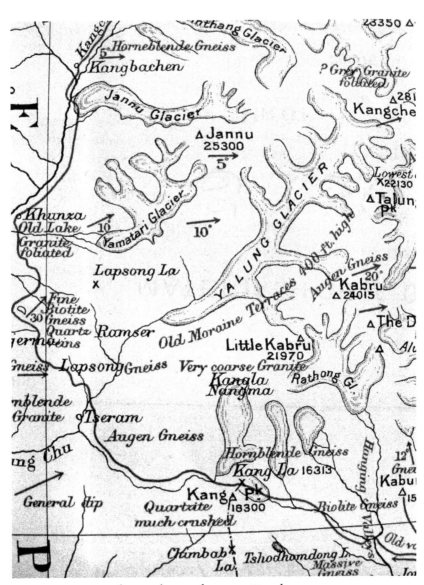

Southwest slopes of Mount Kanchenjunga.

CHAPTER TWENTY

Opening the Gate

'Somewhere over the rainbow
Skies are blue
And the dreams that you dare to dream
Really do come true'

Yip Harburg

So it was, amid tremendous excitement, that Tulshuk Lingpa and twenty of his closest disciples ascended the steep slopes above Tseram in order to find and open the Western Gate to Beyul Demoshong. They took with them bedding, food and pechas. Of the twenty, all were men except for three young women—the khandro, her sister Yeshe and another woman who has since died. The khandro had strapped to her back her and Tulshuk Lingpa's eight-month-old daughter Pema Choekyi. This was in the early spring of 1963. Of the twenty, many have died in the intervening decades. Others—like Mipham, who has been in deep retreat for years in a cave in Bhutan—could not be traced. I was able to speak with eight of those who went above Tseram and piece together what happened.

Years before, Tulshuk Lingpa had been given directions to Beyul by Khandro Yeshe Tsogyal in a vision; so he knew the way. Yet the directions he was given, which he wrote down in his neyik or guidebook—titled *The Great Secret Talk of the Dakinis Showing the Way to Demoshong*—demonstrates that the landscape in which the gate was to be found was not purely physical. While it describes the way to a particular place, the landmarks are clearly visionary as well as cryptic. This terma is after all a treasure map to a hidden paradise full of unimaginable treasures, both physical and spiritual. It reveals secrets while concealing them.

I was given a copy of this guidebook by the lamas of Tashiding only because I was with Wangchuk, Tulshuk Lingpa's grandson. I could have it only after I made the solemn promise that I would not let others see it, publish it in its entirety or publish excerpts that would in any way divulge its secrets. This I have done in the following excerpts:

> Within the fort of the snow mountain there are four trea-sures packed with tremendous wealth that will fulfil your wishes. There is a pond of nectar, and within that pond are eight nagas [serpent gods] protecting a treasure of un-imaginable jewels. There is an unthinkable paradise of the owner of the hidden treasures, as well as a paradise of the protector in charge of the whole world. There are countless natural formations, great hidden treasures of dharma and wealth and some small hidden treasures as well.
>
> At the foot of the snow mountain like a lion, which is full of rocks encircled by rainbows, there is a treasure of innumerable jewels. Within the rock mountain in C there is a treasure of wish-fulfilling gems. In the long cave called L there is another treasure of wish-fulfilling gems. In the East, below Kanchenjunga, are treasures of the three different salts. In the mountain called L there are treasures of life and religion. In the central mountain called T there is a great treasure of immortality. In the northwest, in a great cave at Y, there is a copper horse that will conquer all three worlds. And there is a dagger there that will conquer all illusions. In the holy place of the auspicious dakini there is a granary of corn.

After describing a dizzying and kaleidoscopic array of treasures and secret places, 'paradises of nagas and gods and dakas and dakinis', which are to be found 'on the mountain, in the valley, on the rocks, in trees, as well as in the springs', it says, 'These are the secret places of Padmasambhava, linked like a net.' Lest you think great secrets have been revealed, it then goes on to say, enigmatically, 'These are the well-known secret places.'

About the gates of Beyul, it says,

> In that place there are four main doors, four secret doors, the four cardinal directions and the four corners, which are all held tightly. The eastern great gate is blocked by three natural obstructions: narrow ways, mountain doors and curtains. The three conditions of the southern door are rocky hills, great rivers and innumerable ravines. The western and northern gates are entirely packed with natural barriers. Therefore this beyul is superior to other places.

Some of the directions in the book seem almost practical, as if their true meaning were only slightly veiled. 'The country between the light and dark is blocked by dense snow and three different curtains, one after the other. From the four corners, if you could catch drops of water, then that secret door will not be blocked by the curtains.' This seems to refer to curtains of ice such as you find blocking high mountain ravines and which in the warm season, when you can 'catch drops of water', melt and allow passage.

The guidebook, upon which they relied above Tseram as they neared the western gate, also has many instructions for rituals to be performed to appease the local deities and the deities of Beyul. To enter Beyul is not only a matter of getting yourself to the right place. The timing has to be right. The guidebook says, 'When the world is devoid of happiness, the door of the ascetic valley will open. If one delays, troublesome things will occur and the great and small valleys will be shaken by a red wind of fire, and poisonous hailstorms will drop.'

In the guidebook it says that to open the gate you have to perform rituals and burn incense to the 'deity owner of the treasures. Rituals should be offered to the important hills.' So it was when Tulshuk Lingpa and his twenty disciples left Tseram that day in the early spring of 1963. Again, as he had when they left the nomad above Dzongri, Tulshuk Lingpa announced that from that point forward they would have no contact with the outside world. The only contact would be with the spirit owners of the land and the guardian deities of Beyul.

The directions he had received in the vision years earlier and 'brought down into script' in the guidebook were specific enough for Tulshuk Lingpa to know he had to search for the gate above Tseram but the conscious mind is not a powerful enough tool to locate such a gate. So he performed the trata melong, the mirror divination, and had Yeshe look into the burnished brass. She saw the way ahead of them turning into a green valley of flowers with huge old trees and innumerable waterfalls.

The first night they slept in the area that in Tibetan is known as the *vatsam*, the area above vegetation and below the snow.

The next day they climbed into the snow, and by late afternoon they reached a huge cave surrounded by snow in which they all could fit. There they made camp. From this cave the land dropped off and then rose again on the other side of a little valley, the snowy slope rising to a little notch in a ridge—a pass—across which Tulshuk Lingpa declared was Beyul Demoshong. They were finally within sight of the gate!

The next day, in the morning, Tulshuk Lingpa took twelve of the twenty disciples who were in the cave and led them to the slope rising to the pass. Just as they started their ascent, a cloud came low with a whirl of wind that blew snow from the slope and made the air thick with it. Blinded by the snow and pierced by the wind, they retreated, reaching the cave as a storm came low on the mountain. The storm kept them pinned in the cave for the next two days, during which time they were in the utmost state of concentration upon their pujas and spiritual practices. They needed to purify themselves to the point where the weather would clear and allow them to ascend the snowy slope to the pass leading into Beyul.

On the third day, they awoke to the sun shining into the mouth of their cave. Again, Tulshuk Lingpa headed out to make the ascent. This time he took with him six of those he had left behind on his first attempt. It would be the collective karma of all those attempting the opening that would determine the success or failure of the enterprise. But this time they didn't even make it to the bottom of the slope below the cave when a cloud came in and made further progress impossible.

Thus it went for nineteen days. Some days the weather would look fine when they set out for the slope opposite but never could they even start the ascent before the weather changed. Obviously the guardian spirits were not ready to allow their passage. Some days they didn't even try. Storms raged on the mountain for days at a time, piling snow outside the cave in huge drifts that dwarfed them. On those days, they remained in the cave performing pujas and reciting mantras.

On the twentieth day, they woke up to brilliant sunshine. Again they set out for the steep snow slope leading to the pass, now even thicker with snow than before.

Namdrol stopped Tulshuk Lingpa. Something had been bothering him.

'Master,' he said, 'I am from Lahaul. I've spent my whole life trekking in deep snow. You are from Tibet. You've spent winters down in Pangao, where the snow doesn't build up. What do you really know of deep snow, steep slopes and their dangers? To get to the pass, it is too dangerous to just go straight up. It would be safer to go that way, to the right, where the slope is gentler and the rocks are bare. When we reach the top of the ridge, we can cross to the same place you want to reach. But your way is just too dangerous. It is springtime; the underlying snow is old and crusted in ice. The new snow on it could slip.'

With this, Tulshuk Lingpa became furious. It was prophesied back in Kham that the one to open Beyul would have eyes like a tiger; now he had the disposition as well.

'Who's the lingpa here,' he boomed, his breath condensing into clouds of steam in the frozen air. 'If you're a lingpa, if you know the way, then why are you following me? Why aren't you in Beyul already?'

The slope Tulshuk Lingpa wanted to ascend *was* impossibly steep but when they were leaving Tseram hadn't the others warned them not to contradict him, no matter how illogical he became? Now they had the full fury of Tulshuk Lingpa upon them. To contradict him or to bring in logical thinking or prudence at the very moment he was finding and preparing to pass through a crack in the logic that keeps the world in a seamless web is the greatest sin a disciple can make.

A moment of doubt can crush a lifetime of faith.

As William Blake said, 'If the Sun & Moon should doubt/ They'd immediately Go out.'

It is rare that conditions are right for the opening of a beyul, rarer still that a lingpa takes incarnation at that time. Conditions must be perfect. You need the help and guidance of any number of spirit gatekeepers and mountain deities, who control the weather and the subtle forces that allow the lingpa to discern the way. Those with the lingpa must be as one being in their single-pointed and clear-hearted intention to give up everything. They have to let go of all material possessions, home, family and the very notion of logic that would prevent them from leaping into a realm beyond the constraints of logic that hold them to this world. They must all jump, as a single being, into another dimension. And if at that vital moment—when all those conditions have come together into a single point in time at the prophesied place where a possibility exists for a crack to form—if just as they are to achieve this wondrous step, a doubt arises and is voiced the whole enterprise can be lost.

A very similar event occurred at the decisive moment for Dorje Dechen Lingpa when he came to Sikkim to open Beyul Demoshong in the 1920s. They were nearing this same gate, climbing a snowy slope towards a ridge—probably the very same ridge that Tulshuk Lingpa and his disciples would climb over forty years later—when he suddenly turned to his disciples and said, 'Bring me a white dzo.' A dzo is a cross between a yak and a cow.

'But Master,' they replied, 'we are high in the snow peaks, far away from any settlement. Where are we to find a dzo, let alone a white one? It is impossible.'

This raised the ire of Dorje Dechen Lingpa. 'Don't you understand? Nothing is impossible,' he boomed. 'What we need is a white dzo. Make one, then, out of butter!'

'But Master,' they complained, 'we have no butter. We used the last of it in the tea.'

This was described to me as the 'bad omen' that marked the end of Dorje Dechen Lingpa's attempt to open Beyul

Demoshong. They headed back down the mountain that day and returned to Tibet.

Now, forty years later, Namdrol voiced a doubt about Tulshuk Lingpa's judgment and the very sky itself responded. Suddenly they were engulfed in thick cloud. Freezing winds lashed at them with biting snow. Having spent three weeks above Tseram living in the cave, they would have been unrecognizable to those below. Their faces were thickened like leather by the elements and the skin was almost black. The snow stuck to their faces and turned to ice. Wrapping themselves in their long sheep's wool coats and shawls, they returned to the cave.

That afternoon, Namdrol set out without anyone knowing to try his route and see if it were possible. He didn't make it very far. He slipped on the ice, gashed his forearm and returned to the cave with his arm bleeding.

The next morning the weather was good. Tulshuk Lingpa performed the trata melong, the mirror divination. He announced that the divination bode well. He told some to stay in the cave, while he went with the others to make a reconnaissance of the route they had been trying each day in order to see how the weather was developing. On the way he pulled one of his disciples aside. His name was Wangyal Bodh, a powerfully built man from Simoling in his mid-twenties. Now a retired civil engineer in his late sixties, Wangyal himself told me what happened next.

'Tulshuk Lingpa pulled me aside. "Today we'll let them go by themselves," he said. "You and I will try another route, alone— just the two of us. Too many people make difficult progress. It is good that you have a warm coat—and excellent, you have a climbing axe."

'He sent the others ahead. "We'll go left, up that way," he said to me confidently, indicating a little side valley that angled up to the sky. "That is what I saw in the mirror."

'I followed Tulshuk Lingpa up the valley,' Wangyal said, his voice betraying the excitement he must have felt at the time. The way was steep, icy and dangerous. Water was gushing down innumerable rivulets from a glacier that loomed above them, the ice hard and green.

It was a raw and dangerous place of loose scree and precariously perched boulders balancing over the deep. The glacier was confined to the ravine where the snows of innumerable winters collected and compacted. It had turned an eerie blue. Above the glacier ice gave way to snow- and ice-covered rock rising to a windswept peak with a plume of snow blowing from its summit. The sky at that altitude was so deeply blue it was almost black. Wangyal's heart was pounding—from more than just the altitude. He had the sense that with only the two of them, the way would open.

With a tremendous crack, followed by a resounding roar, a piece of the glacier the size of a house broke off. Scattering boulders and crushing others in its path, it was sliding down the valley directly at them. Wangyal grabbed on to Tulshuk Lingpa to save him but realized there was no way out of the glacier's path. Terrified, he knew this was the end. Though he had first grabbed on to Tulshuk Lingpa to save him, when the lama yelled at him to let go, Wangyal realized he was now hanging on to him out of raw fear. Wangyal released Tulshuk Lingpa from his iron grip.

Tulshuk Lingpa reached under his sheepskin coat and, with the flourish of a knight presenting his sword to a foe, whipped out his purba and held it before him at arm's length as the glacier crashed towards them with a deafening roar.

Holding the purba steady, one arm outstretched and his other arm extended with the index and small fingers pointing towards the onrushing wall of ice, his voice resonated such a profoundly deep note that the rumble of the oncoming glacier reverberated back on itself. His voice was elemental, pre-human. 'Ha-ha-haaa ...' and the glacier broke into two pieces and thundered by them left and right, leaving them unscathed.

Tulshuk Lingpa tucked the purba back into his robe with a calm that was astounding. Wangyal trembled with fright, awed by what he had just experienced, shaken to the core.

Wangyal told me this story from when he was young while we sat drinking tea in his substantial home in Simoling. A more sedate, open and honest man cannot be imagined. I had just been travelling some days with him, visiting people and places connected with Tulshuk Lingpa. I had found him sober, level-headed and very exact in what he said. Exaggeration was not in his character. The way he told the story, I felt it was true. Even though it was embarrassing to do so, I had to ask. I tried to be diplomatic.

Wangyal Bodh.

'People make up stories and exaggerate,' I said, 'especially when it comes to things religious. Did this really happen how you tell it? The glacier split in two and passed you by?'

'Absolutely. I am as amazed today as I was then,' he said, staring me openly in the eye. 'I also probably would not believe it if I hadn't experienced it myself. But it happened exactly as I say.'

Both the man's honesty and his integrity told me it was true.

'The human mind is susceptible to all sorts of things,' Wangyal continued, 'especially doubt. I realized that until this point I had still harboured doubts; now that I had experienced Tulshuk Lingpa's powers, doubt was no longer possible. Beyul Demoshong was now a certainty.'

When the crashing glacier's echoes faded down the valley, Tulshuk Lingpa turned to Wangyal and asked whether he wanted to continue. Wangyal said, 'Yes,' without hesitation. Tulshuk Lingpa was happy. 'Finally,' he said, 'a disciple with enough faith.'

Tulshuk Lingpa took a confident step forward and continued climbing the steep valley. Wangyal followed in a state of awe. Though his mind was calm and confident, his body quaked with animal fear.

Ahead of them was the glacier. Beyond the glacier, where earlier had been a steep slope of snow and ice topped by stone, the ground now appeared bare. Impossible as it might sound, above the bare ground was vegetation and it got greener as it went higher towards what now appeared to be a pass. Even more incredible than that was how the way was marked by rainbows—the most incredible rainbows Wangyal had ever seen, rainbows whose light and arcs were in the patterns of flowers. They looked strangely close—as if he could reach out his hand and touch them. The air was so thin that the rainbows could only be seen where they lay upon the mountains, as if the mountains at these altitudes had the density of air. The air seemed too imbued with the Celestial to contain them.

'When we reached the edge of the glacier,' Wangyal said, 'it was smooth as only melting ice can be and flowing everywhere with water. Tulshuk Lingpa confidently climbed on to it, next to where the piece had broken off. He reached down his hand and lifted me up.'

Wangyal broke his narrative to take a sip of tea and look out the window of his living room at the surrounding mountains. Though it was June, the peaks were still covered in snow.

He told me that when he was a young man here in Lahaul he used to cross the Rohtang Pass in winter. It was dangerous but sometimes they had to do it. Just walking to the next village often meant negotiating snow so deep that houses would be buried in it. Trails were often swept away by avalanches. Since he used to go for treks in the high mountains and walk among the glaciers, he understood as well as Namdrol how treacherous glaciers could be. They were especially a threat in springtime when the ice melts on the surface and the resulting water opens deep crevasses. When the changing spring weather brings fresh snow, the fissures get covered. Under any other circumstance, he would have had more sense than to venture up that glacier. Now he did not hesitate. His awareness was as taut and sharp as the glacier was steep.

He followed Tulshuk Lingpa a few hundred yards up the glacier. The rainbows ahead of them seemed so close he could now practically scoop them up in his hands. The wind swept down the cold surface from the heights and the sky beyond. Suddenly the breeze turned warm and fragrant. The thin crystalline mountain air was bringing with it the scent of the most glorious herbs and flowers. He breathed deeply the fragrant air, and the smell of saffron filled his lungs. Tulshuk Lingpa was walking just ahead of him. His sight, however, was set on the rising greenery beyond the glacier from whence issued this beautiful smell.

Suddenly the ground gave way beneath his master's feet and Tulshuk Lingpa was sliding headlong into a crevasse wide enough to swallow him. Wangyal lunged forward and grabbed on to his ankle. He tried to dig the tip of his boots into the edge of the crevasse to prevent them both from sliding into the dark chasm of ice. Could this be the crack to which they had been travelling so long?

'The ice axe,' Tulshuk Lingpa yelled.

In his panic Wangyal had forgotten that he had one on his belt. He swung it hard and dug its tip deep into the ice, stopping their deathly slide. There he was, lying on his belly with his face hard against the ice, watching his hand slowly slip down the ice axe's handle. His other hand was stretched behind his back holding on to Tulshuk Lingpa's ankle. For the second time that day death seemed unavoidable. How could he ever get his guru out of that crevasse? He turned his head to look at him, and to his amazement Tulshuk Lingpa was standing up! Yes, he was hanging on to Tulshuk Lingpa's ankle but he was standing.

'Hey,' Tulshuk Lingpa said in a jocular voice, 'what are you doing with your face on the ice. Get up!'

Wangyal got up, amazed at his guru's strength. He wanted to bow down and touch his feet but if he did so he'd probably slide right into the crack from which they had just saved themselves.

Though immediately ahead of them it was even more treacherous, Wangyal was ready to follow his master. They were almost there. Just ten steps more, Wangyal told himself, just ten steps and we will be in Beyul. It seemed that close. He heard a sound from above and it took him a moment to realize he was listening to a gyaling, the clarinet-like instrument the lamas use. At first he thought he was hallucinating from the altitude. But he heard it and so did Tulshuk Lingpa. 'It is the gatekeepers of Beyul,' Tulshuk Lingpa said. 'The dharmapala and the dakinis are coming to greet us.'

Wangyal started forward but Tulshuk Lingpa put a hand on his shoulder.

'We can't go, not just the two of us,' Tulshuk Lingpa said. 'The two of us can't disappear. How can we go without the others? There is room for over 2000 in Beyul—this I know. We must turn back.'

'Never did I feel disappointment so acutely in my life,' Wangyal confided. 'We were so close. We were standing in the snow but above us, beyond the glacier, there was no snow. It was so beautiful on the other side, green, and we were almost there. I kept thinking I was hallucinating. I even put my fingers in my ears to see if the sound of the gyalings came from inside my own head. The sound was real. The rainbows were real. And so was Beyul.'

They carefully picked their way down the glacier and descended the valley. By the time they reached the cave dark clouds had once again descended on the mountain.

The others were eager to know what had happened. Tulshuk Lingpa didn't utter a word. He sat a short way off on a large stone, and the others surrounded Wangyal. 'What happened up there?' they asked him. 'Your eyes are glowing. What did you see?'

He related all he had seen and how close they were.

'I know why we couldn't see it earlier,' he told them. 'There were too many doubts in all of our minds. That's why we have been unable to see the Hidden Valley, even though it's right *there!* He pointed up the snowy slope. 'This time we really saw it, for real. Twice we almost lost our lives. It is really there. I saw it with my own eyes.'

The people thought, 'We've travelled so far, from Himachal Pradesh and Bhutan and Tibet. We've come to Sikkim and now to Kanchenjunga, and still have doubts. We have too many doubts; that's why we haven't seen it.'

Tulshuk Lingpa had advised them all along, even before they left Lahaul, that if they had the slightest atom of doubt in their minds they would never see the Hidden Valley.

The others were really excited now. 'We also want to see what you saw,' they said to Wangyal. 'Even if we cannot enter, we want to go to the point where we can see what you saw.'

Wangyal told them that if he hadn't been nervous, if he hadn't been shivering with fear because of nearly dying twice, he would have been able to reach out and touch the rainbows.

That afternoon, Tulshuk Lingpa performed the trata melong.

Yeshe looked into the mirror.

She saw a long pipe coming out of the sky. It was as wide as your outstretched arms, glowing with a golden yellow light like the sun but was also very white. It was coming straight out of the sky.

Though they asked Tulshuk Lingpa what it meant, he grew silent and again sat a short way off on a stone. The moment he sat, four white doves—what they were doing up there amongst the glaciers is anybody's guess—flew low over Tulshuk Lingpa. They circled him three times before cooing as if in salute and flying off into a low-hanging cloud. The cloud came lower and engulfed them. Though it was the middle of the afternoon, a red light glowed through the thick fog they were suddenly immersed in. It seemed like sunset. Then the colour changed, and there were flashes of pulsating coloured light. Those in the cave came out and were staring into the changing, coloured light of a fog so dense they couldn't even see Tulshuk Lingpa. Then the wind blew. The cloud moved up the valley, and they were bathed again in sunshine.

These two events, the circling doves and the multicoloured cloud, were corroborated by everyone I spoke with who was there. When telling me the story, each independently recalled these events with such vividness after four decades that it was as if these events had been etched in their memories.

The next morning Tulshuk Lingpa again did the trata melong and had Yeshe gaze into the mirror.

This time she saw Beyul, a beautiful place of natural wonder. Ancient trees surrounded a field through which water flowed. Waterfalls cascaded through the thick jungle that covered the surrounding mountains, and the field was filled with huge white mushrooms.

The sky was clear over the slope leading to the pass.

Tulshuk Lingpa smiled.

'Today is the day,' he said. 'Today is not like the other days. Today we must be especially careful.'

He chose among his disciples twelve he wanted to take. They wore heavy jackets and scarves wrapped round their heads. Tulshuk Lingpa brought the pechas needed to open the gate and those he'd need once they entered. Wrapped in cloth, he strapped the pechas to his back.

When they were leaving the cave one of those being left behind said to Wangyal, who was amongst the twelve, 'Why don't you stay behind and let someone else go. You've already seen it.'

'That, I thought, was extremely unjust,' Wangyal told me. 'I told the fellow, "That wouldn't be fair. It was only because of all of you that we turned back!"'

Tulshuk Lingpa led the twelve towards the snow slope that rose to the pass.

At the base of the final slope, they stopped on a large flat rock for a final meal of tea and tsampa, after which their food was finished. After this, they would have no food until they entered Beyul.

Tulshuk Lingpa chose three to go with him further: Yeshe and Lama Tashi—both from Lahaul—and the Lachung Lama, not the one by that name still living in Sikkim but a Tibetan lama by that name. 'If we make it,' Tulshuk Lingpa told those he left behind, 'we'll signal.'

The four started pushing their way up through the waist-deep, newly fallen snow towards the pass. Lama Tashi was the *umzay*, the head of rituals, at the Simoling Monastery. In his late thirties, he was a mature man solidly built with years of experience of high mountain snow. He went first to break the trail. Tulshuk Lingpa came second, holding a page from a pecha and chanting aloud certain sacred syllables. Behind him was Yeshe, and taking up the rear was the Lachung Lama.

From a distance, they looked like four little dots slowly moving up the vast white slope.

When they suddenly dissolved into white and disappeared, it took a moment for those on the flat rock to realize that their comrades had been engulfed in a cloud that was pouring down over the pass.

On the slope, the cloud's arrival—like a white and permeable wall—hit them with a sudden vertigo as the steep white plane of snow they were climbing suddenly merged with the air. Everything lost distinction, became uniform and started to spin.

As the snow slope gave way beneath them, the air itself became solid as they were plunged into a darkness that roared.

Each of them found themselves alone—the air sucked from their lungs and a crushing force hitting their bodies. In place of the green valley each expected to suddenly find themselves in, each, alone, found themselves plunged into a world of darkness and profound silence, unable to move—all except for the Lachung Lama who, when the avalanche ended, found himself with only his legs buried in the snow but otherwise unharmed.

He extricated himself and finding himself alone on the slope he started digging frantically, looking for the others. As he neared Yeshe the snow was red and as he cleared her face of snow so she could breathe, he saw blood spurting from a huge gash across the top of her head. When he laid her on the surface of the snow, she was barely breathing and she was unconscious.

Thrashing the snow like a dog, his hands bent like claws, the Lachung Lama dug. He didn't stop until he found Lama Tashi who was bleeding from a gash above his eye, his left hand bent at right angles to the arm. He was in so much pain that he was in shock and barely conscious.

A loose page of one of the pechas that had been strapped to Tulshuk Lingpa's back appeared out of the dense fog and slapped the Lachung Lama on the face in a great gust of wind. Following where it came from with his eyes, he saw more pages. They had been mixed with snow by the avalanche and were waving in the wind. He leapt down the loose slope and clawed at the snow. It was by following the density of pages that he found Tulshuk Lingpa.

Tulshuk Lingpa's body showed no external mark of the accident. As the Lachung Lama dug him out, Tulshuk Lingpa's legs were crossed. He was slumped over, his eyes closed and frosted with snow—and he was dead.

Uncovering but not moving the body, shocked by the magnitude of his discovery, he fell back in the soft snow and stared at the leaves of the pechas. They were blowing in the foggy gusts of wind, sliding by on the snow and disappearing into the steep grey distance.

The Lachung Lama ran down the slope to get help. He went to where the others were waiting and gave them the news. Then together they went up to care for the living and offer homage to the dead.

At first they couldn't tell if Yeshe was dead or alive. The young woman, who had seen the vision of Beyul green and replete with waterfalls only that morning, lay on the snow at the edge of death. The snow beneath her head was red with blood. They wrapped her head in an effort to stop the bleeding. Then, stripping Tulshuk Lingpa of his heavy sheepskin coat, they rolled her in it.

Taking off their own coats, they wrapped Lama Tashi in them. They wrapped the two in whatever hats and scarves they had to keep them warm through the night, for evening was falling and both were hovering too close to the edge of death to be brought immediately down the mountain.

So they left the three of them there, the two living keeping half unconscious night vigil over their dead guide. Lama Tashi slipped in and out of consciousness all night. He thought the two motionless bodies beside him were dead and that for sure he was dying.

He awoke to the rays of the sun striking him from behind a distant peak. Shock soon gave way to pain. His arm was badly broken and his fractured ribs pained with every breath. The continual loss of blood kept him on the edge of consciousness while the shock of the avalanche kept him from remembering what had happened. He didn't know why he was lying on that snow slope with his lama lying dead on one side and Yeshe hovering near death on the other.

When the sun was slightly higher in the sky and their companions reached them, Yeshe was in far worse shape than Lama Tashi. She had bled badly all night and they could hardly bring her to consciousness. They gave Lama Tashi something to eat, hoisted the three of them on their backs and carried them down to the cave to rest. Then they headed down the mountain. That night they slept where they had stopped for the night when they were coming up. The next day they reached Tseram.

The hundreds of people camped at Tseram hadn't heard any news of the expedition since they left three weeks earlier. In a heightened state of excitement, they were awaiting word that the way was open, speculating on whether any of them had had the patience to postpone their entering to tell the others back in Yoksum and at Tashiding.

The sight of the column of climbers wearily descending to Tseram, three of them being carried on others' backs, was enough to set off a collective wail as the cast of their heads let it be known that tragedy had struck.

When they realized Lama Tashi and Yeshe were injured and that the third one being carried was Tulshuk Lingpa and that he was dead, the cries echoing off the surrounding mountains made it sound as if the mountains themselves were crying.

As Dorje Wangmo, Tinley's mother-in-law, told me, 'Only the children weren't crying because they were innocent.'

Tulshuk Lingpa died in his forty-ninth year, a particularly dangerous year by Tibetan reckoning. In Tibetan it is known as a *kak* year, a multiple of twelve plus one. He died on the twenty-fifth day of the third month of the Tibetan calendar, corresponding to Saturday, 18 May 1963.

Death ceremonies for a high lama are very elaborate. For seven days they chanted over the body. They offered incense and butter lamps, and prayed continually. On the seventh day Kunsang, his only son, put a flame to his father's body and it was cremated.

Some of Tulshuk Lingpa's ashes were mixed with earth and formed into a stupa at the spot. Some were scattered on the mountain. The rest Kunsang brought to some of the holy places in India—the Ganga River in Banaras, Allahabad (where the Ganga and Jamuna rivers meet) and to the mouth of the Ganga south of Calcutta.

CHAPTER TWENTY ONE

The Aftermath

'The only paradise is paradise lost.'
Marcel Proust

'When the death ceremony was completed and they cremated the body,' Dorje Wangmo, Tinley's mother-in-law from Bhutan, told me, 'it was like a bomb blast. Everyone just dispersed in every direction, without following one another.' Those from Bhutan returned to Bhutan, those from Sikkim travelled via Dzongri and Yoksum to their villages there.

Dorje Wangmo's husband wanted to return to Bhutan but she said no, and insisted they go on a pilgrimage. So they travelled together with a few monks west towards Mount Everest. In a place called Walung they found an abandoned monastery where they stayed for six or seven months performing pujas and religious fasting. To return to Sikkim they had to sell everything they had, first their meagre jewellery and finally their clothes—everything but what they wore on their backs. When they reached Singtam, a market town in Sikkim on the Teesta River, they had nothing left and could proceed no further. So they collected wild fruits in the forest, laid out a cloth in the market and sold them.

When Dorje Wangmo returned to Sikkim, she was forty years old and pregnant with her first and only child, who was later to become Tinley's wife. She has always considered her daughter a gift from Mount Kanchenjunga.

'There was one couple,' she told me, 'a monk and nun from Bhutan, who decided to attempt opening the door to Beyul by

Dorje Wangmo.

themselves. So when the cremation was through, they carried a sack of tsampa, bedrolls and tin plates with them. They followed the tracks left in the snow by those descending with the dead and injured, and after two days they reached the cave where Tulshuk Lingpa and his followers had lived for three weeks.' Dorje Wangmo started laughing at the recollection, and her eyes got a faraway mirthful look, sparkling with possibility.

'From there,' she said, 'they disappeared. No one knows what happened to them. Their plates and bedrolls were found in the cave but they disappeared without a trace. Perhaps they made it. We'll never know.'

ॐ   ૯૪

Atang Lama was in his early thirties when he first met Tulshuk Lingpa. He was seventy-four when I met him. He had grown up in Sinon and also lived in Tashiding.

'That first trip to Kanchenjunga,' he told me, 'after which everybody thought Tulshuk Lingpa had failed and the rumours started to fly that he was a spy, was the beginning of difficulties. I was on that first trip along with Géshipa, Kunsang and the others. What struck me most was that the khandro had told him in a vision where to go and when he looked down the Kang La Pass into Nepal—and remember, he'd never been there before—he knew the name of the place was Tseram. I was a local boy so I knew. Just when others began to doubt, I knew first-hand the lama's powers. What the others didn't know was that he was only finding the way. That was the purpose of the first trip. Though people spoke ill of him, they were only the people who didn't know him. Whoever came to see him became his followers. Such was the power of his personality. I saw him put his footprint in that stone. It was as if a fire was burning. But then the guy from the king said, "No, I haven't seen it."

'I followed Tulshuk Lingpa to Nepal when he fled Sikkim. I was from a good family. We had a lot of land. Though we didn't plant that year, because we were going, we didn't have to sell our land either. I was in Tseram when news came of his death. When those of us who were from Sikkim were returning home after the body was cremated, we hid in the forest during the day and travelled only by night.

'We weren't afraid of meeting a tiger in the jungle,' he said with a laugh, 'only of meeting other human beings. We sneaked back to our villages because we were afraid of being caught by the king, whom we had disobeyed by going. He had warned us not to go. Our fields were lying fallow. When we returned, you can be sure we were subject to the ridicule of our neighbours who had thought Tulshuk Lingpa mad all along.'

There was something in Atang Lama's tone as he recounted this failure to reach

Seventy-four-year-old
Atang Lama, Tashiding.

Beyul—the way he described sneaking through the forest by night and hiding during the day—that was tinged with embarrassment, as one might have while recounting a childhood prank.

'In those days,' he told me, 'the king would come once or twice a year to Tashiding, and the next time he came he held a public meeting and chided us.

'"Don't go off chasing after every lama that offers you a ladder to the moon from the top of a mountain," the king told us. "It is very cold up there, and you could have died. When Tenzing Norgay climbed Mount Everest, he knew what he was doing. He had the proper boots; he had the proper clothes and equipment. The only miracle is that more of you didn't lose your lives. If the way opens, why should only you from the villages go? I would also be going, believe me! Next time listen to me, and don't go chasing after mad lamas."

'That's what the king told us the first time he visited Tashiding after we returned. He also told us that we were then forgiven, and the matter was dropped.'

஧   ଷ

Baichung Babu was another Sikkimese who went with Tulshuk Lingpa. He was in his late twenties at the time; so he was in his early seventies when I met him. His name often came up when I spoke with the Sikkimese followers of Tulshuk Lingpa. It was not easy to find him, though I did track him down following trails and paths through villages in West Sikkim. When I located his house, I was informed that I'd find him somewhere up the steep slope working on the road. I climbed a trail until I came upon a gravel road under construction. I followed it until I came upon a small gang of boys working on the road with a white-haired man pounding a huge boulder in the roadbed with a maul, trying to crack it. The man was Baichung Babu, and he was the foreman.

It was a brilliant, clear day. Mount Kanchenjunga was glistening to the north not so far away, with its white slopes sharp as a jagged razor piercing the deep blue sky and a plume of snow streaming from its very peak. Baichung Babu was powerfully built, especially for an elderly grey-haired man. He was putting his entire body into cracking the huge boulder. As I approached,

I wondered what it had been like for him to return to his daily life and to live the intervening forty-plus years within sight of the mountain into which he had expected to disappear.

If only that crack had opened forty years earlier and he had entered a land free from toil, he wouldn't be putting his effort into cracking this boulder. I wondered whether this realization had turned him bitter with the years. So I approached him, and he let the head of the maul come to rest by his feet.

Baichung Babu and his road crew.

I told him my business, that I was interested in his feelings about his trip to Beyul when he was a young man. The boys gathered round, and he spoke rapidly—for them as much as for me—as he told the story of going with the lama up the mountain in order to find a place where you'd never have to lift a shovel or pound a maul. To the boys, such a trip made immediate and intuitive sense. Had a lama appeared at that moment who knew the way, I'm sure they would have left their shovels on the side of the road and followed him. Baichung Babu's faith had not diminished with time. He didn't seem embittered that here he was, white-haired and over seventy years old, still pounding rocks to earn his daily fare. His only regret was that the lama died at the crucial moment. 'I won't get the chance again,' he said. 'Such a chance only comes once in a lifetime. Now I'll have to wait till another.'

ॐ   ☙

I asked Rigzin Dokhampa, the researcher at the Namgyal Institute of Tibetology outside Gangtok and teenage disciple of Tulshuk Lingpa, why he thought Tulshuk Lingpa failed.

'Tulshuk Lingpa was the right person to go,' he said. 'But there were many other people involved. Too many. Not all of them had the right karma. Without practice and accumulating merit, you cannot go. You have to be clean. If those who go with the right lama have good karma, they can certainly make it. Even then, it depends on time. Timing is everything.'

'How can it be one's destiny,' I asked, 'to open a beyul and fail? Both Tulshuk Lingpa and Dorje Dechen Lingpa were tertons, both found terma and both knew from within the way to Beyul Demoshong. It appears they were even attempting the same gate on the same snowy slope. How can you fail your destiny?'

Rigzin sat silently collecting his thoughts before speaking. 'Seeds—like wheat or corn—have the power within them to grow. But what is within the seed is not enough. Doesn't every seed need the proper soil and the right amount of water and sun? As it is for the seed, so it is for the terton. To discover terma, the terton must have the proper conditions. Both of these lamas had the karma to find the Hidden Land but nothing stands in isolation. Buddhism teaches the interdependence of all things. For the seed within any of us to grow, it needs proper conditions. Seeds need water. Tertons need not only a female consort, or khandro, to open a beyul. They also need disciples with unflinching faith.'

'Were Dorje Dechen Lingpa and Tulshuk Lingpa the only tertons who have attempted to open the Hidden Valley?' I asked.

'Many tertons have tried, over the years.'

'Were they the last two?'

'Yes, as far as I know.'

'What would you say to the typical Westerner,' I asked, 'who would argue that there are no hidden lands to be found, that by now satellites have photographed and mapped every inch of the earth?'

'So far,' Rigzin said, 'even great scientists can only see germs with microscopes and other modern-day machines. With only their eyes, these microbes would have remained invisible and they would never have discovered them. Beyul is much the same. For the practitioner of Buddhism the instrument is consciousness itself. We develop our consciousness so we can see what does not appear to the common eye. That is the lens that allows us to see what remains hidden to your airplanes and satellites. Besides, Beyul is protected by a "circle of winds" that would prevent an airplane from even flying over it. There are many things that cannot be seen by scientists. No machine will show you Beyul. None will take you there. Anyone can look into a microscope and see the microbe. Only those who have developed their consciousness have a chance of entering Beyul. Developing such a level of consciousness, we Buddhists believe, takes many lifetimes. It is extremely rare. If everybody could go there, why would it be called the Hidden Land? It would be called the Open Land. Wouldn't it? Those who have the karma to go there can go in this life.'

'You were lucky to be born in Tashiding,' I said. 'I was born outside Boston.'

'You were born in the richest country,' Rigzin said. 'Here in India, and in Sikkim, we are the poorest country but the holiest.'

'Which would you choose?'

'For the next life,' he said, 'our world is better. For this life, your world is better.'

'Having been in both countries,' I said, 'what I see is that people are happier here.'

'Really?' Rigzin said. 'That is the blessing of Padmasambhava.'

৪৩   ৫৪

Wangchuk and I spent a lot of time together while tracking down his grandfather's story, and we grew quite close in the process. We travelled together to Sikkim twice, and over the course of two or three years we spent a lot of time crammed together in the backs of jeeps bumping down rough roads clinging to mountainsides in the quest for 'grandpa's' disciples.

When meeting Tulshuk Lingpa's disciples, Wangchuk's presence gave me an immediate stamp of legitimacy that opened people to telling their tales. It was often a deeply emotional experience for those who had courageously followed Tulshuk Lingpa to the Gates of Paradise to find on their doorstep the grandson of their beloved lama and a foreigner wanting to hear what they had to say. As the gates opened to memories of what was for many their greatest adventure and their closest brush with something transcendent to their own selves, the spectre of the beyul appeared before them. They described the reality not of how it *felt* to be on the threshold of another world but how it *feels*.

Wangchuk.

Such was the immediacy they still felt after over four decades. I
was always grateful to repay Wangchuk's gift of accompanying
me and opening doors by his presence and translating for me
by having him present to receive the stories. He had grown up
knowing his grandfather was a lama and had died in an avalanche
but as is often the case, he had scant idea of his ancestor's story
or the extraordinary way his father had grown up.

ℬ   ℭ

The last of Tulshuk Lingpa's disciples that Wangchuk and I
spoke with was a woman named Passang Dolma. We had long
been through with our interviews when Wangchuk told me that a

friend of his, to whom he had been telling his grandfather's tale, had told him he had once heard Passang—his mother's friend— say she had been a disciple of Tulshuk Lingpa. Since she lived in Darjeeling, it wasn't difficult to visit her. Passang must have been in her early or mid-sixties, which would have made her a very young woman when Tulshuk Lingpa was in Sikkim. She was neither learned nor particularly religious. She seemed in all respects a normal woman who had happened to participate in these extraordinary events.

'From the town of Darjeeling,' she told us, 'only two families went with Tulshuk Lingpa. It was my family and the family of my uncle, who was a big sponsor of Tulshuk Lingpa's.'

'How did you become Tulshuk Lingpa's follower?' I asked.

'My uncle had met him. He became a follower and told us about him. Then my husband and I heard Tulshuk Lingpa was at Chatral Rinpoche's monastery in Jorbungalow. We heard that he was taking everybody to the Promised Land, and you wouldn't have to work there. We were very excited. So we went to see him—my husband, our two-year-old daughter and I. When we saw him I was struck by how young he appeared—how young and how handsome! He was in the temple and there were so many people it would have been impossible to actually speak with him. We could only file past him and receive his blessing. I was in his presence only for about ten seconds, and never even heard him speak. That's the only time I ever saw him but it was enough. Such was his power. It was some time later that we heard he had gone up the mountain to open the gate. We were so excited we sold off everything. We *had* to follow him. We felt we had no choice. People had been waiting for generations. We felt so fortunate just to be alive at the right time. We didn't have much but we sold off what we had. Our bronze alone got us sixty rupees—a lot in those days, at least for us. My sister lived in Yoksum, so we went there to wait to hear that the gate had opened. Tulshuk Lingpa didn't want everybody to come to Nepal. I was in Yoksum when word came that Tulshuk Lingpa was dead.'

'How did it feel,' I asked her, 'to be on the verge of entering another land?'

'I was very happy,' she said. 'My husband and I had severed all attachments; we didn't have anything when we went to Yoksum. All I had was one set of thick clothing, which I wore all the time, ready to go up into the snow at a moment's notice. To give up everything was to have one foot already in the Hidden Land. There is no way to describe it.'

'What did you expect to happen when the way opened,' I asked. 'Did you think it would be a cave, a gate?'

'Behind the mountain there would be a gate. Once you were through the gate it would be locked and you could never come back. We would become immortal inside, and would not age. That place would be filled with flowers. If you planted a grain of rice in the morning, it would be ready by evening. You wouldn't have to work. Everything would be very easy. You wouldn't have to sow seeds again; they would just keep growing.'

'Did Tulshuk Lingpa himself tell you what it would be like there?'

'No. As I told you I never even heard him speak. I only received his blessing, and that was enough for me to abandon my life. The thing about the sowing of the seeds—that came from his followers. I don't know anything he himself actually said about the Hidden Land.'

'Do you know why the king was against Tulshuk Lingpa?'

'We were only small people. How could we know about the king's feelings?'

'Has anyone ever made it to Beyul?'

'I haven't heard of anyone. But I still firmly believe in it.'

'Do you still think of Beyul, in your daily life?'

'Every day. Especially when times are difficult. Then I dream of what it would have been like. Even today, I would abandon everything again in an instant if the right lama came.'

'The fact that Tulshuk Lingpa's attempt failed and ended in his death doesn't make you doubt the existence of Beyul?'

'How could it? It was because of him I had the most beautiful time of my life. There is no way to describe what it is like to give up everything. I was never so high in my life. When I came back after Tulshuk Lingpa died I had no sense of regret at all. I'd do it all again.'

ℰ ℭℛ

After Tulshuk Lingpa died and everybody was dispersing, the people from Lahaul tried to convince the family to return with them to Lahaul. But they did not go. As Kunsang put it, 'Why should we have gone back? Father wouldn't have been there; we'd only have sad memories.'

'Besides,' Kunsang said, whistling his breath through his teeth like a cold wind howling through cracks in walls, 'in winter— damn lot of snow.' He burst out laughing.

'The Lahaul people even sent a lama to convince us,' he continued in a more serious vein. 'Since I was Tulshuk Lingpa's only son, he told me the monastery would be mine. But I did not want it. Mipham also felt the same. He never returned to Lahaul either because of the memories. After my father died, he went to Bhutan and he's been there ever since living in a cave. He's in deep retreat. After I refused to go back to Lahaul to take over my father's monastery, the lama from Lahaul went to Bhutan and found Mipham in his cave. He asked him to come with him to Lahaul to take over the monastery but Mipham also refused. When he asked Mipham why, he said, "If I come, you'll be having me do house pujas!" He also finds that life very boring. As far as I know, Mipham is still alive and living in his cave in Bhutan. He is always in deep meditation.

'My father's other close disciple, Namdrol, caught TB and died young. He was from Lahaul and left behind a wife and a daughter. He was such a learned lama that people really mourned his passing.

'Zurmang Gelong, the lama from Kham who was working on the road crew when he discovered that my father was the one prophesied in the scripture, was also a very good and learned lama. After my father's death the Karmapa brought him to Rumtek and then sent him to America, where he died in Los Angeles.

'Tenzing Norgay never knew my father's true reason for going to Sikkim. It was much later that he found out, after my father's death, and he thought, "Why didn't he tell me? I know all the routes around Kanchenjunga." But then he'd laugh. "Tulshuk Lingpa himself knew the way; why should he have asked me? He knew very well." Tenzing Norgay's wife, by the way, died near Pemako. She was poisoned by kapat.

'After the cremation, my family went to Chatral Rinpoche's monastery and he was very kind to us. We had nothing. He gave us land outside Darjeeling, in Tinchulay, and somehow we managed to survive. It was not easy. We were so sad at our loss. Some years later my older sister, Kamala, married Chatral Rinpoche. He is now well over ninety years old.

'It was some years later, in the mid-1970s, that Chatral Rinpoche proposed constructing a stupa for my father at his monastery in Salubari. It would be like a monument to him: a repository for his relics that would hold and emanate their power. We had wanted to construct one ourselves but didn't have the money. Chatral Rinpoche did, and he asked us for whatever relics we had from my father so they could be sealed inside.

'I've told you about my father's purba, that magic dagger he pulled out of a vision in Tibet, the one that split the glacier above Tseram and used to spark in thunderstorms. He was famous for it. Well, I had that purba after my father's death. When Chatral Rinpoche said he'd construct the stupa for my father, we gave him the remaining ashes from his cremation as well as texts and other ritual objects that had belonged to him. I also gave him my father's purba. I had no choice. It was the most difficult thing for me to give up. Now that I am a practising lama, it would have enhanced my work. That purba had tremendous powers. No matter how drunk my father was, he always had it with him. He'd take it out and you would see fire sparks coming out of the tip. Sometimes he'd let people touch it, and they always said it felt like water. You could dry your hands and again touch the purba, and your fingers would be wet. Yet it would be glowing, like incense.

'Tarthang Tulku was a great friend of my father's. Sometimes I see him in Bodh Gaya, the pilgrimage place where the Buddha attained enlightenment. He remembered well my father's purba. A few years ago he asked me what happened to it, and I told him it ended up inside the stupa.

'Tarthang Tulku became angry with me. "How could you have allowed it to be put into a stupa?" he said. "It was a powerful object. You need three lingpas in the family, in the lineage. First there was your grandfather, then your father. You would be next. If you had the purba you'd gain tremendous *lungta*, good fortune.

You'd have the ability to receive revelations and prophecies. Why did you ever give it up?"

'I explained to him how we were poor and didn't have the money to construct my father's stupa and how great an honour it was that Chatral Rinpoche was constructing and financing it—and how we actually had no choice. I described to him how I watched it being wrapped up in a special cloth and lowered in through the top of the stupa before it was sealed. It is in the position that represents mind and consciousness. I told him how disturbed I was that it was sealed in that stupa.

'Tarthang Tulku told me, "You are the son of a great lingpa. You know all the rituals. You should be carrying that purba with you every day. You could be a lingpa yourself. You should get the purba!"

'But breaking into a stupa is a very bad thing to do, and he knew it too so I don't think he really meant it.

'But still, he was angry at me. "What are you doing here?" he asked me. "You should go back to Tibet!"'

        ဆ   03

Kunsang became quite emotional talking of the period after his father's death. 'Before my father died,' he told me, 'people in Lahaul who didn't follow him always said, "Tulshuk Lingpa, he is a mad lama, drinking all the time." Then, after he died, the same people said, "Tulshuk Lingpa—he was a high lama, and a lama like this doesn't come often. We didn't know before. We thought he was mad." They were crying.'

I asked Kunsang whether he ever returned to Kullu or to Lahaul.

'Since we left for Beyul,' he said, 'I've never been back over the Rohtang Pass. I've just never been able to. But I did return to Kullu twice. It was some years after my father's death. As the only son, I was the head of the household, you see, and I had to earn money. So I decided to go into the apple business. The Kullu Valley is famous for its apples. So I returned.

'First I went to Pangao, to see the cave where we had lived the better part of eleven years. Walking down the steep, overgrown path I felt a mixture of excitement and dread. I had left my mother and sisters in Darjeeling a thousand miles away and ventured back on my own. I had been but a boy when I left, just sixteen. As I angled down the path from the village to the cave, I had to wipe the tears from my eyes. When we left for Beyul, we left from Pangao. We were going to a place we'd never leave. It didn't cross our minds that we'd ever return. That's why it took so many years for me to dare face it.

'We used to maintain the path to the cave. I used to run down it from the village. Now it was all overgrown, the brambles catching my clothes as if the guardian deities of the place were warning me to go no further and let the past lie. I had to hang on to clumps of grass not to slip and plunge into the river far below. It wasn't until I was directly in front of the cave opening that I realized I was home. Memories of that happy time, the time of my childhood when my father was alive and everything was hope and promise, flooded my mind and spilled out through my eyes. My cheeks were flowing with tears. So many years; so many changes.

'Jinda Wangchuk had so lovingly walled in the front of the cave, put in windows and internal walls. Now the door was both ajar and askew, hanging by a single hinge. The glass in the windows had been stolen or smashed by stones, the frames left broken and rotting. Stepping inside, I felt as empty as the house itself. The wood-frame walls were all leaning dangerously to the side, the very image of desolation. Not one cup remained on a shelf. Not one spoon. It was empty and damp; leaves crunched beneath my feet. Blinded by tears images flashed through my mind of our departure, of how we had already felt triumphant by the fact of our leaving.

'My eyes were now smarting from the salt of my tears. I fled back outside where the sharp sun blinded me completely.

'I heard a voice: "Hey, aren't you the Prince of Shambhala?"

'Wiping my eyes with the back of my hand, I saw a young man hanging back. His body was half-hidden by a bush. I recognized him dimly. He had been changed by the intervening years as I too must have been changed.

'I didn't know what to answer. "Y-yes," I finally said. "I am."

'"You're back? What happened?"

'Suddenly I felt dizzy, as if my entire life was spinning and I was in danger of falling off that cliff directly into the Beas River.

'"I've got to get out of here," I told him, "It's all so changed. Help me, please. Help me back up the hill. I never should have returned."

'He thought I was crying because I wanted to move back into the cave and had nowhere to sleep the night. "Don't worry," he told me. "You can sleep in my family's house, and if you want, we'll rebuild the cave."

'I slept that night in Manali.

'The real purpose of my visit wasn't nostalgia but business— the apple business. The next day I bought woven sacks in the market and I thought I'd be smart and buy my apples directly from the farmers. So I walked down the valley with the empty sacks on my back until I came upon an apple orchard and I bought enough ripe red apples to fill my sacks. It was difficult after that to transport both myself and my sacks but I managed to find a truck that brought me to the railhead on the plains, some eight hours away. I bought a second-class ticket that would take me the thousand or so miles to the railhead below Darjeeling and sat with my sacks on the slowly moving train, feeling rather satisfied with myself for being so smart as to even think of going where apples were grown in order to get my supply.

'There were no direct trains, so I had to switch trains often. It was not easy with sacks of apples, each weighing as much as I did. I ended up in the passageway of one train, sitting on my sacks. A man sitting next to me on his suitcase started up a conversation.

'"What is your work, my friend," he asked me.

'"Business man."

'"What kind of business man?"

'"Fruit business man," I told him, proudly patting the sacks of apples.

'"I see," he said, and by the smile on his face I could tell he meant trouble.

'"Where did you buy your fruit?"

'"Manali."

'"Where will you sell it?"

'"Darjeeling."

'"Ah," he said, laughing at me and pointing out the absurdity of my venture to everyone else in the compartment, "that's very near!" Even the poorest beggar in that second-class compartment laughed at the absurdity of my venture.

'I hadn't factored in the cost of my tickets and my time when I figured out my profit, so of course I made none. I guess I was slow, for after selling those apples in Darjeeling at a loss, I returned to Kullu to do it again. I wanted to make sure it was a complete failure, which of course it was.

'In the end, I figured it out: No profit in apples.'

༄   ༅

Lama Changchup was with Tulshuk Lingpa all the way back in the Pangi days, even before Tulshuk Lingpa cured the people of Simoling of the leprosy and moved there. He remembers Kunsang as a young boy. He used to play with him in the snow and taught him to write in Tibetan.

I met Lama Changchup in Kalimpong, where he moved after Tulshuk Lingpa died to be close to his root guru Dudjom Rinpoche. He has the reputation of being a very serious practitioner.

I asked Lama Changchup whether he followed Tulshuk Lingpa to Sikkim.

'I didn't go,' he told me. 'I was at his monastery in Simoling when Tulshuk Lingpa left for Sikkim. He knew I wasn't going, and he asked me to stay in Pangao so I went there. I never saw him again.'

'Why didn't you go?'

'I didn't believe in it. I didn't think it would work.'

'Were there many people in Simoling who didn't believe?'

'I think I was the only one! Beyul exists for sure. It exists in Sikkim, near Kanchenjunga. But who will go there—that's another story. You hear that two or three people have gone. One hears stories but nobody really knows. There are many beyuls. It all depends on your karma. Guru Rinpoche wrote about it. I had read in the scriptures that it isn't so easy to go. You have to be very good in your dharma practice. The time has to be right. You cannot just go there with hundreds of people. Tulshuk Lingpa was a very great lama and he carried his lineage but when it came to Beyul ...

'Tulshuk Lingpa's mind was pure, and he had good intentions. But there were too many people around him, and they didn't all think the way he thought. Everyone has a different mind. How

Lama Changchup, Kalimpong, 2006.

could they all have the same mind like him? Though many of those around him weren't prepared, his mind was quite good and pure. Dudjom Rinpoche and Chatral Rinpoche—they both warned Tulshuk Lingpa not to go so fast but those around him forced him to go.'

'Kunsang said Tulshuk Lingpa was a crazy lama, always having visions and falling into a trance,' I said. 'Was he like this?'

'How can we know what a lama as high as Tulshuk Lingpa sees inside, what visions they have? They are big lamas, and they see things; but unless they write them down we cannot know. The work we do with our hands—that we can know. I don't know what is happening in your mind. If you can't see it with your eyes, how can you know?'

'Many of Tulshuk Lingpa's disciples say he made it to Beyul when he died,' I said. 'Could this be true?'

'When you are dead there is no Beyul.' Lama Changchup said curtly. 'You go to the Shingkam, the pure land, like a heaven. What would you need Beyul for?'

ॐ   ☙

Géshipa's yearning for Beyul has not dissipated in the years since Tulshuk Lingpa's death. If anything, he has become more ardent. For him, the events of the early 1960s did not put an end to his quest to find that elusive gate. To this day he is considering making the journey. When we were visiting him, he even asked Kunsang and me to go with him and attempt an opening of the Eastern Gate. He pointed to a tent and a sleeping bag hanging on a nail by his door, encrusted in sooty cobwebs, ever ready should the opportunity arise. Even though he has a heart condition—his doctor tells him it would probably cause his heart to stop if he attempted high altitudes—he does not care.

'Even if I die on the way and the bears eat my flesh,' he said with emotion, his old eyes sparkling, 'I would gladly offer it to them. Better to die on the way to Beyul than to shrink back in fear.'

His eyes—at once open, childlike, and ancient—peered out of his deeply wrinkled yet innocent face and fixed Kunsang in their gaze. 'You are Tulshuk Lingpa's only son,' he said softly.

Then fixing upon me the same gaze he said, 'Now your life too is linked to Tulshuk Lingpa's.'

He looked deeply into each of our eyes in turn.

'Let us go together to Beyul,' he suddenly said, his voice quivering with excitement. 'I've been doing the astrological calculations, and next October will be a very auspicious month for opening the Eastern Gate. This could be the last chance within our present incarnations. It is written in one of Padmasambhava's ancient books of prophecy that once the Nathula Pass is open again for trade with Tibet, it will be next to impossible to get to Beyul. I've just been reading it.' Géshipa pointed in a vague sort of way to a jumble of Tibetan scriptures on a high shelf over his bed wrapped in cloth that were so encrusted in cobwebs and dust that it was clear they hadn't been touched in years.

'But your heart,' I said, 'your doctor said your heart will stop if you go to high altitudes.'

Géshipa brushed away my concern. 'Tulshuk Lingpa was attempting to open the Western Gate of Beyul Demoshong,' he said, his voice at once eager, confident and confidential. 'Even *he* said the Western Gate was the most difficult to open. The Eastern Gate is the one with least obstructions; it is the easiest.

'Some years back, two Bhutanese lamas came to see me. They had a scripture I'd never seen before about Beyul Demoshong, and they wanted to discuss it. They weren't very learned. They were asking me questions and writing down notes. They spent two days with me, discussing the various routes and gates. Early on the third day, they arrived with their bags and told me they were going to make an attempt on the Eastern Gate. That was the last I ever saw of them.

'It was some time later that I got a visit from some other Bhutanese. It was these two lamas' families looking for their missing relatives. Since I knew the route they had gone and I couldn't ask their relatives to risk their lives—the way to Beyul

Géshipa.

must be kept secret—I told them I would go looking for them. So I did. I went to Mangan, Dzongu and Tolung. Then I climbed into the high mountains through thick forests until I got above the trees. There was a lake there and it was very salty, and blue as the sky. There I met a nomad. I spoke to him of Beyul, and he knew the stories. He knew about the Eastern Gate and remembered talking to the missing Bhutanese about it. He had watched the Bhutanese climb a particular valley but they never came down, which was strange to him since the only way out of that high valley was to retrace their steps. But he was a nomad; he had his yaks to attend to, and he never went up to investigate.

'The nomad and I went together up the valley. Following the instructions from the ancient books, we came to a cliff. There was a ladder made of trees lashed together leaning against it. The ladder led to a cave. We climbed the ladder, and inside the cave we found the Bhutanese lamas' clothes, their bags and even their shoes. All the things you don't need in Beyul. I know they had the scriptures with them but they were gone. They had made a fire, and with the blackened end of a stick they had written the name "Tulshuk Lingpa" on the back wall of the cave.

'The nomad returned to his animals and I stayed in the cave. Because I had studied the scriptures, I knew exactly where I was. The gate was just above the cave. The next day I climbed farther and got to the gate but I became afraid. It's easy to have no doubts when you are down here. But when you are up in the snow it isn't so easy. I wasn't ready.

'I've wanted to go to Beyul my whole life. It is my last chance in this lifetime. Because I am old I cannot make it alone.

'But if you come,' he said, looking at Kunsang, 'you can take out ter.'

Turning to me he said, 'If you don't have any doubts, you too can come.'

'I am Tulshuk Lingpa's son, not Tulshuk Lingpa,' Kunsang protested. 'I cannot take out ter.'

'But your father taught you,' Géshipa said. 'Together we know all the pujas. The deities who guard the way get easily angry. That's why we'll have to do lots of pujas, to make them happy. Together with you, surely the way will open! In October, the time will be right. After that, it won't be possible. Time is running out.'

Kunsang winked at me. 'This is not to be taken lightly,' he said in a confident tone. 'Géshipa is a great master of prognostication. When he says the time is auspicious, the time is auspicious. My father always had Géshipa divine the dates for things. He always said once we were in the Hidden Land Géshipa would be the main prognosticator. But still,' he said under his breath, 'I don't think so. Very difficult. He's nearing ninety. With a heart his doctor says will stop beating at high altitudes, it does seem rather *crazy*!'

It did seem an incredible form of suicide—not out of desperation but out of hope.

Kunsang turned back to Géshipa, 'In October the time is right—*you* go!' and he burst out laughing.

Géshipa realized we would not be joining him.

'I am too old now to go on my own,' Géshipa said undeterred. 'I have two boxes of scriptures I must take to Beyul.' He indicated two wooden crates he uses as low tables. 'Since I am not a terton, I'll need them in Beyul. I'll have to get someone to help me. I've been thinking about it. I might be able to find someone with sufficient faith, here in the village. But as we near the gate and the way gets rough, most people's faith would waver. As you near the border of Beyul, you have a chance of dying. But if I didn't tell him, if he didn't know where we were going there'd be no obstacles ...'

⁖ ⁗

Of all the people I met who were with Tulshuk Lingpa above Tseram, Yeshe left the greatest impression on me. It was Yeshe who paid the greatest price. The openness she possessed at the age of nineteen that allowed her to see in the mirror, that deeply intuitive sense by which she could discern images in the burnished brass, had been tempered by time into a deep and open sadness. Her love for the man who was to open the way to Beyul had obviously succeeded in opening her heart.

I met Yeshe in her tiny house in Koksar, her home village in Lahaul just down the valley from Simoling. Hers was the last old-style house in the village. It consisted of two rooms with walls of mud and stone over three feet thick. Her neighbours were all tearing down their houses and constructing larger, two-storey concrete houses, a mark of modernity, prosperity and status—none of which she possessed. She was dressed in a traditional Lahauli dress of deep burgundy with red lacework and large looping earrings. Her warm and engaging smile made me feel at home as I sat on a cushion on the floor and watched her heat water for tea on the wood-fired stove. At sixty-two years old, there was still something of the young woman in her face. A beauty shone through, an innocent quality tempered by suffering. Her aged mother lay wrapped in blankets next to the stove for warmth, sleeping most of the time I was there during my many visits.

I asked Yeshe what happened above Tseram and about the death of Tulshuk Lingpa.

'The night before the avalanche,' she told me in her soft voice, 'I was alone with Tulshuk Lingpa, and he told me something he told nobody else. This was after Namdrol doubted his route—after Tulshuk Lingpa and Wangyal had almost been killed by the glacier, and I had looked in the mirror and seen the white pipe coming out of the sky. This was after the doves had circled him, and the multicoloured cloud had descended. The others had asked him what all these signs meant but he had kept his silence. Now, when we were alone, he told me that these were all signs that he was going to die.

'You would think I would have felt upset at hearing this but he was entirely calm, as if looking down at himself from a tremendous distance. I also felt calm, even knowing he was going to die.

'"I will take rebirth," he told me. "But it will be at the end of this age, when everybody is dying in battles and destruction is upon this earth. It will be at the time of the death of mankind."

'It was the next morning that we set out for Beyul.'

'Weren't you afraid to follow him up that steep snowy slope,' I asked, 'especially after he predicted his own death? It wasn't difficult to guess how his death would come, especially after Namdrol pointed out the dangers of the route.'

'I didn't even think of it,' she replied. 'I was not afraid. He said, "We are going," and we went.'

Yeshe replenished our tea. Then she sat quietly, looking into her cup. It was painful for her to recall what happened next.

'I don't remember the avalanche,' she said in her soft voice. 'I remember going up the slope towards the pass. I remember the cloud coming down over us. And I remember everything turning white. When everything turned black, my light went out and I lost consciousness. What happened after that I only know from what others have told me. I know now that there was an avalanche, and that I was buried. When the Lachung Lama dug me out, I had lost so much blood from the cut on my head that the snow was red all around me. It looked like an animal had been slaughtered. That is how he described it. Though I started breathing again when he uncovered my face from the snow, he thought I would die at any moment. The cut on my head went right to my skull. The scar still causes me pain to this day.' She leaned over and parted her hair to show me the scar, which ran from above her right temple right to the crown of her head. It was thick and misshapen from not having been properly stitched.

'After the Lachung Lama dug me and Lama Tashi out and found Tulshuk Lingpa's body, he went for help. When they returned, they tell me I was drifting in and out of consciousness, though I don't remember this at all. They wrapped me in Tulshuk Lingpa's sheepskin coat. Since he was dead, it wouldn't be doing him any good. Then they took off their own coats and wrapped both Lama Tashi and me as well as they could. Since we were both so badly injured, they couldn't move us till the next day. They didn't expect to find me alive when they returned. But I was. Unfortunately they didn't cover my feet well enough and I got frostbite on all my toes. They took turns carrying Lama Tashi, me and the body of Tulshuk Lingpa down the mountain. It took two days for us to reach Tseram.

'It was while I was being carried on someone's back that I looked over and saw a lama carrying Tulshuk Lingpa on his back. I saw his glazed eyes and realized what had happened and that Tulshuk Lingpa was dead. My entire world was shattered, and I started crying. That is the first thing I remember. I started crying, and I don't think I stopped for six months. They carried me down to Tseram, the tears flowing from my eyes. I stayed there through the cremation. Then they carried me on their backs back over the pass to Sikkim and to Yoksum. There the others just left. They left me with my mother and husband. They just left us alone. My toes were black by then and the flesh was beginning to rot. So they brought me to the Gezing hospital but the doctor said it was too serious a case for them to handle, so we went to Darjeeling. I spent six months there in the hospital. They amputated all my toes. I had lost so much blood that it took me all that time to recover.

Yeshe.

'I cried for six months in that hospital. I was so sick. I just remembered how they carried me down the mountain. The doctor was so nice. He used to wipe my tears.

'Slowly, I learned how to walk.'

Yeshe opened the stove to throw in another piece of wood, and I took the opportunity to look at her feet. She was wearing tiny children's sneakers.

'My husband returned to Lahaul before I did,' she continued. 'When I got there and he realized I could no longer work in the fields, he divorced me. Only my mother was there to help me. We had to sell everything we had. We had a little bit of gold jewellery, and we sold that. We had no other money.'

'Didn't the people in the village help you?'

'Not really. Only two families from Koksar went to Sikkim. When we left, we sneaked out of the village. We left after midnight and walked over the Rohtang Pass. The others in our village didn't believe in Tulshuk Lingpa. When we returned, nobody said bad things about our going—not in front of us. Only behind our backs.'

'You were Tulshuk Lingpa's khandro, weren't you?'

'Yes.'

'Didn't the monastery help you?'

'No. After some time I got married again to another of Tulshuk Lingpa's disciples, but before long he died. I've been alone ever since. Now it's just my mother and I.'

She was silent for some time, staring into her teacup.

'Some say Tulshuk Lingpa was crazy,' she said, looking up from her teacup and looking deeply and hauntingly into my eyes. 'But it's just that he didn't follow the rules. He didn't believe that one man was big and another small. He would talk with anyone, rich or poor. To him everyone was equal, and he helped them all. He was full of compassion. You could feel it. Chatral Rinpoche thought Tulshuk Lingpa was the only man who could open Beyul. The Dalai Lama couldn't do it because he was the head, like a king. Dudjom Rinpoche couldn't take you because he was the head of rich people. Since he was a rich person himself, he couldn't go. Chatral Rinpoche said Tulshuk Lingpa was the one.

'In the end, we couldn't go to Beyul. Everybody has his own karma. If you have the karma, you can go to Beyul. Definitely. We

couldn't go because there were too many people and everybody
didn't have full belief. If everybody had that faith, we definitely
would have made it. But because some had doubts, others began
to doubt. We didn't have the karma, so we couldn't go. Sometimes
I think about it. I dream about him often, that he is doing the
rituals and blessing me.'

There was in Yeshe's voice both sadness and that unmistakable tone of a woman who has kept alive in the secret cavern of
her heart a love that defies both time and death.

'Do you often think about those times?' I asked.

'Yes. But it was so long ago. What's the good of thinking about
it?'

She wiped a tear from her eye, thinking of all the pain she's
endured since that fateful day on the mountain. That tear was
followed by another and yet another, and she started to weep.

'Sometimes I think I should have just died in that avalanche
with Tulshuk Lingpa. I've wondered why I've been living ever since.'

'I'm sorry that my coming here and asking these questions
brings up so much pain,' I said.

Yeshe got up. She wanted to make us more tea. She didn't
have a cow but her neighbour did. She lifted a corner of the rug
she was sitting on and took out a few coins.

'I've got to go get milk,' she said.

₧   ₨

When I went to Simoling to investigate this story, I was greeted
and instructed there by Lama Tashi. He was a large and powerfully
built man who, at the age of eighty-one, exuded authority in
everything he said and a strength of mind that matched his
almost superhuman size. A close disciple of Tulshuk Lingpa and
a learned lama in his own right, Lama Tashi was the umzay,
or head of rituals, at the Simoling Monastery during Tulshuk
Lingpa's time. He holds the position to this day. I had met others
who were close to Tulshuk Lingpa—others who had studied the
ancient writings concerning Beyul. But they only scratched the
surface of their experience when they spoke of such matters and
were sworn to secrecy concerning the depths. None spoke with the
weight, command and certainty of Lama Tashi. Tulshuk Lingpa
had chosen him to break the path through the deep snow on that

fateful day, and I understood why. His faith was as solid as an ancient tree, his learning well-founded. It was over forty years since that fateful day when he gashed open his head, broke his arm and three ribs in the white tide of snow. But his large-boned frame was still wrapped in a musculature like that of an athlete's. His high cheekbones and prominent eyebrows made me feel as if I were in the presence of an American Indian elder.

Over the course of the two extended visits I made to the monastery in Simoling, Lama Tashi and I spent hours sitting in the monastery courtyard wrapped in jackets to keep out the frosty summer wind that swept off the surrounding peaks. Whenever we got too cold we'd move to the monastery kitchen and drink large cups of salted and buttered Tibetan tea. He not only answered my questions carefully but thought deeply about our discussions and raised issues and topics he thought would be important for my research. He spoke with the reasoned authority of a learned professor, one for whom the reality of Beyul was an unshakable truth.

Writing this book put me in the presence of many who had given up everything to go to Beyul: those for whom the tragic ending of the expedition caused not the slightest diminishment of their faith, for whom Beyul remains a reality greater than the world we inhabit. It was by being in their presence, more than any reading I did on the subject or discussions I had with people whose knowledge was from books, that I came to understand what it means to be on a quest for Beyul. Among all those I sought out in both the eastern and the western Himalayas, it was in Lama Tashi's presence that Beyul was the most palpable, an unmistakable and unshakable reality.

Never did I feel closer to that crack than in his presence.

'On that last day on the mountain,' he told me, 'the four of us had no doubt that we could make it. I think that is why Tulshuk Lingpa especially chose us to go with him. Not everyone had that belief, and that made conditions difficult. For twenty days we were practically at the gate, within sight of the pass to Beyul. Every day it would be sunny towards the pass when we left the cave but every day obstacles arose, storms of clouds, snow and wind.

'Something wasn't right.

'If we were to make it, I began to think to myself, why such hindrances? Though I've not spoken of this, I can tell you that by day sixteen a tremendous conflict arose within me. Nobody understood better than I that one's faith in one's teacher must be total and that one must not contradict him, especially when he is preparing to open the way. My faith, both in him and in the reality of Beyul, was and is unshakable. I had been with Tulshuk Lingpa since he first arrived in Simoling and rid our village of the leprosy. This was long before he spoke of Beyul. He had made me the umzay, and left me in charge of his monastery when he left for Sikkim—a post I hold to this day since he never returned. He summoned me to Sikkim only when he felt the time was ripe for the opening. Yet after so many attempts and after each attempt failed when the weather turned bad and beat us back off the mountain and into our cave, the conviction began to arise in me that we should turn back, that we should return to Tseram or calamity would strike. Our rations were running out. Not everyone had the faith I had, which I knew was causing the disfavour of the guardian spirits and causing the obstacles to arise.

'If one truly believed in the reality of Beyul, if one believed that Tulshuk Lingpa was the one chosen by Padmasambhava, if one *knew* that he had the key—then one would have no trouble turning back to await the right time and conditions. Pushing forward, it seemed to me, was a sign not of faith but of doubt. Since it was this lack of faith that was causing the obstructions, I felt I had to tell Tulshuk Lingpa that we should turn back. But I did not have the courage. Though I feared—and even foresaw— disaster, how could I contradict him? Wouldn't this in itself be a sign of a lack of belief? Isn't the ultimate test to follow the guru no matter what, even as conditions spiral out of control?

'I was torn within myself those last days, unsure whether I lacked the courage to tell him my conviction or whether it was my faith that was lacking. While I was thus torn, the others were pushing Tulshuk Lingpa ever harder into going—especially after Wangyal returned from his excursion with Tulshuk Lingpa having seen the snow give way to fragrant greenery.

'Did I correctly sense that Tulshuk Lingpa was himself wanting to turn back but was being swayed by his disciples? While I

couldn't muster the courage to speak to Tulshuk Lingpa, I tried
to convince the others that we should turn back.

'"Wangyal has seen it," I said to them. "We can no longer
doubt its existence. Since Tulshuk Lingpa is the one destined to
open the beyul, as long as he is with us, we will always be able
to go. The obstacles tell us that this is not the time. Therefore we
should not push Tulshuk Lingpa, and we should turn around."

'The others were thinking differently. Since we had come so
far and had left our homes and were willing to lay down our lives,
they thought we should keep going at least to have a glimpse like
Wangyal had.

'"The need to see it can only come from doubt," I pleaded with
them. "Since Tulshuk Lingpa is with us and he is definitely the one
destined to open Beyul Demoshong, we can go there any time. At
any time it is accessible to us—so forget it. Don't have this doubt
of 'Is it there, is it not there? Oh, I want to find out.' Forget it. Our
supplies are being depleted. We all know the dangers of melting
springtime snow. If the time is not right to go now, the time will
surely come. The key lies in Tulshuk Lingpa's hands. Don't doubt
that for a second. When the time is right, there will be no obstacles."

'Nobody would listen. They could only reiterate: "Even if we
don't enter Beyul," they said, "at least we want to see it from a
distance like Wangyal did."

'It was like a wheel: once set in motion, it was very difficult
to stop.

'Tulshuk Lingpa heard us arguing that afternoon when he
returned with Wangyal, and it was as if a cloud descended not only
on the mountain. Tulshuk Lingpa's face also became very dark.

'The next day we tried again. That was the last day, the day
Tulshuk Lingpa died.

'If I had had enough courage to tell Tulshuk Lingpa, probably
he wouldn't have died. Perhaps we would have tried it later—
secretly, with less people whose faith was great enough. Then we
would have been successful.'

Lama Tashi looked away. His gaze rose over the snow-capped
mountains on the other side of the valley from the courtyard where
we were sitting, with our shawls flapping in the cold wind. He was
silent for a few long moments. Then he turned to me and spoke.

'Actually Beyul was a secret. No one should have known, just those who were prepared by their own inner work and by the teachings of Tulshuk Lingpa.

'Faith in Beyul is not enough. It also depends upon your motivation for going there. The fact that Beyul is a place of unimaginable riches where everything will be provided can itself cause impurity. Even the purest of heart can be corrupted by riches. Those who are not prepared can easily find themselves going there for material reasons and not for the dharma. They say three quarters of the world's wealth is in Beyul. So what we see here in this world is merely a quarter.'

I had heard this before. Géshipa had told me that Beyul Demoshong is so large you'd definitely need a chariot just to get around. Dorje Wangmo had told me that Padmasambhava had said half of the wealth of this world is hidden underneath Kanchenjunga. Kunsang had told me that Demoshong, which was the inner secret land within Sikkim, was three times larger than the outer Sikkim or Demojong, the Valley of Rice.

Don't the pronouncements of the modern physicists echo a similar idea? Physicists can only account for a fraction of the matter that their theories and measurements tell them exists in the universe. They dub the rest 'dark matter' because they cannot see it, taste it, weigh it or in any way account for it. Though they know it exists, it cannot be measured as we measure things of this world. Even though they can only infer its existence, they know it exists—every bit as much as Tulshuk Lingpa's disciples know of Beyul's existence. As with Beyul, no one's ever seen it. No one has 'been there'. The physicists go even further than the seekers of Beyul. They say the visible world of electrons, protons, neutrons, quarks and all the subatomic particles, electromagnetic forces and everything existing in the three dimensions including you and I, all the matter subject to gravitational force—what Kunsang would call the 'outer' Sikkim—makes up only *2 percent* of the universe.

Lama Tashi was adamant about why Beyul exists, and what Padmasambhava's purpose was in hiding it.

'Beyul isn't a place to simply sit back and enjoy oneself be-cause all one's needs are taken care of,' he told me. 'It isn't as if upon entering Beyul you suddenly become a millionaire and live a life of worldly pleasures. Padmasambhava hid Beyul in the eighth century as a place free of care so those who enter could have uninterrupted practice. Practice has one goal: to develop compassion for others. Here we don't have time to practice. It is extremely difficult to develop compassion. The entire world conspires for the strengthening of the ego and its drive to put itself first. How rare it is for someone to be developed to the point of putting *others* first!

'Now times are difficult. Everywhere we look we see war. Everything brings distraction and destruction. Padmasambhava foresaw these dark times. The search for Beyul is only important at the end of time, when the world is coming to an end. It is for that we have the lineage of the lingpas, those destined to find the ter concerning Beyul.

'Now it is difficult even for those with a pure heart to help others. We are conquering the material world but we are destroying it as well. Soon we will have nowhere to run. They are building an eleven-kilometre tunnel through the mountains that will connect Lahaul directly to the lush Kullu Valley. Twelve months a year you'll be able to drive to Simoling. The opening of the tunnel will be right there, on the other side of the valley. We'll be able to come and go at will. Since people first came to this valley, we've been snowed in half the year. Now they will "improve" our situation. But what will it bring us? Maybe a lot of tourists.

'You cannot make this world a Shangri-La. No improvement will ever get you there. To reach that state of happiness, you must let go of this world. 100 percent. Maybe it will soon be time again to attempt an opening. It is written in the ancient books that when the dharma is becoming lost, when there is nowhere else to run, the Great Door of the Secret Place will open. Times are getting rough.

'But you can't just go there. I know the way. I spent twenty days at the base of the slope to the pass which opens to Beyul. I could take you there. But what's the use? I cannot do it alone. We have to wait for the lama to come. You have to believe in Padmasambhava. Beyul does exist.'

Looking into the old, calm eyes of Lama Tashi I had the wish to see what he had seen.

'Once I had the opportunity,' he continued. 'I cut the path through the deep snow for my lama. We were just approaching the top of the pass when the cloud descended and everything turned white and then blackness descended. I got this gash over my eye and lost litres of blood. You can still see the scar. I broke my arm. Three ribs were broken. I vaguely remember the La-chung Lama wrapping the sleeve of his shirt around my head to stem the bleeding.

'I lay for a night on that mountain wrapped in the others' coats and scarves. The dead Tulshuk Lingpa was on one side, Yeshe on the other. She didn't move all night; I thought she too was dead. Drifting in and out of consciousness I sometimes thought I was also dead, staring into that bright mountain sky illuminated by a myriad of stars, my body in pain and numb with cold. I didn't yet comprehend what had happened. I remembered neither the avalanche nor being dug out from under the snow. I just wondered why we were lying there alone—the dead and half-living on a steep white cold slope when the young woman I thought was dead beside me had just that morning seen a vision of a green valley in the mirror.

'In the morning, I saw the others coming up the slope to rescue me. I could hardly move but I waved my good arm. "Over here," I called to them. "I'm not dead."

'It took us two days to reach Tseram. In Tibetan tradition, it isn't good to cry at the death of a high lama but the people couldn't help it. Since I was the umzay of Tulshuk Lingpa's monastery, it should have been my job to perform the death ceremony. It was all I could do to stand up, offer a khata to my dead lama and prostrate one time before collapsing again. There were no doctors in Tseram, though there was a lama from Bhutan who knew how to set bones. He made a brace out of pieces of wood and bound them to my arm with cloth. When the death ceremony was over, most of the people just left. I stayed on with Tulshuk Lingpa's family for a month, healing enough so I could travel.

'It took us five days to walk from Tseram to Tashiding, and from there two more to Darjeeling. I went to see Chatral

Rinpoche. He asked me what happened. When I told him, he told me to return to Simoling to take care of my land and take charge of the monastery.

'I returned to Simoling. It took me two years of bed rest to recover from the avalanche and to take charge of the monastery. The monastery was in disrepair. The stupa was crumbling. I had to rebuild it. I have devoted the second half of my life to maintaining both Tulshuk Lingpa's monastery and his memory.'

I asked him what it was about Tulshuk Lingpa's character that led him to devote his life to Tulshuk Lingpa, even after his death.

'Tulshuk Lingpa was spontaneous,' Lama Tashi said, smiling with the recollection. 'He didn't follow rules. He would say one thing and then do something else. He didn't believe one person was high caste, or one low. If he met a high caste person, he would treat him the same as he'd treat anyone else. He did as he wanted. He was a free man, the freest man I've ever met. He didn't listen to what anyone else said. In Buddhism everyone is equal. Buddhists are very compassionate, helping others. That is the ideal.'

Lama Tashi squeezed his forearm as if to test his own strength. 'Now I'm over eighty years old,' he said. 'I'm grateful for my good health. It is very important to keep this monastery well. We are accumulating merit. Even the fact that we are sitting here is the fruit we have generated.

'Someone like Tulshuk Lingpa comes only once in very many years. Just to meet him and to be in his presence—even just to hear about him—you need special merit.

'He wrote his guidebook to Beyul, which you have a copy of. Only a few people have

The 'new' stupa,
Simoling Gompa.

seen it; it has been kept secret. Not everyone can write such a work. You need a mind as clear as the sky to understand it. Consider it a blessing that you have this book. Just be careful. Say you show someone a photograph of the footprint Tulshuk Lingpa left in the stone in Sikkim. Not just any lama can make such a footprint. Even the Dalai Lama hasn't done such a thing. If you show it to someone who doesn't believe in such things and if you don't explain it well, his reaction will be to think it was a fake. This will cause him problems. It will create obstacles for him.

'It is very difficult now to go to Beyul. You have to practise dharma, and keep practising. But it should be in our minds. We must pray that we can go. If we pray for this now, even after we die, when we come back there will be the conditions. We will meet the right lama at the right time. We have to generate great love and compassion for human beings and then the fruit will come.'

'Do you often think about Beyul?' I asked.

'I will think about it till the day I die,' was his simple reply.

'Just that you are writing this book,' he continued, 'and have come here at this particular point means that we have karma together from our previous lives. There are many people these days who don't have pure motivation. It is best not to speak of it with them. We are like one family, those who believe in Tulshuk Lingpa.

'Now we don't have the opportunity to go to Beyul. But we have the belief. No matter how many years it may take, we have to keep the belief alive—and keep it secret. If we keep it really well in the cave of our hearts and keep our belief pure, then in our next lives we will all meet again and we can then go to Beyul.

'I am very happy that you have come,' he said. 'May we meet again!'

Lama Tashi.

Tulshuk Lingpa.

Epilogue

While most accounts of a life story end with the protagonist's death, Tulshuk Lingpa's story has a breadth and depth to it that mere death cannot end. As with all stories of Tibetan lamas who have passed on, one must consider the reincarnation.

I met quite a few who said they wished they had died with Tulshuk Lingpa on that snowy slope, claiming he had made it to the Hidden Land. Some of these ones drew the logical conclusion that Tulshuk Lingpa's case was unique and there would be no reincarnation. Breaking with traditional notions as laid down in Tibetan tradition, they claimed one cannot take one's body to Beyul. Having left his body behind on that snowy slope in order to enter the Hidden Land, he had not died and therefore would not be reincarnating. This view was clearly in the minority. For the others, the topic of his incarnation was and is of keen interest.

In May 2003 Phuntsok Choeden, Tulshuk Lingpa's widow from Tibet, had an operation for colon cancer in a hospital in Kathmandu, Nepal. It was a condition she was to die from three years later. Two days after her operation she was lying in her hospital bed surrounded by her son, three daughters and some of her grandchildren. Suddenly the door flew open and in strode a tall, slim Westerner with short hair dressed in a polo shirt.

Approaching the convalescing Phuntsok Choeden, he said, to the shock of everyone present, 'In my last life, you were my wife.' Turning to her children Kunsang, Kamala, Penzom and Kunsun, he said, 'You were my son, and you were my daughters.' To Wangchuk, he held out his hand. 'We've not met,' he said. 'I was your grandfather Tulshuk Lingpa!'

Turning to Kunsang, he said, 'How does it feel to meet your father for the first time in this life?'

'Very happy,' Kunsang replied, eyeing the stranger cautiously. 'Very happy.'

'If you are really Tulshuk Lingpa,' Kunsang said, no doubt laughing, 'tell me what happened in Simoling. Surely you must know,' and he proceeded to ask the Westerner a series of questions about the life of Tulshuk Lingpa, for which the Westerner had not a single correct answer.

'You don't seem to know anything about Tulshuk Lingpa,' Kunsang said.

'I will educate myself,' the Westerner said, opening a bag and giving Kamala some brocade and placing a wad of rupees on the little table next to Phuntsok Choeden's bed.

He turned to Kunsang. 'The last time I said I would take you to the Hidden Land. This time I will take you to Mongolia!'

'Mongolia?' Kunsang gasped. 'Why Mongolia?'

'I will take you to Mongolia because you are a lama, and in Mongolia lamas are rare. If you come with me to Mongolia you can ride a cart pulled by reindeer! In Mongolia people live in felt tents, they have excellent butter, and the women there—ah, the women in Mongolia are beautiful beyond compare. You will have a wonderful time in Mongolia. It is most auspicious to go in June or July. I will be going then, and I want you to come with me.'

So saying, the strange Westerner strode out of the room with as much suddenness as he had entered. They neither saw nor heard from him again.

When Kunsang told me this story I could hardly believe it was true. But Wangchuk, who was translating for me, assured me that he was present in his grandmother's hospital room when this Westerner made his cameo appearance. Crazy as it may sound, it occurred exactly as his father said it. Though the way they told it—howling with laughter—made it obvious that though the story was true, the crazy Westerner was not to be taken seriously as the reincarnation. It was just another crazy episode in a story that attracts a certain madness.

There is, however, a serious contender for the post of the reincarnation of Tulshuk Lingpa.

In 1970, practically a decade after Tulshuk Lingpa died, the daughter of Jinda Wangchuk—the big sponsor of Tulshuk Lingpa from Pangao who prepared the cave on the cliff face there for Tulshuk Lingpa and his family—had a son. As soon as the boy was able to speak, he started saying, 'I am Tulshuk Lingpa. I have a monastery.' Jinda Wangchuk went to Lama Tashi in Simoling to tell him the news. Lama Tashi had of course been on the lookout for Tulshuk Lingpa's reincarnation. He went to Pangao, offered the boy a khata and was quite impressed. But the determination of whether a boy is a true reincarnation, especially of such a high lama, can only be made by a lama of very high standing. He advised Jinda Wangchuk to bring the boy to a learned and wise lama named Gelong Tenzing, a former secretary of Dudjom Rinpoche living in Manali, which is not far from Pangao.

The night before Jinda Wangchuk brought the boy to see Gelong Tenzing, Gelong Tenzing had a dream in which he saw many lamas being given mandala offerings. There was a small stupa made of glass in the middle of the offerings. He picked it up and thought, 'What a nice stupa.' In the dream, it was said that an election was to be held between the lamas to see who the true lama was. The time came to vote. He picked up a piece of paper in order to write down his vote, and on the paper it was written 'Tulshuk Lingpa', then he woke up.

It was later that day that Jinda Wangchuk announced to Gelong Tenzing that he wanted to bring the boy to meet him.

Gelong Tenzing put photographs of many lamas on a large low table and he placed a piece of glass over them. Tulshuk Lingpa's photo was amongst them. Jinda Wangchuk had scrubbed the boy clean and he was wearing new clothes. When the boy came in, the old lama said, 'It's been a long time since I've seen you,' and he offered the boy a cup of tea. The boy only laughed at his words. He wasn't interested in the tea. With a serious look on his face, he went directly to the table with the photos. He looked at the photos, and then he looked at Gelong Tenzing. Again he looked at the photos, and again he looked at Gelong Tenzing. He had never met Gelong Tenzing, and he was shy. So he turned to Jinda Wangchuk and said, 'Look Grandpa, there I am. That's me.' He was pointing to the photo of Tulshuk Lingpa.

After Jinda Wangchuk and the boy left, Gelong Tenzing thought long and hard about whether the boy was the reincarnation of

Tulshuk Lingpa. He later contacted Jinda Wangchuk. 'It is still too early to tell whether he truly is the reincarnation of Tulshuk Lingpa,' he said. 'For now put him on a pure diet—no meat, no eggs.' He sent the boy a golden robe.

News of this spread throughout the valley. Lama Tashi came down over the Rohtang Pass and said to Jinda Wangchuk, 'Now we must bring him to Simoling for his coronation. His monastery has stood empty for over ten years. It is time for him to return.' They went to Gelong Tenzing but Gelong Tenzing refused to declare the boy the reincarnation.

'Choosing the reincarnation of a lama as high as Tulshuk Lingpa is too big a decision for me to make,' he said. 'I cannot do it. I will write to Dudjom Rinpoche. He was Tulshuk Lingpa's root guru. It should be up to him.'

He wrote a letter to Dudjom Rinpoche in Kathmandu with a photograph of the boy, explaining that since he uttered his first words he was saying he was Tulshuk Lingpa and that he had a monastery. He described how he witnessed the boy choose Tulshuk Lingpa's photo.

There was tremendous pressure on Gelong Tenzing to accept both the boy's statements and his choosing the photo of Tulshuk Lingpa as enough evidence to declare him the reincarnation and to get on with the coronation. Unwilling to take on the responsibility himself and distancing himself from the decision, he told everybody that he was awaiting the return letter from Dudjom Rinpoche. 'When I get the reply,' he told everybody, 'I will make the announcement.'

Then the reply came from Dudjom. Relieved that both the long wait was over and the decision was made by anyone but himself, Gelong Tenzing tore open the envelope and to his tremendous dismay read, 'You are the one who has met the boy. You are there and

The photo of the boy that was sent to Dudjom Rinpoche.

you have both the knowledge and the wisdom. You knew Tulshuk Lingpa. Therefore you are in a better position to make the decision than me. Decide for yourself whether to coronate the boy.'

When Gelong Tenzing read this, he started to cry. 'I can't possibly decide,' he thought to himself. 'If something goes wrong with the incarnation, everybody will blame me.'

He travelled to Kathmandu to see Dudjom Rinpoche. Kunsang was then living in Kathmandu, so Gelong Tenzing first went to find Kunsang. They went out for a drink. It was after the third drink that Gelong Tenzing got the courage to tell Kunsang why he was there, that he might have found his father's reincarnation. He explained how he had sent a letter to Dudjom Rinpoche. Then he showed Kunsang Dudjom's reply. He started to cry. 'If I knew how to decide,' he said, 'I wouldn't have asked Dudjom in the first place. Dudjom has the powers necessary to make such a decision. He is supreme. If I could look into that boy's soul and tell his past as well as his future, I would have decided myself. This is just too big of a responsibility for me.'

The next day they went together to see Dudjom Rinpoche, who was then living in Thamel. This was before Thamel was the tourist area of Kathmandu. Dudjom was very happy to see both Gelong and Kunsang. He hadn't seen either of them in many, many years. He started asking them mundane questions, as if there was nothing to discuss of any importance. He asked them when they had come to Kathmandu, about the weather on the Plains and many other things. Then Gelong could stand it no longer. He broke down and started to cry. 'Your letter said that I have to decide about the coronation of the reincarnation of Tulshuk Lingpa,' he said, 'Please, Rinpoche, please! I don't have any idea about the future. When Tulshuk Lingpa was living amongst us, there was no one as educated as he was, not a single lama in the whole area. We knew he was learned but many of us didn't know of his greatness. Now that he is gone and we know about the Hidden Valley, we know how precious he was. Now we realize. I have met the boy and, as you instructed, I try to guess whether this little boy will be as learned as Tulshuk Lingpa, whether he has that quality that would make him a lingpa. In your letter you told me to decide whether he should be coronated—but I cannot do it. I just don't know. That's why I travelled all the way here to talk to you and to ask you one more time to make the decision. Only a lama with your greatness can make such a decision.'

Gelong Tenzing and Kunsang stood in silence before Dudjom, with their heads bowed in reverence, awaiting his pronouncement. It took some minutes for Dudjom to respond.

'I agree with you that the previous Tulshuk Lingpa was very learned,' he said, 'and his knowledge cannot be matched. But he was not lucky. He knew the way to Beyul, and still couldn't make it. The world is worse than it was before. Times are even darker than they were before. People are not as lucky as they were before, so this boy will not be as learned or as lucky as the previous Tulshuk Lingpa.'

'Are you saying he *is* the reincarnation?' Gelong asked.

'Yes,' Dudjom Rinpoche said. 'But it is better to just leave it. It is better not to coronate him. He will not turn out well. Just forget him and do not search for another reincarnation.'

Gelong felt a tremendous relief. Now he knew that the boy was in fact the reincarnation of Tulshuk Lingpa but the correct course was to take the unusual step of *not* coronating him. If he had given in to the pressure and had coronated the boy, things would have turned out bad and people would have blamed him.

When Kunsang told me the above story, it was thirty years after he and Gelong had met with Dudjom Rinpoche in Kathmandu. I asked him if he knew what had happened to the boy.

'Though I never returned to Simoling after my father's death,' he said, 'and though I didn't return to Kullu and Pangao after my apple business, from time to time I do speak with people from there. Sometimes we meet when I'm in Kathmandu and they've told me what became of the boy.

'Dudjom was right. The boy turned out bad. He used to beat up his parents when he was young. He was wild and unruly. He quit school at an early age. This was when all the young foreigners started flooding into the Kullu Valley and getting into drugs, and he fell into drugs as well. He got into bad company. Who knows what he did to make money when he was young but eventually he started driving a taxi. The last I heard he was in a little town not far from Pangao, working in an auto parts store. Maybe when you go you can find him there. But really it would be better if you also took Dudjom Rinpoche's advice and forgot about him. He doesn't have to appear in your book.'

I asked Kunsang how it could be that a great lama like Tulshuk Lingpa, who had the ability to direct his consciousness into his next incarnation, could chose an incarnation who was not only unable to fulfil his role but would turn out crazy and sell auto parts?

'These are the dark ages,' Kunsang replied, 'and people will slowly stop following the dharma. Everything is degenerating. It doesn't get better from here on. Every tulku, or reincarnation, should have increasing knowledge but it is not happening because of these dark ages.'

'Still,' I said, 'if he is really the incarnation of Tulshuk Lingpa surely there must be something special about him.'

'Yes,' Kunsang said, laughing. 'He beats everyone up!'

'I guess it's true,' I said. 'Tulshuk Lingpa was also a madman.'

I completed the research for this book in Sikkim and Darjeeling, which is where Kunsang lives, before I went to the Kullu Valley and to Lahaul to meet Tulshuk Lingpa's older disciples. Kunsang had called ahead, and when I arrived there I was met by Tulshuk Lingpa's grandson Gyurme, the son of Tulshuk Lingpa's daughter by his khandro. There was also his close disciple Wangyal Bodh, the retired civil engineer who witnessed the splitting of the falling glacier. They took me under their wing and brought me around to other old disciples of Tulshuk Lingpa's, the cave in Pangao and the monastery in Simoling.

Already foreseeing this Epilogue, I asked them if they knew the story of the reincarnation and whether he still worked in an auto parts store. They told me his name, Raju, and their opinion was much as Kunsang's had been. They said I'd better forget him. After it was decided not to coronate him, he was still trained as a monk. So from the age of three or four they shaved Raju's head, dressed him in a robe and tried to train him in the monastery that had been built just above the cave in Pangao. But it hadn't worked. He was crazy. He used to run out of the monastery in the middle of winter and climb up and down the mountain without shoes. Their description of his life after leaving the monastery was much as Kunsang had described it.

When I insisted that I still wanted to meet Raju, that he was part of the story whether he was a 'success' or not, they told me he had quit his job selling auto parts and now lived in a city far away across the mountains near Shimla. He was driving a van to earn his meagre fare and living in his vehicle. With no fixed address and no way of contacting him they advised me to forget him entirely, which I had no choice but to do.

I lived for three months in the Kullu Valley in a house in the middle of an apple orchard with my wife Barbara. She was working on her doctoral thesis in social and medical anthropology at Oxford, and I was conducting my research and writing the first draft of this book. She travelled with me to meet some of the old disciples of Tulshuk Lingpa's and we journeyed together to Simoling. Because she spoke Tibetan, she was not only my lovely companion but acted as interpreter.

Towards the end of our stay, we were discussing any loose ends I might not have tied, areas I should look into further before leaving the place, stories I hadn't yet gotten. I had just finished writing about the avalanche and Tulshuk Lingpa's death, so it was natural that my thoughts would turn to the reincarnation. I looked over my notes and realized that though my informants had told me Raju had moved to a town near Shimla, none of them really seemed to know him. What they told me was based more on hearsay than on first-hand knowledge. It seemed that Raju was something of an embarrassment to the disciples of Tulshuk Lingpa. It was clear they would rather he did not appear in the book. While Kunsang seemed more open about the story of his father's reincarnation, and though his story concurred with the others', he had never met Raju and hadn't even known his name.

Suspicious that Raju might still be selling auto parts, Barbara and I went to the small market town people had mentioned on the Manali road. It wasn't difficult to walk from one end of the town to the other and to see there weren't any auto parts stores. But there were two mechanic shops: one specializing in broken-down buses and the other in derelict jeeps. I had visions of a grease-smeared man sliding out ass first from under a jeep with a cigarette dangling from the corner of his mouth, looking at me with suspicion, jutting his jaw out and asking me in a threatening tone what I wanted. I did want something from him. I didn't know what but perhaps a last word for this book, some pearl of wisdom from Tulshuk Lingpa's reincarnation delivered by a thug.

At neither shop had they heard of Raju from Pangao and they concurred that there were no auto parts stores in the town and never had been. Our last chance was to go to Pangao and see if we could find any surviving members of his family there who might know of his whereabouts. I had been to Pangao with Gyurme and Wangyal to see the cave but we hadn't had much time there. I had only met a few monks at the monastery. So we jumped a bus and hitched a ride and landed in Pangao, where we followed narrow paths down steep slopes by houses and the nunnery until we came to the house of Raju's aunt, who was herself a nun.

'Raju?' she said. 'You want to meet Raju? No, he's not near Shimla. He lives just down the valley in a village at the base of the mountains.' The place she described was but twelve kilometres from where we had been living for the better part of three months. She knew he had a mobile phone—he'd call once or twice a year—but she didn't know his number. She brought us up a side path to the house of her mother, the widow of Jinda Wangchuk, but she also didn't have her grandson's phone number. I tried to get from them something of Raju's story, whether he was still crazy but they were reticent. It seemed they preferred saying nothing than speaking ill of a family member. All they would say was that he was now married and had two children. They claimed not to know much about his life. Since we had arrived in

Raju as a teenager.

Pangao so late in the day, it was too late to leave so the family put us up. In the morning they gave us a photo of Raju as a young boy. We made our way to Raju's village and found ourselves in front of his door.

Raju lives in a low concrete building surrounded by other concrete dwellings. His was perhaps smaller than the others but otherwise it was a home indistinguishable from thousands of others across the width and breadth of modern India.

We knocked on Raju's door. It was opened by a fairly short, fairly round man with a big moustache and very warm eyes.

'Are you Raju?' I asked.

'Yes, I am.'

'We've come to see you.'

He seemed completely unfazed by two Westerners appearing unannounced on his doorstep.

'Please,' he said, 'come in.'

It was then I noticed the words written on his T-shirt: 'Positive People Don't Put Others Down.'

He led us into the one room where he lived with his wife and two children, who all happened to be out. The room was simple and clean. One could tell they were living with tremendous dignity on precious little. He graciously invited us to sit on the bed but we preferred to sit on the rug in the centre of the room. One would have thought he would have asked us at the door what we wanted with him, or perhaps upon inviting us into his home. But first he asked if we wanted tea, which he then prepared on a gas ring in the corner of the room that served as a kitchen by pouring water from a plastic jug (they had no running water) into an aluminium pot into which he threw one handful of tea and two of sugar. Once it was brewed, he poured the tea into two unmatched glasses and a chipped cup.

It wasn't until he gave us our tea and sat in front of us with his own that he smiled broadly and asked us with a quizzical look what we wanted.

I answered in a very deliberate manner, 'We've been living here in the Kullu Valley for almost three months,' I said. 'Barbara is conducting research for her doctoral thesis at Oxford on Tibetan Medicine. Her topic is longevity.' Raju nodded his head

Raju, incarnation of Tulshuk Lingpa.
'POSITIVE PEOPLE DON'T PUT OTHERS DOWN'

thoughtfully at this, obviously trying to imagine what that might
have to do with him. Pausing to take a sip of tea, I continued. 'I
am a writer,' I said. 'And I'm writing a book. The book is about,'
and I let a little silence intervene so I could look closely at his
face for the reaction before I uttered the name, 'Tulshuk Lingpa.'

At the mention of the name, Raju burst out laughing and
almost spilt his tea. He looked at me out of the corners of his
mirthful eyes, shaking his finger playfully. 'So that's it!' he said.

I explained to him how I heard about Tulshuk Lingpa in
Sikkim, and how I'd spent time with Tulshuk Lingpa's disciples
there and in Darjeeling. I told him about my close association with
Kunsang and Wangchuk, and how we'd travelled to Tashiding and
to Yoksum. I told him how we'd met with Tulshuk Lingpa's oldest
disciples here in the Kullu Valley and over the Rohtang Pass in
Lahaul, how we had visited the cave in Pangao and the monastery
in Simoling. Finally, I told him how I'd been writing the story and
had just written about the avalanche and the death of Tulshuk
Lingpa. 'The last piece of the story,' I explained, 'is yours.'

Raju had an obvious sense of playfulness; yet he was also
extremely serious. One could sense it in the intense focus of his
eyes as I told him of my project, the way he strained to understand
my English, the way he was obviously deeply moved to have us
suddenly sitting with him on his rug sipping tea awaiting his
story, which he was obviously eager to tell.

Because it was difficult for him to fully express himself in
English, he switched to Tibetan which, he explained, he had
learned during many years of living in monasteries. So with
Barbara interpreting, he told us the following story:

'I remember when the whole thing started. I must have been
no more than three years old. I had a recurring dream in which I
saw an old bell and dorje, the ritual thunderbolt the lamas use in
their Buddhist practices.

'It would be dark when they'd appear, and always the thought
would come to me, "These are mine." I would have this dream
at night, and during the day I would forget it. Night after night
I'd have this dream, always with the thought that these items
reserved for the lamas belonged to me. It was at this time—
not long after I had learned to say the words for mama and

Tulshuk Lingpa's dorje, or ritual thunderbolt,
given to his daughter Pema Choekyi after his death.

papa—that I started saying I was Tulshuk Lingpa. I don't know
how his name came to me. I cannot explain it, and to tell you the
truth the memory is only dim in my mind. The dream is what I
really remember, not the outer events that followed.

'I do remember that a lama came to the house. He put me on his
lap and gave me candy. I took the candy but then I gave it away.
He asked me if I was a lama, and I said yes. I also remember
looking at the photos under the glass table and choosing the
photo of Tulshuk Lingpa.

'I had long hair then, and they shaved it. I was sent to the
monastery in Pangao. They started training me as a lama.
Sometimes I used to sneak away and go down the trail to the
cave where Tulshuk Lingpa had lived. Whenever I went there,
I'd feel very happy.

'When I was quite young, my father died. He was an alcoholic
and died from too much drink.

'There were many of us young novice monks at the monastery
but I was always singled out, given special attention and I always

had the feeling of being watched. My status as Tulshuk Lingpa's reincarnation was controversial. I was expected to both show the powers he possessed and to go bad, as predicted. It was too much for me. Even then, while I was so young, I had an inner feeling. I felt I couldn't develop at my natural pace if everything I did was being watched and compared to Tulshuk Lingpa, who was such a high lama. The more they tried to put me into a box, the stronger was my instinct to break free. I knew, in my childish way, that my nature couldn't be put to school.

'I stayed in the monastery in Pangao until I was about thirteen. I think I was too much trouble for them, so they sent me to the monastery of Mindroling, the high Nyingma lama outside of Dehradun. In Mindroling's monastery I learned to read the pechas, and I attended many *wangs* or blessing empowerments performed by Mindroling himself. It was at this time, when I was thirteen-fourteen, that many dharma obstacles arose within me. It was all because people were talking about me and who I was. It affected something in my mind, and I went the other way.

'I came home for a vacation to see my mother and little sister, and on my way back to the monastery something snapped inside me. I didn't feel like studying to become a lama. I didn't want to practise. I just wanted to go away. Where did I want to go? Anywhere! I was on the bus to Dehradun when the bus stopped in a little town on the way, and I just got off the bus and started walking. It was completely unpremeditated. I just couldn't return to the monastery and all the talk and other people's expectations and their ideas of how to channel me. After all that was pent up inside me, I went a bit crazy. I wandered without aim, staying a month here, a month there. This was out of the mountains on the Plains.

'Was it dangerous? Sure! But I was a bit crazy and did a lot of crazy things. I slept on the side of the road. Of course I had no money, so I had to be very quick-witted. It was some months later, after I simply didn't show up at the monastery, that the monastery secretary contacted my mother to see why I had stayed home. She thought I was at the monastery. Together, they figured out I must be dead. I suppose for them I was. I was harsh, just taking off and telling no one.'

Raju laughed at the recollection of his wild years. His daughter came in, a delightful seven-year-old. He got her a glass of milk and she plopped down on his lap, looking at us with wide, open eyes as he told us how he ended up in the Punjab where a Punjabi family took him in and raised him as one of their own. The warm way Raju wrapped his arms around his daughter as he spoke showed that the cruelty of not telling his mother where he was, which must have caused her untold pain during his teens, was not an innate quality in him. It was an act borne of necessity, his total disappearance being the only way he could survive the attention drawn on him at too tender an age. 'The Punjabi family was wonderful,' he said with a smile. 'They simply accepted me as they would a son. They didn't know my background, that I was a monk. They had no idea about the story of the reincarnation. I think I told them I was an orphan.'

Raju was silent for some moments, a painful memory crossing his brow.

'When I was about eighteen,' he continued, 'I decided it was time for me to go home. At the beginning, I didn't think anything of the pain I must have been causing my mother. But I had studied enough of the dharma to know about the law of karma and that if I caused her such pain, I couldn't escape similar pain myself. I knew it was simply wrong to cause pain. What pain is worse than that of a mother who loses her child? So I left the Punjabi family. They gave me the bus fare and I returned to the Kullu Valley. I walked into Pangao for the reunion with my mother. I was so happy my self-imposed exile was over.'

Raju's eyes filled with glistening moisture.

'When I returned, they told me my mother had died of tuberculosis a year earlier.'

Raju's arms tightened lovingly around his youngest child.

'Of course, this was a tremendous blow to me. I was agonized, not just because I could never see my mother again or because I was not there when she died but also from the knowledge that she had died grieving for me. I had a younger sister. She was about the age of this little girl here.' He ran his hand over the top of his daughter's hair. 'She was staying with relatives but nobody had money to take care of her. We were both orphans now. I realized quickly that I was now responsible for her. All I knew was how to be a lama but I didn't want to do that, so I slowly learned how to do all sorts of work. Because she was an orphan, I was able to get my little sister into a government boarding school where they gave her food, clothes and books. With my guidance, she was able to complete class twelve.

'Now I know lots of things. I know carpentry, the apple business. I never owned my own apple orchard—it always belonged to others. But I know the business.

'Then I thought I had to do something else. A friend of mine was driving a taxi and he said, "Come to Manali, and I'll teach you how to drive." Because we only did it little by little, it took me three years to learn to drive. Now I can drive a lorry, a bus, a car. It was much later that I got my own car.

'I never thought I'd marry because on the inside I still considered myself a lama. But everybody, my auntie and all, were telling me "Get married, get married." But I said, "How can I get married? I don't have a house. I don't have fields. I don't have any money. How can I feed a wife?"

'My auntie said, "You get married, and I'll help you with the house and everything. You get a job, earn money and slowly-slowly you'll learn to look after your wife and then a family."

'I was twnety-five when I got married. It was a love marriage.

'For five years after marriage, my wife was really ill. Then our son was born.

'During the winters while my wife was sick, I didn't have work. I had nothing to do. I had to stay inside. So I worked my way back towards the knowledge of being a lama. I had many pechas, and I had learned how to read them. So I started reading. I offered butter lamps every day.

'I started going to Rampur, near Shimla. I was doing business, small business only. Small business is OK. With big business, big tension. Small business, no headache—family happy, I'm happy.

'My whole life has been coloured by Tulshuk Lingpa. Back when I was a child in Pangao, there was an attendant of Tulshuk Lingpa's who used to watch me closely. I was pretty crazy even then. He used to say to me, "You are Tulshuk Lingpa. I knew him well, and you have the same tulshuk nature." Then I would say, "No. I am not Tulshuk Lingpa. I am just a kid." I would run away from him. I just wanted to be left alone.

'Of course I've always asked myself whether I *am* the reincarnation of Tulshuk Lingpa, and there are times I look deeply within and think, Yes, I am.'

'I've spoken with many people about Tulshuk Lingpa,' I said, 'and from what I know about him it was impossible to put him into a box, to say, "You are a lama; you are this or that." He would break whatever box others tried to put him in. He was well suited to the name Tulshuk. He was always changing and contradicting himself.'

'I am just the same,' Raju exclaimed. 'I'm of two minds. I often set out in one direction and end up going in another. Just ask my wife! It drives her mad, but that's just how I am.

'When I was living in Rampur, I met a Tibetan nun who was very sick. Her body was full of scars and wounds. I had heard the story of Tulshuk Lingpa curing the lepers in Simoling. While a child at the monastery I had learned how to read the pechas and recite the mantras. Even though I was driving a taxi at the time, I was also feeling the pull back to the dharma. My friends were drivers and some of them were rough people but I was living a pure life. I was waking up early every morning and taking a bath. Before eating anything I'd read the pechas and recite the mantras. I'd do the same every evening. None of my friends who drove taxis and rickshaws had any idea about this aspect of my life. I had to wonder about it myself. In a way, I was just a driver. But then I've always had this pull towards the inner life. And I've always wondered why.

'I decided to test it. I told the nun I would try to help her. So one morning I did my morning practice and I went to her. I recited the mantras over her and much to my amazement and to her great joy, she was cured. The boils on her body simply disappeared. It frightened me, and left me with a sense of awe.

'My wife was also sick at the time. I thought I could try curing her too. I was trembling, afraid to do so. But I did it, and she too was cured. This left me shaken. I never asked for all this attention, though I've felt sometimes that I really am Tulshuk

Lingpa. Pema Choekyi, Tulshuk Lingpa's daughter by the khandro, used to come to me when I was a kid. She used to call me Father. I've never tried curing people again. Once people get the idea you can cure them, they'll be lining up outside your door. Wasn't that Tulshuk Lingpa's problem, too many people? Wasn't that why he failed to enter Beyul?

'Now I'm in my late thirties. I feel something maturing in me. I've got these inner feelings, and maybe even abilities, which I've never allowed myself to develop. Sometimes I feel the time is coming. I'd like to go on the three year, three month and three day retreat that the lamas go through as part of their training. But I don't want to do it with the set routine of the practice as it is traditionally done. I want to go somewhere quiet, maybe to a cave, and I want to become a nagpa. I want to let my hair grow long and not cut it. I want to wear it in a knot on my head. I will let my fingernails grow. This urge comes from deep inside me. I want to go there and be quiet and let what is inside me come out.'

Raju's wife walked into the room. She had been at a neighbour's. Behind her walked in their twelve-year-old son wearing a T-shirt with a tiger on it with the caption 'Family'. His wife gave a quizzical look, wondering what these two Westerners were doing sitting on the floor with him sipping tea. Raju introduced us, in much the same way I had introduced Barbara and myself to him.

'They've been living in the Kullu Valley for almost three months,' he said. 'Barbara is an anthropologist working on her thesis on long life in Tibetan medicine.' He paused just long enough for his wife to wonder what that had to do with him. 'And Thomas,' he said, winking at me, 'he's a writer. He's writing a book,' he paused for the theatrical effect. 'He's writing a book about ... ME!'

Mount Kanchanjung, as seen from Sikkim.

Glossary

Beyul — *Tibetan*. Literally Hidden Land.

Beyul Demoshong — *Tibetan*. The hidden land in Sikkim (see Demoshong).

Bonpo — Often regarded as the original Shamanistic religion of Tibet, whose spirits and gods were subdued by Padmasambhava and turned into 'protectors' of the dharma or Buddhist teachings.

Chorten — *Tibetan* (*Stupa* in Sanskrit). These sacred monuments originally derived from cairns and burial mounds in ancient Asia. Stupas are found throughout the Buddhist world. The Tibetan chorten is usually filled with the relics of a lama or other realized being or with holy objects, texts, etc., and is situated in auspicious locations. Their geometric structure with a square base, hemispherical dome and conical spire crowned by a crescent and disk signifying the moon and sun represents the Buddhist cosmology. Chortens are often found near temples, though they may stand alone, and they usually have a well-worn path called a *kora* around them along which the faithful circle in a clockwise fashion reciting mantras.

Daka — *Sanskrit*. Male *dakini* (see below).

Dakini — *Sanskrit* (*Khandro* in Tibetan). Literally: Sky Goer, or Sky Dancer. A female spiritual entity that sometimes takes human form. She can appear to a lama as a vision and act as a guide or revealer of hidden knowledge. If she takes human form, she can not only act as a guide to hidden stores of wisdom but can be his physical consort as well.

Demojong — *Tibetan*. Literally: Valley of Rice. This is the Tibetan name for the Kingdom of Sikkim, so named because the kingdom's fertile valleys falling away from the high Tibetan Plateau are well suited to the growing of rice.

Demoshong — *Tibetan*. Literally: The Great Valley of Rice. This is the name for the Hidden Land, or *beyul*, that Tibetan tradition maintains is hidden within the Kingdom of Sikkim. Paradoxically, this hidden land is supposedly many times larger than the kingdom itself.

Dharma — *Sanskrit* (*Dhamma* in Pali). Literally: that which upholds or supports. In its widest sense, it refers to the order that upholds the cosmos. In the context of this book, it refers to the teachings of the Buddha, especially as understood in a Tibetan Buddhist context.

Dip shing — *Tibetan*. Literally: invisibility stick. A concoction made from a variety of materials that confers invisibility, so named for one of the main ingredients, a stick from a crows' nest that when thrown in a swiftly moving stream flows upstream.

Dorje — *Tibetan* (*Vajra* in Sanskrit). Means both thunderbolt and diamond. Sometimes used as a name, it refers to the double-sided brass implement used by lamas during religious ceremonies.

Dungsay — *Tibetan*. An honorific title for the son of a high lama. Thus, Tulshuk Lingpa's son Kunsang is known as the Dungsay Rinpoche.

Golok — A relatively small region of eastern Tibet between the Kham and Amdo regions. Some consider it part of Kham, others, part of Amdo.

Gompa — *Tibetan*. Monastery.

Jinda — *Tibetan*. Sponsor, especially of a lama or monastery.

Khata — *Tibetan*. A ceremonial scarf, traditionally of silk, now commonly synthetic, which is presented to lamas or other respected members of the community as a greeting or sign of respect.

Kham — *Tibetan*. A region of eastern Tibet known for its fierce warriors.

Khampa — *Tibetan*. A person from Kham.

Khandro — *Tibetan*. See *Dakini*.

Kora — *Tibetan*. The circular trail or way around a monastery or other sacred site in the Tibetan world, around which the faithful circle in a clockwise direction reciting mantras. Used also to describe a circumambulation.

Lama — *Tibetan* (similar to Sanskrit Guru). Loosely analogous to a priest. Strictly speaking, a monk or practitioner of a certain standard. Lamas can be married or not, depending on which branch of Tibetan Buddhism they belong to. The Dalai Lama is the head of the Gelukpa branch of Tibetan Buddhism; he was also the temporal leader of Tibet. His position as compared to other lamas would be roughly analogous to the position of the Pope to other priests.

Lepcha — The indigenous people of Sikkim and the Darjeeling Hills. Also the name of their language. Known for being a peace-loving people, they rarely put up a fight when others encroached on their land. Thus they often ended up living in the most inaccessible land and were subsequently named the Rong by the invading Nepalis. Rong means 'Ravine Folk'. The Lepchas believe themselves to have been created from the high pristine snows of Mount Kanchenjunga. They call themselves the *Matanchi Rongkup*, or Mother's Beloved Children.

Lingpa — *Tibetan*. A special class of lama with the gift of being able to find hidden treasures (*terma*: see below) and hidden lands. The more common title for treasure-revealing lamas is *terton* (see below). While there is no consensus on exactly how a lingpa differs from other tertons they are generally seen to be the elite of the tertons.

Mala — *Sanskrit*. The ubiquitous rosary of Tibetan Buddhists with 108 beads, used to count the recitation of mantras.

Mantra — *Sanskrit*. Sacred syllable or set of syllables repeated in meditation or while circumambulating sacred sites. The most common mantra in the Tibetan world is the mantra of Chenresig, the Buddha of Compassion, *Om Mani Padme Hung*. Another common mantra is that of Padmasambhava, *Om Ah Hung Vajra Guru Pema Siddi Hung*.

Mayel Lyang — *Lepcha*. Literally: Hidden Land. The indigenous Lepchas' name for their land, which comprises modern Sikkim, the Darjeeling Hills and adjacent parts of Nepal and Bhutan.

Melong — *Tibetan*. Mirror. In the context of this book, referring to the convex polished brass mirror used in divination.

Myonpa — *Tibetan*. Crazy person.

Naga — *Sanskrit*. Serpent deities, often connected with water, springs and moist places.

Nagpa — *Tibetan*. A Tibetan tantric yogi who doesn't cut his hair, commonly wears a white robe instead of the burgundy robe common to other lamas and often has sexual relations.

Nyingma — *Tibetan*. The oldest of the four main branches of Tibetan Buddhism. The others are the Kagyu, Sakya and Geluk.

Neyik — *Tibetan*. Guidebook to a hidden land.

Pecha — *Tibetan*. Unbound religious scripture written on long rectangular sheets, which are stacked between wooden blocks and wrapped in cloth.

Puja — *Sanskrit*. Ritual.

Purba — *Tibetan*. Ritual dagger, often made of brass and whose blade has three surfaces, used in Tibetan ritual and during the religious dances.

Rinpoche — *Tibetan*. Literally: precious one. The term reserved for highly respected and spiritually accomplished lamas, often appended to their names.

Sang — *Tibetan*. Incense made from the needles and branches of various pine and cedar trees.

Shambhala — *Sanskrit*. Literally: source of happiness. Mystical kingdom of Tibetan tradition hidden behind a ring of snow peaks somewhere in the Himalayas or perhaps north of western Tibet. First known to the West in the writings of the seventeenth century Jesuit missionary Estevao Cacella, this hidden kingdom has fired the imagination of the West ever since. Such mystics and artists as H.P. Blavatsky, Alice Bailey and Nicholas and Helena Roerich wrote of the kingdom and even claimed to be in touch with the hidden adepts there. A very important Tibetan religious text, the Kalachakra Tantra, is said to have originated there.

Shangri-La — The hidden mystical valley of lamas and wisdom in central Asia that the survivors of a plane crash find in James Hilton's 1933 novel *Lost Horizon*. Now synonymous with any hidden place of refuge or Utopia, it was even the name first given to the US presidential retreat now known as Camp David.

Stupa — see *Chorten*.

Tamic — *Tibetan*. Literally: picture eye. The special ability to see prophetic images in the burnished brass mirror during the divination known as *trata melong* (see below). This ability is most often found in girls and young women.

Tantra — *Sanskrit*. Literally: thread or continuity. Esoteric and often secret spiritual teachings, many of which are at the root of Tibetan Buddhism.

Ter, Terma — *Tibetan*. Literally: treasure. These treasures, which may take the form of a scripture, ritual object, or insight, were hidden by great masters of the past, most notably the eighth-century mystic often credited with bringing Buddhism to Tibet, Padmasambhava. Hidden in the earth, mountains, water, sky, or the mind itself, they await the auspicious time for their discovery, even centuries later. They are found by a special class of Tibetan lamas called tertons (see below).

Terton — *Tibetan*. Literally: revealer of hidden treasure. An incarnate lama with the spiritual ability to find hidden treasure.

Thangka — *Tibetan*. Tibetan religious scroll painting usually painted on cloth depicting Buddhas, deities, mandalas and other religious subjects.

Trata melong — *Tibetan*. A form of divination using a convex brass mirror, or *melong*, typically propped up in a bowl of rice. Following this ritual, which is performed by a lama, people with the *tamik* (see above), a special intuitive ability—typically girls or young women—gaze into the mirror and see images in it, which are then interpreted by the lama.

Tsampa — *Tibetan*. Roasted barley flower, the staple of Tibetan diet, typically mixed with water or tea and butter into a paste or dough and eaten raw. Tsampa is a highly concentrated food that is easily transported and prepared on the high Tibetan Plateau and in the remote regions of the Himalayas.

Tulku — *Tibetan*. An incarnate.

Tulshuk — *Tibetan*. Changeable or mutable, and by inference crazy.

Umzay — *Tibetan*. The master of rituals at a Tibetan *gompa*, or monastery.

Yogi — *Sanskrit*. A practitioner of yoga. One who aspires to direct experience of the divine by means of meditation, physical exercises or esoteric ritual practices.

Dramatis Personæ

This is not an inclusive list of the people (and Buddhist figures) found in this book. It lists those who appear at more than one point in the narrative and—since so many of the names will be new to readers not familiar with Tibetan culture—the reader might need assistance in recalling.

Atang Lama — Atang Lama was in his late teens at the time Tulshuk Lingpa lived in Tashiding and Sinon, which is where he grew up. He died in 2009.

Chatral Rinpoche — An accomplished yogi of the Nyingma branch of Tibetan Buddhism, Chatral Rinpoche was born in Tibet and is now in his late nineties. Older than Tulshuk Lingpa, he was something of a teacher and advisor to him. At the time of the events depicted in this book he had a monastery in Jorbungalow, about 8 miles (12 kilometres) outside of Darjeeling. He now has monasteries south of the Darjeeling Hills in Salbhari and in the Kathmandu Valley of Nepal. He is married to Tulshuk Lingpa's eldest daughter Kamala, with whom he has two daughters.

Chenresig — *Tibetan* (Avelokiteshvara in *Sanskrit*). Literally: see with the eyes. The Buddha of Compassion.

Chimi Wangmo — Tulshuk Lingpa's *khandro*, or consort, from the village of Koksar in Lahaul, with whom he had a daughter, Pema Choekyi.

Chokshi — At the time of the events depicted in this book, he was a young man from Simoling, where Tulshuk Lingpa had a monastery in the high mountains of Lahaul.

Dalai Lama — Born in 1935 the present Dalai Lama, Tenzin Gyatso, is the fourteenth incarnation in the lineage. Considered the head of the Gelukpa branch of Tibetan Buddhism, he is said to be the incarnation of Chenresig, the Buddha of Compassion. The Dalai Lamas were also the temporal leaders of Tibet from the seventeenth century until 1959 when the present Dalai Lama was forced to flee the Chinese invasion. The Dalai Lama's position as compared to other lamas would be roughly analogous to the position of the Pope to other priests. Still considered the leader of the Tibetan people, he is also a moral force in the world and deeply committed to non-violence. He won the Noble Peace Prize in 1989.

Dorje Dechen Lingpa — Also known as the Domang Tulku. He coronated Tulshuk Lingpa at the Domang Gompa in eastern Tibet and gave him his name. He made an attempt to open Beyul Demoshong in the 1920s, which failed. He died on his return journey.

Dorje Wangmo — The mother-in-law of my friend Tinley Gyatso, the thangka painter from Gangtok. She was the one who first told me of the expedition to Beyul Demoshong. In 1961, while she was in her mid-thirties, she heard the lama had arrived who would open Beyul Demoshong. She left her native Bhutan, never to return. She is now in her late seventies. A few years ago she shaved her head, donned robes and became a Buddhist nun.

Dudjom Rinpoche — Born in Tibet in 1904, Dudjom Rinpoche was the 'root' guru, or main spiritual teacher, of Tulshuk Lingpa. Himself a terton, or revealer of hidden treasure, Dudjom was also a great scholar and the author of many books on the Nyingma tradition of Tibetan Buddhism. He died in 1987.

Gonde Drungyig — An official of the Sikkimese Ecclesiastical Department. He was at the head of the first delegation sent by the Sikkimese king to investigate Tulshuk Lingpa.

Géshipa — With a name that translates to Four Hundred, he is sure to be an unusual character. Once the rainmaker for the king of Bhutan, Géshipa is now in his mid-eighties and is actively working on a potion of invisibility.

Gyurme — Tulshuk Lingpa's grandson, now in his early twenties. His mother is the daughter of Tulshuk Lingpa and his consort, or khandro, Chimi Wangmo. Gyurme acted as my guide and interpreter during my journey to the Kullu Valley and Lahaul.

Jinda Wangchuk — The sponsor who provided Tulshuk Lingpa and his family with a place to live in a cave above the

Beas River in the Kullu Valley of the Indian state of Himachal Pradesh.

Khandro Yeshe Tsogyal — The main spiritual consort of Padmasambhava (see below).

Kunsang — The only son of Tulshuk Lingpa, also known as the Dungsay Rinpoche, an honorific title for the son of a high lama. Through the many hours I spent with Kunsang both at his home in Darjeeling and while travelling together in Sikkim, he provided me with the thread that held all the disparate stories together.

Kyechok Lingpa — The father of Tulshuk Lingpa. He was a lama at the Domang Monastery in eastern Tibet until he was forced by the invading Chinese to flee over the Himalayas to India with his wife, Kilo. He then had a monastery in Patanam, a few days' march from Tulshuk Lingpa's monastery in Simoling in Lahaul until he died.

Lama Tashi — A lama from Simoling. He was and is the umzay, or head of rituals, at Tulshuk Lingpa's monastery in Simoling, Lahaul, in the Indian state of Himachal Pradesh.

Lobsang — A close disciple of Tulshuk Lingpa and a very learned lama.

Mipham — A close disciple of Tulshuk Lingpa and a learned lama in his own right. Originally from Lahaul, and a great practitioner of chod, a practice performed at charnel grounds in which the practitioner imagines himself flaying the flesh from his bones, Mipham now lives in deep retreat in a cave in Bhutan.

Namdrol — One of Tulshuk Lingpa's closest and most learned lama disciples. He was often the one to hand-copy the texts that Tulshuk Lingpa wrote or received as terma, hidden treasure. He was also a practitioner of Tibetan medicine.

Padmasambhava — *Tibetan*. Literally: The Lotus Born. Also known as Guru Rinpoche. The eighth-century mystic credited with establishing Buddhism in Tibet.

Pema Choekyi — The daughter of Tulshuk Lingpa and his khandro, or consort, Chimi Wangmo. She was born shortly before Tulshuk Lingpa went into the snow mountains to open Beyul Demoshong. Her son Gyurme acted as my guide and interpreter in Himachal Pradesh.

Phuntsok Choeden — Tulshuk Lingpa's wife. She was from central Tibet and went with Tulshuk Lingpa to India at a very young age. She died in Kathmandu following a bout of colon cancer in 2006.

Rigzin Dokhampa — The senior researcher at the Namgyal Institute of Tibetology outside Gangtok, Sikkim. He was a disciple of Tulshuk Lingpa and learned thangka painting from him from the age of fourteen. He died in 2005.

Senge Dorje — The birth name of Tulshuk Lingpa.

Tamang Tulku — The boy who lives with Tulshuk Lingpa's son Kunsang and his family in Darjeeling. Originally from Nepal, he is learning Tibetan and the dharma from Kunsang and helps run the family clothing shops. Whether he is really a *tulku*, or reincarnated lama, is an open question.

Tarthang Tulku — A reincarnate lama born in Golok, eastern Tibet in 1934. He fled to India in 1958, where he met and spent time with Tulshuk Lingpa in both Pangao and Simoling. He moved to California in 1968, where he founded the Nyingma Institute and Dharma Publishing.

Tashi Lhamo — Tulshuk Lingpa's half sister.

Tenzing Norgay — He and Edmund Hillary were the first to successfully climb Mount Everest, the highest mountain in the world, in 1953. Though born in Nepal, he was the favourite son of his adopted home, Darjeeling. After Tulshuk Lingpa cured Tenzing Norgay's wife of a fatal illness, he became a sponsor of Tulshuk Lingpa's, even though he never knew the real reason for Tulshuk Lingpa's journey to the area. He died in 1986.

Tinley Gyatso — The thangka painter from Gangtok whose mother-in-law first told me of Tulshuk Lingpa and his expedition to Beyul.

Tulshuk Lingpa — Literally: Crazy Treasure Revealer. The main character in this book. Born in the Golok region of eastern Tibet with the name Senge Dorje, he was recognized as a revealer of hidden treasure at an early age and received this name. He moved to India in his early twenties, lived and had monasteries in Himachal Pradesh, in India's western Himalayas. After receiving visions that indicated he was the one to open the hidden valley in Sikkim, Beyul Demoshong, he went to Sikkim with many followers.

Wangchuk — The grandson of Tulshuk Lingpa, son of Tulshuk Lingpa's only son Kunsang. Apart from acting as my interpreter, he became a close friend. In many ways we investigated the story of 'Grandpa' together.

Yabla family of Yoksum — An influential landholding family from the village of Yoksum in West Sikkim. Once with high positions in the government of the chogyal, or king, of Sikkim, they now own hotels and the biggest beer brewery in Sikkim. Of the six sons in this family, five were followers and sponsors of Tulshuk Lingpa in his quest for Beyul Demoshong—all but the youngest, who was on a quest for his own promised land and made it, to Bollywood, where he is well known for playing the dark villain under the stage name of Danny Denzongpa.

Yab Maila — The eldest son of the Yabla family of Yoksum, Sikkim, who were major sponsors of Tulshuk Lingpa. He was a tax collector for the king, and very influential.

Yeshe — The sister of Tulshuk Lingpa's khandro, Chimi Wangmo, and herself a khandro to Tulshuk Lingpa. Yeshe had *tamik*, the special intuitive ability to see images in the burnished brass ritual mirror known as a *melong*.

Places

This annotated list of places mentioned in the book is by no means comprehensive. Rather, it lists those places a reader unfamiliar with India and Tibet, particularly the obscure places in which so much of the story takes place and which recur throughout the book, might find difficult to remember.

Bhutan — A Himalayan Buddhist kingdom situated in the eastern Himalayas south of Tibet, and bordered on the west, south and east by India.

Darjeeling — A town of a hundred to a hundred-and-fifty-thousand people in the Himalayan foothills of the Indian state of West Bengal. At an elevation of about 7000 feet (2200 metres), it was established as a hill station by the colonial British in 1835 and quickly became a centre of tea production. Situated just south of Sikkim and Tibet, it has a sizeable Tibetan Buddhist population.

Domang Gompa — A monastery in the Golok region of eastern Tibet where Tulshuk Lingpa was trained and to which his father Kyechok Lingpa was attached. It was also the monastery of Dorje Dechen Lingpa, also known as the Domang Tulku, who both coronated and gave Tulshuk Lingpa his name and who tried to open the way to Beyul Demoshong in the 1920s.

Dzongri — At 13,200 feet (4000 metres), this small nomad settlement is on the main trekking route from Yoksum, in Sikkim, to the massif of Mount Kanchenjunga.

Gangtok — Literally: hilltop. The capital of Sikkim at about 4750 feet (1450 metres). With a population of approximately 30,000 people, the culture of Gangtok is heavily influenced by Tibet, which lies just to its north.

Golok — The region of eastern Tibet where Tulshuk Lingpa grew up and was trained.

Himachal Pradesh — The Indian state in the western Himalayas just south of Kashmir where Tulshuk Lingpa lived for many years before travelling to Sikkim to open Beyul Demoshong.

Jorbungalow — A small town about 8 miles (12 kilometres) from Darjeeling where Tulshuk Lingpa visited his spiritual teacher Chatral Rinpoche.

Koksar — The first village in the high mountains of Lahaul after crossing the Rohtang Pass. At 11,000 feet (3300 metres), Koksar is where Tulshuk Lingpa's *khandro*, or consort, and her sister Yeshe were from. It is situated on the banks of the Chandra River.

Kullu — The capital town of the Kullu district in the Kullu Valley (see below) of the Indian state of Himachal Pradesh in the western Himalayas.

Kullu Valley — A roughly north- to south-lying valley in the western Himalayas through which the Beas River flows and has its source. Located in the Indian state of Himachal Pradesh, this is where Tulshuk Lingpa lived in the winters in a cave outside the village of Pangao.

Ladakh — A region of high mountains in the western Himalaya. With over half its population Tibetan Buddhist, it is part of the Indian state of Jammu and Kashmir and lies just north of Himachal Pradesh.

Lahaul — [Pronounced 'Lahool'] A high-altitude region in the Himalayas from roughly 10,000-17,000 feet (3000-5100 metres) in the Indian state of Himachal Pradesh. It is accessed from the Kullu Valley by crossing the 13,000-foot (4000 metre) Rohtang Pass.

Manali — A town in the Kullu Valley, now quite popular with tourists.

Mount Kanchenjunga — The third-highest mountain in the world at 28,169 feet (8586 metres). It straddles the Nepal-Sikkim border. Long regarded as sacred by people who have lived in its vicinity beginning with the indigenous Lepchas, it was on the slopes of this mountain that Tulshuk Lingpa went to find the hidden valley of immortality, Beyul Demoshong.

Pangao — The village in the Kullu Valley where Tulshuk Lingpa and his family lived during winters for the years preceding his going to Sikkim to open Beyul Demoshong.

Pangi — The village in the further reaches of Chamba where Tulshuk Lingpa had his first monastery.

Rohtang Pass — Literally: Plain of Corpses. The approximately 13,000-foot (4000 metre) pass at the head of the Beas River that connects the Kullu Valley with Lahaul and Spiti in the Indian state of Himachal Pradesh.

Simoling — Also known as Telling. The village in Lahaul where Tulshuk Lingpa cured the inhabitants of leprosy then lived for many years and had his own monastery.

Sikkim — Formerly an independent Himalayan kingdom and British protectorate, Sikkim became the twenty-second state of India in 1975. It is bordered by Nepal to the west, Tibet to the north and northeast, Bhutan to the southeast, and the Darjeeling Hills of India's state of West Bengal to the south. Its western border with Nepal is dominated by the third-highest peak on the planet, Mount Kanchenjunga.

Sinon — A village in West Sikkim with a historic monastery, a few kilometres from Tashiding. This village, connected to the ancient history of Sikkim, is where Tulshuk Lingpa moved when things got difficult for him in Tashiding. He performed a miracle here on the outcropping of rock just below the monastery.

Tashiding — A village in West Sikkim; also the name of the monastery perched on a hilltop outside the village. The name is Tibetan and means Auspicious Centre. Believed to have been blessed by Padmasambhava, the founder of Tibetan Buddhism, the monastery is considered the spiritual centre of Sikkim. It was here that it was prophesied the lama who would open Beyul Demoshong would announce himself, and it was here Tulshuk Lingpa came when preparing to open that hidden land.

Tseram — The nomad encampment at 12,300 feet (3770 meters) on the slopes of Mount Kanchenjunga in Nepal where the journey to Beyul Demoshong began.

Tso Pema — The Tibetan name for a sacred lake in the Indian state of Himachal Pradesh. It is known locally as Lake Rewalsar.

Yoksum — The first capital of Sikkim and the last village before the trail rises to Mount Kanchenjunga. At 5800 feet (1780 metres), the name comes from the Lepcha language. It means the Three Great Ones in commemoration of the three Tibetan lamas who met there in order to found the Buddhist kingdom of Sikkim in 1642.

Padmasambhava.

Acknowledgements

I've always felt gratitude for this story falling into my lap, and for those who gave generously of their time, knowledge and experience. Without the willingness, kindness, generosity of time—and often tea, meals, accommodation, transportation and patience—of innumerable people spread across the Himalayas this book simply would not be.

Without the help of Tulshuk Lingpa's family, especially his son Kunsang Bhutia and grandson Wangchuk Bhutia, I would have felt like Theseus in the Minotaur's labyrinth without the thread. Kunsang's enthusiasm, wit, humour and friendship are all lodged as deeply in my heart as his spirit and stories are lodged in the very fabric of this book. To Wangchuk, my interpreter, travelling companion and fellow explorer of 'Grandpa's' story, my most sincere thanks for your time and passion.

If a fire could feel grateful for the spark that gave it life, then thanks should go to Tinley Gyatso of Gangtok for recognizing how my imagination would be fired by this story and to his mother-in-law Dorje Wangmo who, through her spellbinding story so full of crevasses and determination, was the first to take me along on that long-ago journey to the Hidden Land.

To the lamas of the Tashiding Monastery and the others of that remarkable community I offer my most sincere thanks for their support in writing this book. Special thanks go to Géshipa, the closest I'm ever likely to get to knowing a living wizard. The purity of his vision of the Hidden Land gave me my closest glimpse. I thank Garpa for the innumerable times he offered me a tiny stool at his side behind the Tashiding Monastery where I could watch his chisel coax Tibetan letters from stone and hear what it was like to be the Messenger of the Hidden Land. The late Atang Lama of Sinon will be remembered as the one who brought to life the perspective of a teenager from Tashiding when the prophesied lama came.

To the late Rigzin Dokhampa I owe much of the accuracy in this book in terms of the Tibetan dharma and its peculiarities as found in Sikkim. With one foot in the traditional world and another in scholarship, he was an ever-patient bridge between worlds, elucidating points alluded to by others with the accuracy of a researcher and the heart of a true practitioner. While the world will produce many scholars, the very world Rigzin Dokhampa grew up in and so artfully melded into his scholarly life has all but vanished. With his passing, something irreplaceable has been lost.

I offer my thanks to all the others of Sikkim and Darjeeling who gave clues and guidance and told me their stories during my years of research between 2001 and 2008.

When I arrived in the Kullu Valley in 2006 to research Tulshuk Lingpa's early years in India and to meet his oldest disciples, Kunsang had called ahead and I was met there by Tulshuk Lingpa's grandson Gyurme Chand and by Wangyal Bodh, who hired a vehicle to take me to many of the people from Kullu and Lahaul connected with this story. I thank Gyurme's mother Pema Choekyi, Tulshuk Lingpa's daughter in Lahaul, for showing me the few precious things she had inherited from her father, and who, together with her husband Amar Chand, gave Barbara and me our base in Lahaul. Their hospitality still warms.

I am grateful to the monks at the monastery in Pangao for beating the ground before us with sticks to scare away cobras as they brought me down the treacherous slope to Tulshuk Lingpa's cave. And to Jinda Wangchuk's family in Pangao, thank you for giving Barbara and me a place to stay and for the old photos of Raju.

To Khandro Chimi Wangmo I offer thanks for taking her stuffed snow leopard down so she could pose with it. Chokshi of Simoling gave me his story, and the other monks and head lama of Tulshuk Lingpa's monastery in Lahaul offered me their hospitality, for which I am grateful. Yeshe's story of the love and the pain she has endured over the years moved me greatly, and I thank her for her openness in expressing the beauty she harbours deep in her heart.

As the head of Tulshuk Lingpa's monastery in Lahaul for over forty years, Lama Tashi's deep understanding of Tulshuk

Lingpa's history, which he shared with a voice at once authorita-tive and deeply human, shed a unique light on the story.

To Raju, Tulshuk Lingpa's reincarnation, I offer thanks not only for the book's last words but also for the frankness of his story. May this book not become an obstacle for you.

I've had the good fortune of having a number of very good readers and editors who have had an important hand in shaping this book. I want to thank Mark Canner in Cambridge, MA, for his thorough read and penetrating insight, Geoffrey Samuel in Cardiff for his precision, and Didi Contractor in Sidhbari, Dharamsala, for the sharpness of her critique. Tashi Tsering of the Amnye Machen Institute in Dharamsala provided corrections that only a Tibetan scholar of his calibre could have given, and for that I am grateful, as I am to Alex McKay for important historical fact checking. I want to thank Raymond Lowe in Vermont and Anna Hopewell in London for their feedback, which helped shape the first draft. Any mistakes that remain are entirely my own.

For the translation of Tulshuk Lingpa's writing from the Ti-betan I thank Gyurme Tsundu, Professor Samten Norbu and the late Khen Rinpoche, all of Darjeeling.

To all those anonymous photographers of yore whose old black and white photographs are reproduced in this book: thank you. If any of you want to come forward, you will be raised from the ranks of the *anonymous*, and be given full credit in future editions.

My ignorance of Tibetan, Nepali and Hindi would have been an insurmountable obstacle if it weren't for those who acted as my interpreters. First among them was Wangchuk, Tulshuk Lingpa's grandson, who not only interpreted his father's stories over the course of innumerable afternoons but also accompanied me twice to Sikkim, during which trips he was not only a wonderful companion but also a superlative interpreter. His sister Yeshe also spent many an afternoon interpreting her father's stories for me, and for that I am grateful. During my trip to the Kullu Valley and Lahaul, Tulshuk Lingpa's grandson Gyurme was my guide and interpreter. Thank you.

At Oxford University I had the help of two scholars: Charles Ramble who was generous with his time, pointing out important literature on the tradition of the Hidden Lands, loaning me obscure texts and setting up my first lecture based on the book; and Saul Mullard, whose help shining light on the tight knot of Sikkim's history was invaluable.

It was Jetsunma Tenzin Palmo of the Dongyu Gatsal Ling Nunnery whose kind words and enthusiasm concerning the manuscript at a crucial juncture helped this book see the light of day.

To all those not mentioned here but who had a hand in shaping this book, either through scholarly expertise, edits or experience, a heartfelt appreciation is hereby sent out to you.

Thanks also go to my parents, Henry and Vivian Shor, who, while not having always understood what made me tick, have always believed in me as a writer.

I save for last the one who fulfilled all the above-mentioned roles and more. She not only interpreted for me innumerable times, translated from the Tibetan, steered me to pertinent literature, read and edited various drafts of the book, offered sage advice and accompanied me to remote valleys and innumerable lecture halls in India, Europe and the USA: but also offered her encouragement when needed, and her love always. I'm speaking of course of my wonderful companion on this earth, my partner and wife, Barbara.

Photo Credits

All photographs were taken by the author, Thomas K. Shor, except for the ones on the following pages:

p. (ii), from *Himalayan Journals* by Sir Joseph Dalton Hooker, Ward, Lock, Bowden and Co., London, New York, and Melbourne, 1891.

p. (vi), from an old photo, photographer unknown.

p. (viii), from *Himalayan Journals* by Sir Joseph Dalton Hooker, Ward, Lock, Bowden and Co., London, New York, and Melbourne, 1891.

p. (xii), map modified from *The WorldFactbook*, CIA.

p. 19, from an old photo, photographer unknown.

p. 29, from an old photo, photographer unknown.

p. 56, from an old photo, photographer unknown.

p. 66, from an old photo, photographer unknown.

p. 69, (bottom left) from an old photo, photographer unknown.

p. 72, from an old photo, photographer unknown.

p. 94, map modified from *The WorldFactbook*, CIA.

p. 146, map modified from *The WorldFactbook*, CIA.

p. 162, image in the public domain.

p. 183, from an old photo, photographer unknown.

p. 210, map from *Round Kangchenjunga* by Douglas W. Freshfield, London, Edwin Arnold, 1903.

p. 264, from an old photo, photographer unknown.

p. 268, from an old photo, photographer unknown.

p. 273, from an old photo, photographer unknown.

ABOUT THE AUTHOR

Writer and photographer Thomas K. Shor was born in Boston, USA, and studied comparative religion and literature in Vermont. With an ear for unusual stories, the fortune to attract them, and an eye for detail, he has travelled the planet's mountainous realms—from the Mayan Highlands of southern Mexico in the midst of insurrection to the mountains of Greece, and more recently, to the Indian Himalayas—to collect, illustrate, and write stories with a uniquely personal character, often having the flavour of fable.

Shor has lectured widely on his writings and has had solo exhibits of his photographs in Europe and India. He can often be found in the most obscure locales, immersed in a compelling story touching upon fundamental human themes.

He is also the author of *The Master Director: A Journey through Politics, Doubt and Devotion with a Himalayan Master* (HarperCollins 2014) and *Windblown Clouds* (Escape Media Publishers 2003 and Pilgrims Publishing 2006).

Visit him at www.ThomasShor.com

Lightning Source UK Ltd.
Milton Keynes UK
UKHW011852111219
355199UK00001B/211/P